Desire in Ashes

Also available from Bloomsbury

Bloomsbury Studies in Continental Philosophy presents cutting-edge scholarship in the field of modern European thought. The wholly original arguments, perspectives and research findings in titles in this series make it an important and stimulating resource for students and academics from across the discipline.

Breathing with Luce Irigaray, edited by Lenart Skof and Emily A. Holmes
Deleuze and Art, Anne Sauvagnargues
Deleuze and the Diagram: Aesthetic Threads in Visual Organization, Jakub Zdebik
Derrida, Badiou and the Formal Imperative, Christopher Norris
Egalitarian Moments: From Descartes to Rancière, Devin Zane Shaw
Ernst Bloch and His Contemporaries, Ivan Boldyrev
Why there is no Post-Structuralism in France, Johannes Angermuller
Gadamer's Poetics: A Critique of Modern Aesthetics, John Arthos
Heidegger, History and the Holocaust, Mahon O'Brien
Heidegger and the Emergence of the Question of Being, Jesús Adrián Escudero
Immanent Transcendence: Reconfiguring Materialism in Continental Philosophy, Patrice Haynes
Merleau-Ponty's Existential Phenomenology and the Realization of Philosophy, Bryan A. Smyth
Nietzsche and Political Thought, edited by Keith Ansell-Pearson
Nietzsche as a Scholar of Antiquity, Helmut Heit
Philosophy, Sophistry, Antiphilosophy: Badiou's Dispute with Lyotard, Matthew R. McLennan
The Poetic Imagination in Heidegger and Schelling, Christopher Yates
Post-Rationalism: Psychoanalysis, Epistemology, and Marxism in Post-War France, Tom Eyers
Revisiting Normativity with Deleuze, edited by Rosi Braidotti and Patricia Pisters
Towards the Critique of Violence: Walter Benjamin and Giorgio Agamben, Brendan Moran and Carlo Salzani

From the same author
The Poetics of Sleep, Simon Morgan Wortham
Derrida: Writing Events, Simon Morgan Wortham
The Derrida Dictionary, Simon Morgan Wortham

Desire in Ashes

Deconstruction, Psychoanalysis, Philosophy

Edited by Simon Morgan Wortham and Chiara Alfano

Bloomsbury Academic
An imprint of Bloomsbury Publishing Plc

B L O O M S B U R Y
LONDON · OXFORD · NEW YORK · NEW DELHI · SYDNEY

Bloomsbury Academic

An imprint of Bloomsbury Publishing Plc

50 Bedford Square	1385 Broadway
London	New York
WC1B 3DP	NY 10018
UK	USA

www.bloomsbury.com

BLOOMSBURY and the Diana logo are trademarks of Bloomsbury Publishing Plc

First published 2016

British Library Cataloguing-in-Publication Data
A catalogue record for this book is available from the British Library.

ISBN:	HB:	978-1-47252-913-8
	ePDF:	978-1-47252-574-1
	ePub:	978-1-47253-351-7

Library of Congress Cataloging-in-Publication Data
Desire in ashes : deconstruction, psychoanalysis, philosophy / edited by
Simon Morgan Wortham and Chiara Alfano.– 1 [edition].
pages cm– (Bloomsbury studies in Continental philosophy)
Includes bibliographical references and index.
ISBN 978-1-4725-2913-8 (hb)– ISBN 978-1-4725-3351-7 (epub)–
ISBN 978-1-4725-2574-1 (epdf)
1. Deconstruction. 2. Desire. 3. Derrida, Jacques. I. Wortham, Simon, editor.
B809.6.D48 2016
149'.97–dc23
2015014780

Typeset by Fakenham Prepress Solutions, Fakenham, Norfolk NR21 8NN
Printed and bound in Great Britain

This book is respectfully dedicated to the memory of Pleshette DeArmitt

Contents

Contributors

Chiara Alfano is a Leverhulme Early Career Fellow in the School of Humanities at Kingston University, London. Previously, she was a postdoctoral research fellow at The Institute for Advanced Studies in the Humanities (IASH) at the University of Edinburgh. She is currently working on a monograph-length study that looks at the figure of the infant in post-war literature, philosophy, psychoanalysis and feminist texts. She has published on the cross-fertilizations between literature, philosophy and psychoanalysis, in particular in relation to Stanley Cavell, Jacques Derrida and Shakespeare. She is also reviews editor at *The Oxford Literary Review*.

Gil Anidjar is Professor in the Department of Religion, the Department of Middle Eastern, South Asian, and African Studies, and the Institute for Comparative Literature and Society at Columbia University. His books include *'Our Place in Al-Andalus': Kabbalah, Philosophy, Literature in Arab Jewish Letters* (Stanford: Stanford University Press, 2002), *The Jew, the Arab: A History of the Enemy* (Stanford: Stanford University Press, 2003), *Semites: Race, Religion, Literature* (Stanford: Stanford University Press, 2007) and *Blood: A Critique of Christianity* (New York: Columbia University Press, 2014). He also edited Jacques Derrida's *Acts of Religion* (London and New York: Routledge, 2002).

Elissa Marder is Professor of French and Comparative Literature at Emory University. She is the author of *Dead Time: Temporal Disorders in the Wake of Modernity (Baudelaire and Flaubert)* (Stanford: Stanford University Press, 2001) and *The Mother in the Age of Mechanical Reproduction: Psychoanalysis, Photography, Deconstruction* (New York: Fordham University Press, 2012). With E. S. Burt and Kevin Newmark, she also edited *Time for Baudelaire (Poetry, Theory, History)*, Yale French Studies Vol. 125/126 (2014). She has published essays on diverse topics in literature, literary theory, feminism, film, photography and psychoanalysis.

Simon Morgan Wortham is Professor of English in the Faculty of Arts and Social Sciences at Kingston University, London. He is co-director of the London Graduate School. His books include *Counter-Institutions: Jacques Derrida and* *the Question of the University* (New York: Fordham University Press, 2006), *Derrida: Writing Events* (London and New York: Continuum, 2008), *The Derrida Dictionary* (London and New York: Continuum, 2010), *The Poetics of Sleep: From Aristotle to Nancy* (London and New York: Bloomsbury, 2013) and *Modern Thought in Pain: Philosophy, Politics, Psychoanalysis* (Edinburgh: Edinburgh University Press, 2014). His latest book, *Phobia*, is due to appear in 2016.

Herman Rapaport is Reynolds Professor of English at Wake Forest University. Among his many books are *Milton and the Postmodern* (Lincoln and London: University of Nebraska Press, 1983), *Heidegger and Derrida: Reflections on Time and Language* (Lincoln and London: University of Nebraska Press, 1989), *Between the Sign and the Gaze* (Ithaca: Cornell University Press, 1994), *Is There Truth in Art?* (Ithaca: Cornell University Press, 1998), *The Theory Mess: Deconstruction in Eclipse* (New York: Columbia University Press, 2001), *Later Derrida: Reading the Recent Work* (London and New York: Routledge, 2004) and *The Literary Theory Toolkit: A Compendium of Concepts and Methods* (Oxford: Wiley-Blackwell, 2011).

Kas Saghafi is an Associate Professor in the Department of Philosophy at the University of Memphis. He is the author of *Apparitions – Of Derrida's Other* (Fordham: Fordham University Press, 2010) and has also published articles on contemporary French thought in journals such as *Bulletin de la Société Américaine de Philosophie de Langue Française, International Studies in Philosophy, Mosaic, Parallax, Philosophy Today* and *Research in Phenomenology*. He is co-translator of Derrida's 'A Europe of Hope' and 'Aletheia'.

Céline Surprenant is an associate researcher to the Chair of Modern and Contemporary French Literature: History, Criticism, Theory (Antoine Compagnon), Collège de France, Paris, and a Visiting Senior Lecturer in French at the University of Sussex. Her publications include *Freud's Mass Psychology: Questions of Scale* (London: Palgrave Macmillan, 2003), *Freud: A Guide for the Perplexed* (London: Continuum, 2008) and articles on Marcel Proust, Charles Darwin and psychoanalysis, among other topics. She has translated Jean-Luc Nancy's *Speculative Remark: One of Hegel's bon mots* (Stanford: Stanford University Press, 2011).

Lynn Turner is Senior Lecturer in Visual Cultures at Goldsmiths, University of London. She is one of the assistant editors of *Derrida Today* and arts editor of *parallax* for which she has also co-edited several issues. Her books include *Visual Cultures as Recollection* (co-authored with Astrid Schmetterling, Berlin: Sternberg, 2013), *The Animal Question in Deconstruction* (edited, Edinburgh: Edinburgh University Press, 2013) and *The Edinburgh Companion to Animal Studies* (co-edited with Undine Sellbach and Ron Broglio, Edinburgh: Edinburgh University Press, 2016). She is currently writing a monograph on autobiographies of the performative in visual culture.

Acknowledgements

The editors would like to acknowledge the following permissions:

Excerpt from *Poetry as Experience* by Phillipe Lacoue-Labarthe, translated by Andrea Tarnowski. Copyright © 1999 by the Board of Trustees of the Leland Stanford Jr. University English translation. All rights reserved. Used with the permission of Stanford University Press.

Excerpt from *The Ear of the Other: Otobiography, Transference, Translation* by Jacques Derrida, copyright © 1985 by Schocken Books, a division of Random House, Inc., used by permission of Schocken Books, an imprint of the Knopf Doubleday Publishing Group, a division of Penguin Random House LLC. All rights reserved.

Excerpt from *The Clinical Diary of Sándor Ferenczi* by Sándor Ferenczi, edited by Judith Dupont, published by permission of The Marsh Agency Ltd on behalf of The Estate of Sándor Ferenczi and Judith Dupont.

Excerpt from *Of Spirit: Heidegger and the Question* by Jacques Derrida, translated by Geoffrey Bennington and Rachel Bowlby, copyright © 1989 by The University of Chicago. All rights reserved.

Excerpts from *The Post Card: From Socrates to Freud and Beyond* by Jacques Derrida, translated, with an Introduction and Additional Notes, by Alan Bass, copyright © 1987 by The University of Chicago. All rights reserved.

Excerpt from 'If There is Cause to Translate I' reprinted by special permission of *Recherches sémiotiques/Semiotic Inquiry*, Copyright © 1984 by RSSI.

Introduction

Simon Morgan Wortham and Chiara Alfano

This collection of essays takes the question of desire as its specific focus in order to re-evaluate deconstruction's continuing importance and future possibility in the field of modern European thought. Why desire? Our starting point was the idea that, rather than reduce deconstruction to a stale and static 'object' of historical importance or memory, something now fit only for the archive deposit or for monumentalization or even hagiography (something that is, in other words, now only a 'ruin' or just 'ashes' in a very simple sense), one might more fruitfully analyse deconstruction's significance in terms of complex matrices of desire in which it continues to figure. Such matrices of desire, in their different forms, ceaselessly provoked Derrida's interest over several decades, forming not just the critical 'object' of deconstructive enquiry, but establishing some of the performative conditions of its own discourse or 'text'. Such a thinking of the significance of desire for deconstruction's 'afterlife' demands, therefore, attention not only to deconstruction's numerous and multiple analyses of desire in a variety of texts, but also careful consideration of deconstruction's 'own' desires, whatever they may be, as well as the acknowledgement and assessment of a complicated range of desires still played out in relation to deconstruction and its various legacies.

Drawing upon – both affirming and resisting – resources that are neither simply its own nor those of 'others' (psychoanalysis, for instance), deconstruction has taught us much about desire. Once the question of desire, a question that is both at the very heart of Derrida's philosophical project and has been irreversibly altered by his attention to it, is evoked, even the desire to attest to the impotence of deconstructive desires today, we contend that the idea of deconstruction's demise seems woefully simplistic. If critical momentum in European philosophy and theory has seemed to shift away from deconstruction over the past decade or so, nevertheless the indebtedness of contemporary key thinkers to Derrida's writing and to the entire project of deconstruction is unquestionable, regardless of whether it is always fully acknowledged, and whether or not Derrida's influence manifests itself as a source of inspiration or the grounds of critical antagonism or opposition. Many of those who now reject deconstruction continue to write texts that engage with Derrida's work, however minimally, whether dismissively or not. Conversely, whilst sharing certain gestures, work that self-admittedly thinks under the banner of 'deconstruction' (whatever that may be) does not always give a uniform account of what its aims and methodologies are. First paradox: deconstruction may be too uniform for its own good, offering the same gestures in a variety of different contexts, and yet it is often not practised with sufficient theoretical consistency to move beyond those gestures. This will certainly get tongues wagging. This then is the second paradox of deconstruction today: whilst it is flexible enough to accommodate a great variety of critical approaches, it is not always patient enough to incorporate criticism productively. It seems that after decades of being besieged by accusations of a lack of rigour and charlatanism deconstruction risks closing its gates to all but the initiated.

In this context, how best to recall deconstruction as a continuing 'voice' across the fields of the critical humanities, theory and philosophy? Looking at the question of deconstruction and desire in this way, as several of our contributors readily acknowledge, means that deconstruction may neither be dismissed as simply 'dead', nor unproblematically defended as still alive and well. Deconstruction never was alive and well; it was always in ashes, and it certainly never spoke with one voice. To some extent its plurivocality is an effect of the fact that deconstruction lives on the very threshold of life-death (about which it always had much to say), on its fundamental refusal to think and even be in terms of ontology, and this in itself poses some challenges just as it opens possibilities. Answering this question – Wither deconstruction? – will therefore involve mobilizing an intricate threshold of desires which profoundly complicates deconstruction's relationship to the 'present' field of critical thought. In this way, what we hope to offer the reader is not just a thoroughgoing account of deconstruction's relationship to the question of desire, encompassing, for instance, Derrida's remarks on metaphysics, religion, philosophy, politics, literature or psychoanalysis, nor even a reinterpretation along strongly thematic lines of the 'origin' or trajectory of deconstructive thought itself. Instead, by bringing together leading authors of international importance, spanning several generations and thus communicating quite different 'memories' of deconstruction in the twentieth and twenty-first century, our principal aim is to provide fresh perspectives that enable us to think about the 'afterlife' of deconstruction in relation to other forms of contemporary thought.

It would be difficult to argue against the contention that deconstruction is, among other things, irreducibly a thinking of desire. From Derrida's earliest readings of logocentrism, phonocentrism and phallogocentrism, right the way through to his description of autoimmunity and his evocation of 'the experience of the impossible', desire has always been a part of the picture. From speech and writing to the gift, from pharmakon to forgiveness, from Hegel, Husserl and Heidegger to hospitality, from phenomenology and ethics to invention, decision and responsibility, from language and metaphysics to institutions and politics, from Plato to Freud and beyond, the very circuitry of deconstruction has been charged with the question of desire, whether explicitly or implicitly. Desire, in other words, may be thought of as the irreducible supplement of deconstruction; or, perhaps better still, yet another term in the unmasterable chain or untitleable series that also includes the trace, *différance*, remainder, writing, dissemination, cinder, and so on.

Desire is indeed so critical to Derrida's project that one could play the parlour game of interrogating key Derridean terms from the perspective of 'desire'. One could ask, for example, about logos and desire. The *logos* expresses the desire for an ultimate origin, telos, centre or principle of truth which grounds meaning. This desire founds the metaphysical tradition, in particular its determination of being in terms of original presence. Thus, the concern of the *logos* is to establish a self-sufficient foundation or transcendental signified, for which God would perhaps be the most familiar name. Yet the deconstructibility of this same tradition consists in part in the very fact that logocentric *desire* is the irreducible supplement of metaphysical 'truth'.

Or, one could assemble some remarks about speech, writing and desire. In 'Plato's Pharmacy', of course, we find Socrates in the company of Phaedrus, discussing a written speech by the sophist Lysias. The manuscript of the work is concealed under Phaedrus's cloak. This furtively kept resource is a dangerous supplement. Phaedrus has not learnt the speech by rote, since he desires instead to convince Socrates of his ability to reconstitute and weigh its reasoning without recourse to mechanical memorization (without recourse, that is, to the machinic). However, the precedence of living philosophical 'speech' over 'writing' to which this gesture aspires threatens to unravel in the concealing folds of Phaedrus's garment, and indeed in the very text of *Phaedrus* itself. The relation of speech to writing (indeed, of life to the 'machine') is not, then, simply a matter of conceptual priority within the philosophical tradition, but is structured by a complex play of desires.

Religion and desire might constitute a further topic. In 'Faith and Knowledge: The Two Sources of "Religion" at the Limits of Reason Alone', Derrida follows a path which leads out from Kant's *Religion Within the Limits of Reason Alone*, in which two types of religion are identified. While, for Kant, 'cult' religions base themselves more passively on prayer and desire ('faith'), 'moral' religion demands (more or less dispassionate) action in the interests of the good conduct of life ('knowledge'). In 'moral' religion, then, the emphasis shifts away from the historical revelation of God and towards the harnessing of the will to moral ends. Thus, practical reason and knowledge are ostensibly preferable to dogmatic faith. (Much could be said here of the complicated desires, and disavowal of desires, on either side.) For Kant, Christianity is the single historical example of 'moral' religion. And its effect is to conceive of and encourage moral conduct that is independent of God's revelation, presence or indeed existence. Thus Christianity as 'moral' religion may be thought to announce the very death of God (rather than the *desire* for God – or so one might think). Judaism and Islam, meanwhile, may be considered the last two monotheisms that rebel against the secularizing Christianization of the world (maintaining therefore a different relation to what might be termed desire). Derrida speculates on the origin of this double origin of religion. In particular, he speaks of a messianicity without messianism, one older than all religions and all messiahs – a messianicity which opens itself, for better or worse, to the wholly other and to an unanticipatable and radically interruptive future, without first establishing for itself a horizon of expectation or without grounding itself in a prophetic discourse. (One might link this messianicity to the 'yes' or 'yes, yes' as both originary affirmation and promise, treated in texts such as 'A Number of Yes' and 'Ulysses Gramophone: Hear Say Yes in Joyce'.) Such messianicity belongs properly to none of the Abrahamic religions yet marks each of them in particular ways. Crucially, it is the desire for justice rather than simply the law that stems from this messi-anicity. Indeed, this basic relationship between the 'messianic' and the 'just' puts in question traditional distinctions between mysticism and reason, pre- and post-Enlightenment, desire and the overcoming of desire.

We may wish to reflect upon desire and the question of secret. In an interview with Maurizio Ferraris conducted during the 1990s, Derrida confesses his taste for the secret. However, one should not be quick to confuse this 'taste' with a desire for a deeper, revealed truth, since for Derrida the construal of truth in terms of revelation remains a determining feature of the metaphysics of presence, and thus of Western philosophy in general. Instead, Derrida's analysis of the structure of the secret may be linked to his thinking of *différance* as the non-signifying, non-present remainder which traverses each mark, every system, every relation or entity, and which thus founds the metaphysical tradition in its very deconstructibility. In *The Gift of Death*, however, the Platonic and Christian inheritance are to be understood in terms of a series of conversions, incorporations and repressions that not only depart from what they seek to replace or overcome, but which reactivate – albeit in unacknowledged ways – certain aspects of a demonic or orgiastic tradition of the secret. This is another way of thinking the history of European responsibility as one that remains tied to an irreducible secrecy. For Jan Patočka, as Derrida notes, Platonism is to be distinguished from Christianity in that it utterly denounces mystery in its idea both of philosophy and politics. To the extent that Europe inherits such Platonism, its traditions of democracy and freedom are therefore bound to be accompanied by a near totalitarian desire for disclosure and mastery – a desire, however, that Europe wishes in other respects to deny or repress. The relationship of the secret (in both 'deconstructive' and 'metaphysical' senses) to desire is therefore a complex matter for Derridean thought.

The question of desire and the familial similarly provokes further thought. In *Glas* the store Hegel sets by the brother–sister relationship problematizes as much as secures dialectical reason. The spiritual and ethical purity of the sister–brother relation seems guaranteed both by the lack of conjugal desire and by the absence of epic conflict between parent and child, so that in going beyond internecine struggle, this very same relation provides grounds for the 'free' dissolution of family into a wholly felicitous civil life. Thus, the brother–sister bond at once provides an exemplary image of filiation in its full plenitude or synthetic possibility, uninterrupted either by longing or resentment; and yet it also places Antigone outside the possibility of dialectical incorporation according to the dominant logic of filiation (that of the masculine in the conventional fatherly or state form, which Antigone powerfully resists in defying Creon as the embodiment of a state substitute for the father). In other words, Antigone represents at once the condition of possibility and impossibility for the synthesizing universality of Spirit, and thus of the Hegelian system itself. She short-circuits, perhaps, the very desire for non-desire.

Desire, deconstruction and the polis: a whole book on Derrida could be written under this heading, beginning perhaps with 'Plato's Pharmacy'. In *Echographies of Television*, to take just one example, Derrida is reluctant to decide between the cultural exception and the market (a national policy of protectionism will hardly defeat global capital, for instance), preferring instead a less simple negotiation among the always-divided borders that not only separate France from the United States, say, but which also disrupt the supposed self-identity of each territory or concept (whether that of the nation or of the market). In *Echographies* the question of television and tele-technologies is also linked to democratic desire, or to the 'democracy to come' that is not reducible to established concepts of citizenship, territory or state-domination, but which instead senses its opportunity in a more dislocated topolitics, albeit one that can equip itself to address the tormented desire for the 'at home' which, amid the global topolitical 'fragments' of today, gives rise to resurgent nationalisms and fundamentalisms of all sorts.

Desire, philosophy, institution – what could be said of this? During the 1970s and 1980s, Derrida defended philosophy against government plans to limit its role within French national education. While he did not frame his intervention in terms of an unquestioning defence of philosophy in its canonical form, Derrida's objection to the attacks upon it was articulated in terms of a desire to question and resist 'a certain unformulated philosophy' which, in fact, spurred government policy (in other words, the 'desires' of the state-machine) from the beginning. For Derrida, there is in this sense no space outside of or free from 'philosophy', but only a certain countering of one philosophy with another (or, better still, a countering of 'philosophy' with the other-of-itself). It is this complex play of desire that shapes a deconstructive approach to institutions. Derrida is not so naïve as to suppose that any claim, demand or desire to suspend absolutely the various forms of legitimacy, authority, competence or tradition that accompany the established university model might produce satisfactorily effective results. On the contrary, he suspects such a purist brand of radicalism may actually buy into (i.e. 'desire') several of the metaphysical assumptions which underpin the inherited order; and thus, through its own naïveté, that such an approach might allow for a surreptitious and thus all the more powerful reinscription of the dominant field. In 'The Principle of Reason', then, Derrida addresses colleagues at Cornell as the occasion to think about the topolitical scenography of the institution as one that is caught – in the aporia of its founding and justification – between the barrier and abyss, between an impossible desire for autonomy and self-protection on the university's part and an uncloseable exposure to what is abyssal in its very grounds. For Derrida, the classical desire of philosophy to attain a meta-institutional or extra-territorial standpoint, to become pure thought thinking itself, is continually confounded by the fact that philosophy remains an indispensable part of the institutional body it institutes. Philosophy cannot hope to transcend the field that it itself partitions. Neither, however, can it wholly belong to the university of which it is inextricably a part, as one discipline among others. Since the university could not have been founded without it, philosophy is never just found on the university's 'inside' as an entirely interior element participating in and contributing straightforwardly to the 'whole', the *universitas*. If the part thus remains larger than the whole of which it is a part, Derrida's analysis calls us to dwell on the question of philosophy's *desire* as itself an irreducible part of this story of institutional deconstructibility.

Desire, 'truth', representation, art, together form another cluster, perhaps. While, in 'Restitutions', Derrida is keenly aware of the political stakes involved in Schapiro's critique of Heidegger's interpretation of Van Gogh's painting of shoes, he nevertheless detects in this dispute between the two not only an oppositional struggle, but a certain correspondence and, indeed, a common interest or desire. As one of the voices in Derrida's polylogue suggests, the disputed question of attribution thinly veils a desire for appropriation on the part of both these noted intellectuals. By investing in the act of attributing the painting 'properly', a certain return is doubtless to be had. Truth is therefore restituted as much to the critic as to the painter or the painting itself. Yet Derrida's point is not merely that Schapiro and Heidegger are somehow disingenuous or egotistical in falling upon these shoes only to assert their own academic credentials. More than this, attribution and restitution are seen to occur only via a series of detours or slippages, by way of mediating interventions and investments of energy, which trouble the very idea of intact return, unstinting reparation and indeed undisputed property. Yet upon such an idea of absolute restitution, it would appear, rests the truth in painting – of either the 'city' or the 'fields', the industrial or rural world – that both Heidegger and Schapiro fervently wish to restitute.

Psychoanalysis itself and desire: pages of analysis beckon on this topic, insofar as Derrida's writings are concerned. To limit ourselves to just one example: in *Archive Fever*, psychoanalysis emerges as a thinking of the archive which struggles to detach itself securely from the desired object of its thought – which is to say, the object of its desire. (Psychoanalysis, then, is irreducibly both archivo-analysis and archive fever.) In one respect, psychoanalysis's desires cannot be read outside of the psychoanalytic interpretation of desire – although equally, the always *supplementary* force of desire means that the analysis of psychoanalytic desire cannot remain confined within the framework of a neat parallel between pyschoanalysis's desires, on the one hand, and the psychoanalytic conception of desire, on the other. (Derrida's *Resistances* suggests just this kind of thinking.) Instead, the analysis – like the desire it wishes to analyse – must itself belong to a more 'obscure economy' (to borrow Derrida's phrase from *Writing and Difference*).

We could continue this parlour game more or less endlessly, asking how these various readings provoke other questions: of autoimmunity and desire, countersignature and desire, language and desire, 'self' and desire, the 'who' and the 'what' of desire, sex, sexuality and desire, gender and desire, politics and desire, film and desire, time and desire, science and desire, animals and desire, and so on. We might also ask, how does 'deconstructive' desire, Derridean desire or Derrida's desire (these are non-identical propositions, of course, hence always already 'other') suggest differences in relation to the 'desire' of others? (Freud, Lacan, Deleuze ... the list is a long one.) How would one go about making such comparisons? On the basis of the 'constative', i.e. by describing the various differences, which help to define a number of conceptions of desire, or which operate at the level of their theoretical or propositional grounds? Or, on the basis of the 'performative', i.e. by looking at what theorists 'do' with desire, or *how* they desire, as much as what they 'say' about it (and asking why)? (The latter would of course redouble the question of desire, indeed triangulate it within a complex force-field of writing and reading permitting no simple position of neutrality or exemption.) Or, would one 'compare' on the basis of a more 'obscure economy' than either of these possibilities – i.e. the constative or the performative – would imply?

We could continue this game of thinking desire within a variety of Derridean contexts without obvious horizon, but we will not. What we are more interested in is interrogating the very possibility of thinking desire through deconstruction as well as the dynamics between deconstruction and desire. If Derrida's work in texts such as *Archive Fever* and *Resistances* suggests that psychoanalysis's own 'desires', for instance, cannot be comprehended simply by recourse to psychoanalytic conceptions of desire, precisely because desire is always also the supplementing force of any conceptual framework or field, how should we understand deconstructive desire 'itself'? What might deconstruction mean by 'desire' (if desire can be made to 'mean' anything, in any simple sense)? What does deconstruction itself 'desire' (if 'it' desires anything, any 'object', in any simple sense)? And what connects these two – non-simple – questions? (Exactly which 'desire' forces them together, for instance?)

Amid the divided traits or complex folds and interlacings that tie and untie these questions, what do we discover about desire 'itself', and what are the limits of any such 'knowledge' that we might hope to produce? And what, once again, do we learn about the continuing legacy of deconstruction, if the complicated question of its 'desires' goes right to the heart of the inheritance it bequeaths? For instance, what does the litany produced by our parlour game express about the desires of deconstruction? We suggested a little while ago that desire is one among an extended chain of non-synonymous substitutions; desire may however be closer to the conditions of such a chain than a link in it. Grappling with deconstruction's desires therefore means not merely giving an account of the many rich and thought-provoking ways in which deconstruction ponders desire, but also to face what desire means for it methodologically.

In a multiple sense, then, the question of desire repeatedly *opens* deconstruction. The volume begins with a series of essays that, while they seem to take stock of the deconstructive legacy, in fact trace its openness – an openness that persists precisely where many have felt it possible to insist on deconstruction's now-permanent closure in the face of contemporary theoretical and political challenges and possibilities. Essays in this section of the volume explore the ongoing resources that may reanimate deconstruction's significance for us today, or at any rate remind us of the lessons it may still be able to teach.

Going straight to the issue that is perhaps most contentious for the modern memory of deconstruction, Gil Anidjar poses the question of the Holocaust insofar as it continues to trouble the legacy of the Derridean corpus. Throughout Derrida's writings, Anidjar detects a profound resistance to mere oratory, received piety or ready answers where the Holocaust is concerned; or, in other words, an abiding distaste for political grandstanding, or for indulging in the simple saying of that which goes without saying, in all good conscience. Attending at length to the complexities of Derrida's texts, Anidjar contends that, unlike some of his intellectual peers from the twentieth century, Derrida refrained from writing a direct or explicit full-length analysis of the Holocaust, often choosing instead to make explicit the rules and protocols of the 'discourse' of the Holocaust, as it has arisen from different – although not totally distinct or separate – political standpoints. In the process, Derrida sought to teach us how *not* to speak of the Holocaust about which we are nevertheless bound to speak, as well as attuning us to the complex political entanglements that ensue from the discursive (although far from just discursive) choices with which we are presented. Anidjar writes: 'It is imperative to recall … that Derrida almost always discussed the Holocaust indirectly, without naming it, or alternatively by using the uncapitalized word *holocaust.*' In the act of dispensing with capitalization, it is as if Derrida hesitates before granting the Holocaust special status in relation to other terrible conflicts, unforgivable crimes or horrific events on the world stage, not at all to downplay its undoubtedly massive significance but instead to put in question the very discourse and rhetoric underlying such exceptionalizaton in the first place, and asking us to think harder about how this may work, and for whom. If, as Geoffrey Hartmann put it, Derrida played with fire in his refusal to adopt readily acceptable or easily recuperable positions in relation to such matters, Anidjar does not simply shield himself or us from the flames. He shows not only the ways in which Derrida mined the linguistic – although far from just linguistic – resources of the term, bringing out its sometimes troubling complexities; but also, as Anidjar himself contends, how Derrida offered his own 'peculiar insistence on – and paradoxical resistance to – the autobiographical' as both 'a site and cipher of reflections on Nazism, anti-Semitism, and the Holocaust'. But where does this leave us? As Anidjar observes, the question of the Holocaust troubles deeply our capacity for decision in the sense that it impedes the ability 'to extricate ourselves by way of our conscience or consciousness'. As Derrida himself noted, the entire matter would become far less 'grievous' if it were possible to simply state what is meant by 'Auschwitz', but the problem is that such a 'referent' is precisely what remains in question here, not at all as a prop or prompt for Holocaust denial but on the contrary as an expression of the (impossible) desire to do justice to the Holocaust itself – of which it may not be possible or even desirable to say that it is a 'thing' in itself. Finally, it is not that Derrida is incapable of distinguishing between Nazis and non-Nazis, on the contrary; but only that the unresolved problem of 'Nazism', which is far from simply 'proper' to Nazism, affects not just the discourse or desires of a subject – Derrida, for instance, or any other, for that matter – but constitutes an unresolved legacy which abides as a powerful, if still inadequately acknowledged, provocation to the 'political' today.

The question of the Holocaust also forms a cue of sorts for the next essay in this collection. Amid the newfound dominance in the theoretical field of positions associated with Marxism, new materialism and approaches which express a mathematical or neurobiological preference (rather than favouring language as founding thought), Simon Morgan Wortham examines the ways in which an 'ethics-of-the-other' position broadly associated with deconstructive or post-structuralist analysis is seen to impede emancipatory possibility in the sphere of politics. According to Morgan Wortham, this ethical standpoint is, thereby, often depicted as 'regressive, bound by the repetition of trauma, and given to a sense of redemptive entitlement', notably in regard to the worst horrors of the twentieth century. Here, as he notes, a certain irony surrounds recent suggestions concerning the deeply pro-Jewish sentiments of deconstruction, when up until recently Derrida was regularly castigated by Zionist lobbyists and other pro-Israeli factions for the critical (although far from oppositional) positions he consistently took on the question of Israel, and behind this the complicated inquiry into the question of the Abrahamic religions which he unstintingly pursued. Morgan Wortham broadens the reading of contemporary theoretical disputes to look at ways in which, in the writings of Jacques Rancière, such a critique of an 'ethics-of-the-other' position as ultimately politically conservative is targeted on the work of Jean-François Lyotard. One reason why Lyotard becomes especially interesting, here, is that in Derrida's mourning text for Lyotard, far from lapsing into the melancholic demeanour of which he is now frequently accused, he in fact dwells on a particular phrase from a short essay by Lyotard included in a collection of texts devoted to Derrida's own work: 'There shall be no mourning'. Reading this phrase, not least in terms of the politics of mourning, Derrida takes the opportunity to think of a certain mourning against mourning: that is, a mourning which actually resists the effects Rancière would wish to impute to a certain 'ethical' mournfulness. Since Rancière makes repeated mention of a short text by Lyotard from the early 1990s, written for Amnesty International, Morgan Wortham undertakes a close reading of this particular lecture, not only to demonstrate that Rancière's take on Lyotard comes down to mere caricature, but to suggest that in performative terms Rancière's discourse – rather than going in the direction of simple or radical equality – may actually repeat the 'differend' of the interlocutionary model that Lyotard detects at the fragile origins of civil life and possibility. The essay closes by examining some of the post-war writings of Emmanuel Levinas, particularly those on Léon Brunschvicg, in order to demonstrate that, when one reads such texts, composed so close to the end of the Second World War, what one finds is the expression of ideas, values and ways of thinking that far from comply with Rancière's depiction of a retrogressive, mournful 'ethics-of-the-other' standpoint. Levinas, often taken as the 'Ur-text' of such an ethics (not to mention, a key source for Lyotard) here writes in ways which therefore very much problematize contemporary critiques.

Staying with the question of the legacy of deconstruction, what of deconstruction's elevation, or reduction, to an 'ism' – 'deconstructionism' – during a certain period of its life in the Anglo-American academy? When Anglo-American academics begin thinking in terms of 'isms', argues Herman Rapaport, they immediately imagine that a body of thought is some sort of social actor that has agency in the public sphere. The model that gives credence to such assumptions is, he suggests, drawn from political philosophy in which 'isms' such as fascism and communism are perceived as doctrines, predicated on philosophical beliefs of various sorts that are inherently political in the sense that in order to realize such doctrines one has to transform the social and political environment. One cannot have a communist or fascist utopia without a thoroughgoing revolution that radically transforms the order of things. Or, to take a more twenty-first century 'ism', environmentalism, one cannot realize an ecological agenda for combating climate change without a politics of legislating serious transformations in how we live and work. In that sense, for Rapaport, 'isms' want something of us; they are desiring (whether attractively or worryingly so). Or, rather, they make demands of us that, for many people, are going to be unacceptable. Rapaport makes the following claims. During the 1970s, when 'deconstruction' was being reified as yet another 'ism', intellectuals on the right, as well as some on the left, immediately began identifying it with a broadly political agenda that was most often characterized in terms of nihilism. This idea of deconstruction's nihilistic tendencies is itself instructive, for if an 'ism' implies a demand or desire, deconstruction's own reluctance to subscribe to various 'isms' (Marxism, for instance), or to form a school or formalize a doctrine, meant that if it were to be attributed a (worrisome) desire or demand – an 'ism-ism', if you like – this had to be configured in largely negative terms. Rapaport traces Derrida's complex attitude to 'isms', which is on the one hand obviously resistant, and on the other unusually complex. For, as he writes, 'Derrida was certainly opposed to the reactionary belief that in essence "isms" are necessarily to be seen as bad political actors engaging in civil and cultural subversion, if only because "deconstructionism" was vilified in the press on precisely such assumptions'. But by understanding that different bodies of thought are far from 'self-organizing in a way that rationalizes antagonism in terms of clearly delineated pitched battles among opposing forces', as Rapaport puts it, Derrida proved highly receptive to the analysis of complicated force-fields – politico-institutional, socio-historical, libidinal, and so on – that determine and over-determine the interplay of 'isms' in a number of ways. If the 'ism' is anything, then, it is a feature of a field of plural forces in which 'theoretical jetties' rather than stable, self-identical 'positions' or 'perspectives' come to the fore. As Rapaport notes, 'this jetty is a leap (*jété*), it is necessarily a pushing out ahead, as well as a projection. Indeed, to project in this way is akin to a drive', which must be analysed as such. Yet it is also, of course, the name for a construction or fortification that, in Rapaport's words, 'only partially organizes a turbulent environment'. If the 'ism' relates to deconstruction in a more complicated way than is usually appreciated, in part this has to do with the complex thinking of 'isms' as inherently dynamic and unstable opened up by deconstruction itself. Rapaport ends by tracing out the (loving) transferential relations that structure this dynamic instability, notably in the theoretical field of which Derrida was a part.

Questions of desire and ashes, of love and of the remains, are brought together in Elissa Marder's essay. In Derrida's *The Post Card*, she argues, reading burns letters in the way that a flame divides into manifold tongues as it consumes the body of what it touches. This erotic and destructive inflammatory encounter inaugurates the event of reading. Reading, Derrida suggests throughout his text, only happens when letters are set on fire; moreover, the *Envois* are love letters because they burn. Meanwhile, fire, flames, tinder, embers, cinders and ashes link the work on mourning (on the crypt and the incalculable remainder) in *Glas* and *Fors* to the pyrotechnic erotic encounter between philosophy and psychoanalysis in the *Post Card* and announce the later writings on translation, poetry and the secret. In French, as Marder shows, Derrida's text already anticipates (and even calls for) the effects of the translation to come. Whenever he invokes the idiom 'tongue of fire' ('*langue de feu*') he is always already writing about how translation teases out what is untranslatable within the body of language by exposing it to the fire of translation. Like all forms of reading, translation burns the body of the text it touches. This is why, whenever Derrida writes about the relation between translation and the untranslatable, he invokes fire and tongues of flame. In 'What is a "Relevant" Translation,' he describes how translation consumes and consummates the unique body of the other in the caress of a burning tongue. If fire is a figure for both reading and translation, it is because the 'tongue of fire' alights on the untranslatable matter in every language (the idiomatic singularity of the word) that renders all languages foreign to themselves. This is another way of saying that for Derrida translation is not primarily a relation between languages, but rather something that happens in language, and to all languages. Translation touches the secret heart of that which in language does not belong to it: its internal other, its non-mattering matter. Translation exposes the material matter of language to the process of signification and, in so doing, destroys it. For Marder, then, burning (in passion and in immolation) is what happens to untranslatable matter in any encounter with the other. Writing harbors secrets in the body of language; it gives a space to literature and a chance for the relation to the wholly other that we call love.

Lynn Turner's chapter 'Fort Spa: In at the Deep End with Derrida and Ferenczi' also turns to questions of the body, albeit not the body of language, but the role of the body in Derrida's reading of psychoanalysis. Turner begins her analysis by suggesting that Szandor Ferenczi's *Thalassa* is a dangerous supplement to the psychoanalytic genealogy Freud wished to establish, not merely because of the significant overlap with Freud's 'Beyond the Pleasure Principle', but also because of the importance Ferenczi gave to the biological. Following Elizabeth A. Wilson's reading of *Thalassa* in 'Gut Feminism', Turner concentrates on Ferenczi's focus not on female sexuality but on the fallibility of the phallus itself, in particular his understanding of male sexuality in terms of amphimixis, namely that the so-called phallic phase remains indebted to a form of group work with other organs. For Wilson, this departure from both a strictly ordered *and* utilitarian biology and a psychic organization of the soma allows for a dynamic understanding of the body, namely Ferenczi's 'biological unconscious'. Thus the body is not merely the writing pad for the psyche but is amenable to 'bioanalysis'. Turner shows therefore that in 'Gut Feminism' and in her book *Psychosomatic,* in which Freud's 'nerves-penis-cortex-psyche' is portrayed as not necessarily self-contained, Wilson draws more or less explicitly on Derrida's notion of différance to give an account of the bioanalytic body. Reading back through 'Freud and the Scene of Writing', Turner finds uncanny hospitality to this notion of bioanalysis through what Derrida there names 'a new psychoanalytic graphology' in brief reference to the work of Melanie Klein. This notion of a psychoanalytic graphology is, Turner suggests by way of concluding, relevant to the project of bioanalysis in as much as it breaches the body and shows how it is already subjected to the trace. It further contributes to the work of deconstruction as the radicalisation of the traffic between insides and outsides, ingestion, identification and sexuality.

In 'The Obverse Side of Jacques Derrida's "Freud and the Scene of Writing"' Céline Surprenant stays with the question of Derrida's account of the body and/ in psychoanalysis by examining Derrida's complex stance towards the neuro-sciences. The vivid and avid nature of Derrida's engagement with psychoanalysis – which spanned more than forty years and through which he refined his notions of, for example, the trace, the inscription and the archive – should not belie the fact that his readings of Freud were also the occasion for the re-examination and confrontation of the psychoanalytic corpus. Yet, Surprenant argues, Catherine Malabou, in formulating her notion of plasticity and in moving towards a neuropsychoanalysis, puts Freud's and Derrida's understanding of trace on a par. Derrida's apparent initial rejection of the neurosciences is founded, Surprenant argues, on the belief in the existence of a Freudian psyche, which is also a condition for his interest in metaphor in Freud. However, by turning to 'Freud and the Scene of Writing' Surprenant shows that metaphor is not only an instrument and technique of representation, but that, not merely illustrating what is known but also exploring what is unknown, it is also a commentary on its own spacing metaphoricity, its capability to open a representational relation between the psyche and its technical models. Moving to Freud's *Project for a Scientific Psychology, Beyond the Pleasure Principle* and *The Interpretation of*

Dreams, Surprenant asks whether Freudian metaphors of the trace, breach or path may thus be understood as the forerunners for Derrida's concept of the trace. In this sense, the terms Freud borrows from neurology to talk about the 'hypothesis of the contact-barriers' are central to Derrida's understanding of metaphoricity. Indeed, it is from these metaphors of the psyche, Surprenant maintains, that the language of deconstruction, with its traces, différances, archives, supplements and so on, emerges. Even the writing machine in the 'Mystic Writing Pad' is not merely a metaphor for trace, but also metaphorizes its own metaphoricity, the process of its representation. This abstract shift of Derrida's is important, Surprenant maintains, because the metaphor of writing and its deconstruction through Malabou and others is at least partly aimed at toppling the dominance of the linguistic in the human sciences. It is also important because, given that Derrida's early encounters with Freud were about the relation between the psyche and technology, the emphasis on metaphor is Derrida's way of addressing questions central to the neurosciences during the 1960s, namely the relation between the brain and the techniques used to find out about the brain. For Surprenant, then, although seemingly detached from or even opposed to the neurosciences, 'Freud and the Scene of Writing' sends us right back to them.

The last two pieces in this collection turn to questions of deconstruction, desire and survival. In 'The Desire for Survival?' Kas Saghafi gives a critical account of Martin Hägglund's *Radical Atheism*, in particular his notions of desire, finitude, immortality and survival, in order to critically examine his reading of Derrida's work. At the heart of Hägglund's project lies the desire to save Derrida's from those who argue for an ethical or religious turn in his thinking. In contrast to this reading of Derrida, which, as Saghafi notes, has never been endorsed by Derrida himself, what is desirable for Hägglund is not the immortality of the soul; quite on the contrary: immortality or infinity cannot be the subject of a deconstructive desire because everything that can be desired must be mortal in its essence. Hägglund's reading of Derrida is, Saghafi suggests, based on a misunderstanding of the workings of the concepts of desire, finitude and infinity in his oeuvre. As Saghafi argues, in Derrida's early works, such as *De la grammalotogie* and *Mal d'archive,* but also in *Psyché* or *Sauf le nom,* desire is always other. Since desire is thus more complicated than Hägglund allows for its relation to finitude must also be re-examined. Drawing on Derrida's usage of finitude in a variety of texts from 'Freud and the Scene of Writing' to *Le Toucher,* Saghafi contends that putting too much emphasis on finitude in Hägglund's manner does not work because Derrida's notion of différance, as Rodolphe Gasché has already suggested, is already a critique of finitude. Derrida thinks about finitude, like desire, as other: Derrida's thinking of finitude is, whether radical or temporal as Hägglund suggests, a thinking together of the finite and the infinite. For Saghafi, Hägglund is in fact so preoccupied with arguing against whom he believes to be conservative religious readers of Derrida that he conflates Derrida's account of immortality and eternity with the history of Western thought rather than acknowledging that his work resists this. Moving to Derrida's discussion of immortality as death in *Demeure,* as emerges in particular from his analysis of Blanchot's peculiar phrase 'dead-immortal' in *L'instant de ma mort,* Saghafi shows that Derrida does not subscribe to the clear distinction between immortality and mortality and finitude and infinitude that pervades the Western tradition. For Derrida, then, *demeurance* or abidance does not remain infinitely but is, like time itself, the time of an interminable interval. For Derrida *demeurance* is in other words not timelessness but an awaiting, a waiting for, a withstanding, an enduring, a bearing patiently. Similarly, as Saghafi shows through an in-depth discussion of Blanchot, his understanding of survival expresses an ambiguous relation between life and death. In this sense, survival does not mean having an afterlife but is already achieved in life: life, which is life-death, is already a survival. Returning to Derrida, Saghafi maintains that his notion of survivance (which is fleshed out through reference to *L'écriture et la différence,* 'Circonfession' and *Schibboleth* amongst others) like Blanchot's 'dead-immortal' fundamentally questions the distinction between mortality and immortality. Saghafi thus maintains that in Derrida surviving indicates that living is always more than one (*sur-vivance*) and always haunted by the oscillations of life-death.

In this book's last chapter Chiara Alfano too turns to questions about deconstruction and survival. In 'The King is Dead! Long Live the King!' Alfano asks how deconstruction should survive Derrida's death in the context of Ernst Kantorowicz's famous notion of the king's two bodies. Through a close study of Kantorowicz's principle – in which the body politic, kingship itself, survives the body natural, a particular king's mortal body – Alfano argues that the effects of corporation and incorporation that follow from such mental acrobatics of the medieval mind are first and foremost in service not of one particular royal lineage, but of the very idea of sovereignty itself. Moving on to the Tenth and Eleventh sessions of *The Beast & the Sovereign,* which contain a discussion of the 1681 anatomical dissection of an elephant at Versailles under the watchful eye of Louis le Grand, Alfano argues that this elephantine anatomy lesson not merely represents a strangely disembodied representation of the king's two bodies, but that in doing so it also dissects or analyses the violence inherent in any exertion of power, sovereignty or mastery. Drawing parallels between the dissection described in *The Beast & the Sovereign* and Derrida's reading in *The Work of Mourning* of Sarah Kofman's interpretation of Rembrandt's *The Anatomy Lesson of Doctor Nicolaes Tulp* (1623), which Derrida mentions only in passing in *The Beast & the Sovereign*, Alfano maintains that what is dissected in all these tableaux is first and foremost the sovereignty of knowledge, which, as Kofman brilliantly shows, depends on its violent severing from the body. Turning to Derrida's pieces on Kofman and Barthes in *The Work of Mourning*, a collection of texts written in the aftermath of the deaths of fourteen philosophers, Alfano argues for the pertinence of Kantorowicz's notion for our thinking about the relationship between a philosopher's mortal body (body natural) and her thought (body philosophic). She in fact suggests that what underlies work on a philosopher is often not the desire for the survival of one philosophical line but a desire for appropriation of the corpus of the philosopher in service of one's own mastery and sovereignty within the corporation in the business of 'keeping alive' this philosopher's thought. This is, Alfano writes, also true of deconstruction today. Taking a hint from Derrida's intriguing claim that only reader-thinker poets may keep his thought alive beyond what is deposited in libraries, Alfano invites the reader to move the understanding of a philosopher's legacy away from the idea of an archival corpus to an idea of a philosopher's corpus as her idiom. Through an engagement with Paul's Celan's reading of Büchner's *Danton's Death* in his 'The Meridian' Alfano shows what such a shift would entail. Here, Lucile's interrupting 'Long live the king!' is the poematic idiom or signature which cuts through the sovereignty of knowledge, as we know it, albeit in a different way than Derrida might have imagined in his reading of 'The Meridian' in *The Beast & the Sovereign*.

What this volume does, then, is to open up afresh the question of deconstruction's legacy (whether from the perspective of Derrida's advocates or his detractors), re-examining both the interconnections and distinctions that supposedly characterize deconstruction in relation to other types or fields of thought, while putting to the test its continuing reception today. In each of these instances, desire offers itself not just as a thematic prism to guide analysis, but instead contributes to the very conditions of possibility for just such critical re-elaboration. Desire is not, therefore, the topic of this book so much as it is a way of re-describing the performative grounds of deconstructive reflection as not merely self-reflection but – according to a multiply charged grammaticality – a thinking of the other. Such a thinking would be not so much transformative of, or for, deconstruction, as it would affirm the dynamic and unpredictable transformations already at work where deconstruction is concerned.

1

Ashes to Ashes: Derrida's Holocaust

Gil Anidjar

For the man returned to earth (catastrophized), such 'unfaithfulness' is the height of 'piety'.

— Philippe Lacoue-Labarthe[1]

Is ash the Good or the Evil of flame?

— Jacques Derrida[2]

Sometime around 1989, Jacques Derrida must have agreed to give the opening lecture at the UCLA conference entitled 'Nazism and the "Final Solution": Probing the Limits of Representation'. Derrida must have agreed since, on 26 April 1990, in front of an undoubtedly sizable audience, he delivered that lecture, a demanding reading of Walter Benjamin's 'Critique of Violence' that has since become one of Derrida's most influential and most generative texts.[3] The academic equivalent of a star-studded event, in Los Angeles no less, the conference was explicitly and centrally organized as a defensive call to arms against those who question – or used to question – the historical profession's strenuous policing of Holocaust testimony, evidence and representation (what the organizer Saul Friedländer describes as 'the imprecise, but no less self-evident notion that this record should not be distorted or banalized by grossly inadequate representations').[4] The conference unfairly singled out Hayden White, himself a historian, as representative of the risks – and negationist, even fascistic, inclinations, however unwitting – courted by 'postmodernist' claims. White consented to participate in the conference and he was duly included, along with numerous detractors, in the published proceedings. But Derrida was not. Otherwise fleetingly mentioned in a bibliographic footnote or two (one of which is by White himself), Derrida is missing from the archive and the historical record. By a strange distortion, a trouble of the archive, his intervention did not register. He was simply and inexplicably left out of the book.[5] No doubt a minor or marginal event, perhaps the result of a mechanical or typographical accident, a non-event, as it were, or better yet, a *machine-event*, this vanished or erased lecture turned major intellectual milestone seems an oddly fitting bequest for the one-time figure of 'Jewish mysticism' (as Jürgen Habermas charged)[6] who inspired, among other things, the 'deconstructive architecture' of Holocaust memorialization, while becoming, for others, something of a Nazi by associ-ation, a fellow traveller, at the very least a significant promoter of 'the blurring of distinction between victims and perpetrators'.[7]

La répétition nazie[8]

Doubtless this was the first desired holocaust (as one says a desired child, a desired girl).

— Jacques Derrida, *The Post Card*[9]

This is the stuff from which headlines – not fairy tales – are made. Yet, 'at the juncture where the unconscious meets history',[10] the two share more than might otherwise be acknowledged: good and evil, for example, the individual and the collective, but also the spectre and management of fear, ambiguous and unambiguous identifications (victim and perpetrator, judge and accused, human and inhuman), the incessant and mechanical repetition of certain motifs (innocence and guilt, memory and forgetting, knowledge and ignorance, atonement and forgiveness), emotional twists and turns that are at once expected and surprising, a primal struggle, a hero's downfall, and, if there is a difference, the rise and returns of seemingly forgotten villains. 'A cultural giant of epic proportions in the 1970s and 1980s, Paul de Man no longer seems to exist', recently wrote Evelyn Barish, herself about to make the headlines, as she embarks on a biographical narrative of discovery into (and resurrection of) that uncertain existence, plumbing 'the double life of Paul de Man' and the depths of one man's multifarious associations with nefariousness itself, with radical evil.[11] Double life indeed, another unreadable allegory of the polarities that, we will see, solicit and unsettle – that should solicit and unsettle – any reception history of deconstruction, any reading of Derrida's Holocaust.[12]

Not that the headlines – or Western governments, whose past and present immigration quotas and policies, judgment mantles and carceral regimes, weapon development programmes or assassination practices might not bear scrutiny (think 'nuclear holocaust') – would let anyone forget. As Naomi Mandel astutely points out, 'claiming history as Holocaust is an identity game. Who gets to call whom a "Nazi"? Who can play the far more popular role of "Jew"? Who gets to participate in a collective psyche that represses the Holocaust or is traumatized by it? Whose history is so horrific that it is, like the Holocaust, unspeakable?'[13] The state of emergency in which we live is garrulous, and it teaches us that evil – itself less unspeakable than it might seem – has many faces (or axes), in truth, many lives. At the same time, the names evil bears appear to have drastically narrowed (Hitler), its referent solidified (Nazism), its crime pointedly identified (genocide), its symbols and colours fused into one, or two (*feldgrau*, grey–green; red and black). All this testifies again and again to the laws of iterability, the necessary possibility of citation, of repetition.[14] De Man and Heidegger aside, we scholars may therefore have been reminded of *the evil of banality* by other means, and by additional headlines. Under the expanded rule of Godwin's law, at any rate, from Saddam Hussein to Slobodan Milošević (and back), to Mahmoud Ahmadinejad and, more recently, Vladimir Putin (I mention only a few among them), 'never again' increasingly seems to spell 'eternal recurrence'.[15]

Considered from a different angle and the more explicit perspective of popular culture (or current fairy tales), the paradoxes and contradictions that solidly bind good and evil, 'complicity, collaboration, and guilt', uniqueness – that is, presumably, chosenness and election – and repetition may be too numerous and widespread (and too 'controversial' too) to recall.[16] It will by no means suffice, for instance, to signal that, before the making of that other movie in which 'the Nazi vs. Jew dichotomy will dissolve in the course of the film',[17] Steven Spielberg's 1981 global blockbuster, *Raiders of the Lost Ark*, uncannily stages the strange and potent association whereby the master race appears as a *substitute* for the chosen people, the power of the latter as the real – and divine – object of the former's desire (for a variation on the theme, consider the *X-Men*'s Magneto and his casually inflected rise – and genocidal inclinations – from the ashes of the Holocaust).

In the following pages, I wish to reckon with (some of) the headlines and attend to Derrida's Holocaust. A challenge in its own right in the expected attention to established binaries or the suspension of judgment and good conscience, it will appear as a largely untreaded path, an unexpected entryway toward such disconcerting associations, toward the 'double life' and the lingering disturbances, the unsettling traces and eerie resonances, the impossible lessons of (collaborations with, and resistances to) Nazism and its crimes. As we saw at the outset, under the cover of permanent education or the promise of lessons learned (what Lauren Berlant calls 'sentimental pedagogy'),[18] scholarly and public discourse confronts us with splits and divisions, and with *the banalization of the exception*, maintaining and enacting both at the same time. As if caught in 'what remains of the still too pious, too respectfully nihilist',[19] beyond the disagreements of intentionalists and functionalists,[20] we find ourselves in a broad but uncertain topography, which spans and cuts across 'the Americanization of the Holocaust', its European transformations or its Middle Eastern entanglements.[21] We seem at any rate torn between endlessly reiterated incommensurabilities and equally incessant identifications ('another Hitler'), between an expanding historical universe and universal (from Holocaust to genocide to extermination, from the singularity of Jewish suffering to an ancient and somehow habitual practice of the human race) and back again, to a general and ubiquitous insistence on the Holocaust's exceptional uniqueness.[22]

Not so long ago, it was Jean-François Lyotard's contention that

> the destruction of Nazism also leaves a silence after it: one does not dare think out Nazism because it has been beaten down like a mad dog, by a police action, and not in conformity with the rules accepted by its adversaries' genres of discourse (argumentation for liberalism, contradiction for Marxism). It has not been refuted.[23]

Lyotard added that this and other silences 'interrupt the chain that goes from them, the deported, and from them, the SS, to we who speak about them'.[24] It may very well be that a definite discursive proliferation, which the headlines (together with Hollywood and other memory machines, along with ISIs and unabated scholarly production) echo and amplify, have begun to restore some of the links in that generic chain, albeit not necessarily those Lyotard envisioned.[25] Are we finally 'thinking out' Nazism? Refuting it? The newly sedimented conflation of Nazism and communism has definitely troubled, it seems to me, Lyotard's easy characterization of Marxism among Nazism's 'adversaries'.[26] In Timothy Snyder's *Bloodlands*, for example, Stalin is as bad, i.e. as massively murderous, as Hitler, and 'totalitarianism' (a regime of terror, and a terrorist regime) is the name of radical evil.[27] A recent *New Yorker* article accordingly conjures the ghost of controversies past: it ups the ante and joins Spielberg (and Arendt?) in volunteering the figure of that other impossible alliance, asserting that 'even without particular regard to *Jews and Nazis*, Heidegger's brilliance was intrinsically political'.[28] Refutation may or may not be forthcoming, in other words, but I intend to show that, with regard to 'Jews and Nazis' as well, there might be reason 'to expect to find in Derrida's writings some innovative approach, some new insight into the Holocaust'.[29]

Let me make clear at the outset that I do not think, as Richard Wolin does, that 'what is especially troubling' about Derrida is 'that the "foundational" deconstructive gesture of overturning and reinscription ends up by threatening to efface many of the essential differences between Nazism and non-Nazism'.[30] As I just mentioned, the category of 'totalitarianism' (among other things) has already achieved a crucial version of that erasure. But Derrida does resist 'isolating the topic of the Holocaust'.[31] He insists instead on 'the general complicity of Europe with the Nazis ... All this concerns European culture as a whole ... European thought as a whole'.[32] Derrida compels us to reflect upon other ubiquitous and covert, general and exceptional, if troubling and seemingly avoidable, binaries that, in and around him, in and around us, *separate and bind* Nazism and Holocaust, victim and perpetrator, exception and banality, and the chain described by Lyotard as yoking 'the deported ... the SS ... and we who speak about them'. In a way that he himself will deem 'terrifying', Derrida forces us to confront contamination and complicity where we fear and reject it most: among the 'adversaries' of Nazism identified by Lyotard (Marxism *and* liberalism). After a manner that could have been obvious from the earliest essays and interviews, Derrida dares 'to show the complicity of the two sides', or the three – and counting.[33]

To begin with, one might return to the UCLA conference and reflect further on the massively contradictory reception of 'deconstruction', which features prominently in the once popular, and still enduring, constellation of ethical commitments of post-Holocaust philosophy from Arendt and Adorno to Levinas and Lyotard, with Derrida as another example of searching reflections on Judaism and Jewishness in their relation to the Holocaust.[34] At a different end of that spectrum, however, deconstruction (or more often, 'deconstructionism') has been famously tainted by its 'enabling' role in the spread of Holocaust denial, its dangerous proximity to Nazism and to anti-Semitism (the famous 'affairs': Heidegger, de Man).[35] 'Is it by chance', asks Geoffrey Bennington, 'that this thought of deconstruction is associated with those of Nietzsche and Heidegger, and that it therefore inherits a relationship with Nazism that is to say the least unclear?'[36] Controversies aside, Derrida's ethical stance is simply indisputable. He has been more than vocal and unequivocal in his opposition to Nazism and his condemnations of racism and anti-Semitism. It is equally true, however, that he has also left a number of traces that should give pause to any pious account of his 'positions' as transparently settled on the right side of history (or on the left side of the political spectrum), as well as to any opportunistic judgment banishing him to the pit of misguided politics and worse. Derrida – 'Jewish Derrida', as some might have it – has been a consistent reader of what he himself registered as a certain Jewishness (Jabès, Levinas, Freud, Cohen, Rosenzweig, Celan, Benjamin, Scholem) all the while scrupulously, often simultaneously, reading (others have said: defending) thinkers whom he explicitly, and rightly, acknowledged as compromised by Nazi appropriations, sympathies or worse (Heidegger and de Man, already mentioned, but also Nietzsche and Schmitt). Derrida has surely displayed a constant, and heightened, sensitivity to anti-Semitism; and his 'immense reading of the Holocaust and the metaphysics of race' cannot be ignored under any circumstances.[37] But with no less considerable obstinacy, Derrida has also resisted abiding by current expectations. Derrida is no imaginary Jew.[38] He has, for instance, refused to endorse in any simple way established claims for exceptionality ('No Apocalypse, Not Now'). Granting the uniqueness of the Holocaust as a historical event ('An Interview'), he spectacularly opposed the claims of incommensurability, or fashionable calls for identifications with the victims.[39] 'What some people have seen as a quite perverse refusal on Derrida's part to decide, condemn, pass a judgment without appeal' on radical evil is paralleled by his avowed reluctance to pronounce on forgiveness (*On Cosmopolitanism and Forgiveness*).[40] Derrida has written on testimony, yet his most extensive meditation on the prevalent issue is a reading of Blanchot's Second World War experience, *not* of the Holocaust (*Demeure*). Finally, Derrida has gone quite far in suggesting that not only Marxism but also Nazism's historical adversary (liberal democracy) may have partaken (and partakes still) of much of 'the worst' it so vocally condemns ('Paul de Man's War', *Of Spirit*, 'Force of Law', *Specters of Marx*). More personally, or seemingly so, Derrida has confessed to feeling simultaneously disturbed by his early expulsion from school (under anti-Semitic Vichy laws in colonial Algeria) *and* by the gregarious *repli* of the Jewish community to whom he ambivalently but unapologetically belonged (*Post Card*, 'Circumfession', 'Avowing'). In a gesture that, 'prior to all separation between communitarian separation or discriminating separation',[41] recalls the violence of this early association, Derrida repeatedly insists on 'the correspondence between Meyer Schapiro and Martin Heidegger' ('there is here something like a pairing-together in the difference of opinion, the enigma of a complementary fitting-together of the two sides, of one edge to the other').[42] Later, Derrida will also point to the horizon shared by Husserl and Heidegger with regard to the '"spiritual" determination of European humanity' (*OS*, 120). Husserl would, after all, have excluded 'Eskimoes, Indians, traveling zoos or gypsies permanently wandering all over Europe' (ibid.). At the UCLA conference, Derrida further invoked an equally troubling proximity between Walter Benjamin ('the German Benjamin hunted by the Nazis and repulsed by the Occupation forces') and the National-Socialist programme of extermination ('Force of Law').[43] Explicitly addressing Heidegger's engagement with National-Socialism, Derrida concludes by suggesting that the ashes of 'spirit in flame', as Heidegger deployed it, may have to be thought together with a historiality that ambiguously includes 'the Hebraic *ruah*' (*Of Spirit*). As well, Derrida, who rarely uses the canonized appellation 'Shoah' (or the privileged signifier 'Auschwitz'), quite systematically resists capitalizing the word 'holocaust'. That very word, as we shall see, is deployed through his writings in a variety of contexts, at times recalled to its original Greek sources, as if current usage could (or should) be ignored (*Glas*), at other times shockingly decontextualized. In Derrida's work, 'holocaust' is in fact subjected to iterations that could almost be said to aim at or, more precisely, to tend toward banalization – unless it is the precise opposite ('Schibboleth: For Paul Celan').

Derrida, as a number of his readers (and detractors) have recognized, appears to travel 'so obliquely, so indirectly' on the expected pathways of Holocaust discourse.[44] Everything is as if, always describing two sides or paths (the Jew and the German, for instance), Derrida held fast 'only to what can still say something to us .. about *our* steps, and about a certain crossing of *our* paths. About a *we* which is perhaps not *given*' (*OS*, 107). Derrida thus infringes upon the very limits and divisions of what Karyn Ball has called 'the disciplinary imaginary' of Holocaust discourse.[45] He makes manifest the protocols and rules of this discourse, which Ball probingly identifies, but, displacing and transforming them, Derrida also exposes their vanishing.

The Jew, the German

I am still dreaming of a second holocaust that would not come too late.
— Jacques Derrida[46]

It would be absurd to suggest that this difficult, even impossible, couple – the Jew, the German – which operates on the very surface of Derrida's writing (beginning, no doubt, with 'Violence and Metaphysics' and 'Edmond Jabès and the Question of the Book', both in *Writing and Difference* and all the way to 'Kant, the Jew, the German', *Béliers*, and beyond), could exclusively or exhaustively sustain the burden of an engagement, on Derrida's part, with the

Holocaust and with Nazism, with victim and perpetrator, much less with the substitutability of one term for the other. As Derrida would later go on to cite Paul de Man, elaborating with him on another figure of substitution, 'nothing in the text suggests a concatenation that would allow one to substitute' the Jew, the German, the Holocaust and Nazism, much less, as the *New Yorker* has it, 'Jews and Nazis'.[47] Derrida's reservations with regard to the phrase 'nothing in the text' do, however, apply. For, Derrida asks, 'what does "nothing" mean here? And "nothing in the text"? How can one be sure of "nothing" suggested in a text? Of a "nothing in the text"?'[48] Derrida continues:

> The mere concatenation of places, the sequential juxtaposition of the two accounts is not nothing, if one wanted to psychoanalyze things. The juxtaposition of the two accounts, even if nothing but chronological succession seems to justify it, the mere mechanical association of an 'à-propos' is not 'nothing in the text'. It is not a textual nothing even if there is nothing, nothing else, in the text. Even if nothing else were posed, nothing positive, a force would be at work there and thus a potential dynamic. From ... one attachment to the other, this topology of sequential juxtaposition, this à-propos, this displacement of the à-propos can by itself have a metonymic energy, the very force that will have suggested ... the hypothesis of the substitution that [one] nevertheless excludes vigorously and with determination. In order to be excluded, it must still present itself to the mind with some seduction ... So even if there was nothing *in* the text of these two accounts, the simple topographic or sequential juxtaposition is 'in the text', it constitutes the text itself and can be *interpreted*: it is *interpretable* ... One must and one cannot not interpret it; it cannot be simply insignificant.[49]

As I have already mentioned, a number of readers have alluded to the oblique, even silent, presence of the Holocaust in Derrida's writing.[50] One might justifiably propose therefore that, whether or not they are found 'in' the text, 'the very categories or vocabulary out of which he has wrought his reflections, may be read as deriving from his experience as a Jew', and proceed to a concatenation of that 'Jewish experience' with the Holocaust, suggesting that 'much of what Derrida has to say in his writing bears specifically on the Jewish experience of the Holocaust'.[51] One can then proceed to refer to 'Derrida, survivor', and more.[52] What will be missed, however, is at once the distance *and* the proximity Derrida maintains between the Jew and the German, between the Holocaust and Nazism, Nazism and its others, opening and closing in one gesture the possibility (and therefore the impossibility) of the very juxtaposition, substitution and concatenation that nevertheless operate through and around his writings. By the conclusion of the text I have quoted, a text dedicated to confession, avowal, excuses and forgiveness, a text also devoted to a reading of de Man reading Rousseau, Derrida strikingly concludes by confessing his sadness over de Man's absence, while imagining a 'spectral machine', a prosopopoietic answer to what he, Derrida, has said. In a gesture that, perhaps *pace* de Man and for reasons spelled out by Derrida himself, cannot simply be called autobiographical (at stake is that 'spectral machine' that would answer for de Man, for 'the exemplarity of de Man's autobiographico-political texts'), Derrida implicates himself along with de Man in the mesh of confession and forgiveness he identifies toward an innocence to come. Sooner or later, Derrida writes, 'our common innocence will not fail to appear to everyone's eyes, as the best intentioned of all our machinations'.[53] The complexity of Derrida's gesture of part taking is, of course, as massive as his provocation (or the remarkable lack of historical *ressentiment* it suggests), as great as the shock his assertion should not fail to elicit (though it has of course failed to do so). Distance and proximity; substitution and concatenation.

Accordingly, I am going to contend that it is not possible to pass over the proximity or the distance, the distinction and even the innovation, that are inscribed within the first explicit deployment of the word 'holocaust' – in lower case – in Derrida's work. To the best of my knowledge, this 'first time' (which is not, and cannot be, the first time: 'Repetition and first time: this is perhaps the question of the event as question of the ghost. What is a ghost?')[54] occurs in *Glas*, originally published in 1974, and it initiates a striking, plural and disseminated iteration of the word.

Now *Glas* is a notoriously demanding text, two columns without a beginning or an end (to say that the text or texts begin *in media res* would be an understatement) that offer readings and citations, and one extended juxtaposition, perhaps a concatenation, between Hegel and Genet, along with numerous other associations, one of which could easily be subtitled, in fact, 'the Jew, the German'.[55] I speak of course of Kant and Hegel, and of Hegel's treatment of Kant as 'Jewish' ('Kant is Jewish', writes Derrida after Hegel).[56] But Genet too cuts a Jewish figure on multiple occasions, so that, along with 'Jewgreek and Greekjew', or 'Christians or Jews', and even 'Hegel and Judaism', this title might easily function, by way of a precise invagination, as a title for the book as a whole – if the word 'book' had any chance of applying to this volume.

As he reads Hegel's reflections on 'natural religion', Derrida is particularly attentive to the formless and figureless beginnings of spirit (*Geist*) in its rise to self-consciousness as religion ('the first figure of natural religion figures the absence of figure', *G*, 238a). This 'figureless figure' is light ('das Lichtwesen',

Hegel calls it), an all-consuming light that burns all. Derrida elaborates on this burning light, which 'burns itself in the all-burning it is, leaves, of itself or anything, no trace, no mark, no sign of passage' (ibid.). This 'pure consuming destruction', a 'pure effusion of light' burns everything and predictably constitutes, for Hegel, 'torrents of fire destructive of figuration', or, as Findlay's translation has it, 'streams of fire destructive of [all] structured form'.[57] Yet the 'all-burning (*brûle-tout*)' which Derrida invokes here is at once Hegelian and non-Hegelian. Iterability therefore demands that we pay attention to Derrida's re-staging of this figure which is not one, this all destructive figure of absolute incineration in its uniqueness. The echoes and resonances for what concerns us here are unmistakable and they anticipate many a phrase in Derrida's more explicit engagements with the Holocaust and its aftermath, memory, monument and the trace. And with spirit too (in *Of Spirit*, obviously). 'The all-burning – that has taken place once and nonetheless repeats itself ad infinitum – diverges so well from all essential generality that it resembles the pure difference of an absolute accident' (*G*, 239a). Here too, here again, 'subjectivity always produces itself in a movement of occidentalisation' (the movement and direction of the sun, according to Hegel). But how to understand this 'pure destruction' from which something must nonetheless remain? 'How would the purest pure, the worst worst [*le pire du pire*, the worst of the worst], the panic blaze of the all-burning, put forth some monument, even were it a crematory [*fût-il créma-toire*], some stable, geometric, solid form, for example, a *pyramid* that guards the trace of death?' (240a).

We shall soon be able to confirm that the lexicon here deployed (the worst of the worst, crematoria) leaves little to the Holocaust imagination.[58] But the juxtaposition of these elaborations with the other column of *Glas* and its own vocabulary further heightens, as it must, the reader's sensibility. From the mention of a 'louse' to the 'last station' and 'the monumentalization of the wound' (237b; 238b), the column (but which column is this really about?), 'the column is wounded, otherwise it would not be a column. It is truncated, marked, covered with scars and legends' (238b). Something is 'mixing the black of the ink and the red of blood' (239b). Something is mixing Hegel and Genet, Christ and his tormentors, the German and the Jew. Was Genet Jewish? The Holocaust Christian? Allusions to circumcision, to the Torah, in his text and in Derrida's, are here accelerating. They are at any rate facing and confronting the references to the destruction, the all-burning and 'the worst worst'. The Jew, the German – interpretations at war. Before taking us to Algiers (and to another synagogue), Derrida quotes Genet: 'When the rabbi slowly unrolls the Torah, a mystery sends a shudder through the whole epidermis' (240b). It is at this moment that, across the page (reading from right to left, that is), Derrida finally deploys the uncapitalized word 'holocaust'. Derrida is making an argument, by way of a philosophical lesson or correction, for the necessity – the *proper* or *appropriate* necessity – of the word in a text from which that very word is, in German, missing. *Il n'y a pas de hors-texte*. 'The word *holocaust*', which Derrida has discreetly introduced or reproduced a few lines earlier in the body of a citation from Hegel, 'that happens to translate *Opfer* is more appropriate to the text than the word of Hegel himself. In this sacrifice, all *(holos)* is burned *(caustos)*' (241a). The pure light 'offers up itself as a sacrifice' (as the Findlay translation of Hegel has it [420]). 'The sacrifice', Derrida explains in turn, 'the offer or the gift do not destroy the all-burning that destroys itself in them; they make it reach the for-(it)self, they monumentalize it' (240a). The sacrifice and the monument, the numbers too – these all belong 'to the double register of its accounting, accountable calculus' (241a). But what exactly is it, Derrida asks, 'what puts itself in play in this holocaust of play itself?' This is the question of the gift, the name of which, the word for which, is inadequate, as Derrida is careful to point out. It is an event, but 'an event that no more has any relation with what is currently designated under this word' (242a). This event, let me hasten to add, is not – or not explicitly, not exclusively – the Holocaust, whose name or names Derrida will go on to interrogate in later works. Nothing in the text. It is a gift, for now, that Derrida brings or acknowledges, and proposes to name, translate and call 'the holocaust'. And 'without the holocaust', he explains, 'the dialectical movement and the history of Being could not open themselves, engage themselves in the annulus of their anniversary, could not annul themselves in producing the solar course from Orient to Occident' (ibid.). 'I readily acquired from the Judeo-Christian …'. Derrida seems to explain as he cites Genet in the right column, while remembering on the left the history of Being, which leaves Heidegger's name barely implicit. Derrida goes on: 'The process of the gift (before exchange), the process that is not a process but a holocaust, a holocaust of the holocaust, *engages* the history of Being but does not belong to it. The gift *is not*; the holocaust *is not*; if at least *there is some such*'. Was there a holocaust? Is there some such? For Heidegger? For Hegel or Derrida? Yet, who would doubt that 'this reflection (in both senses of the word) of the holocaust engages history, the dialectic of sense, the speculative'? Who could doubt it? Has it not been said and repeated, by Adorno and others, that 'the speculative is the reflection *(speculum)* of the holocaust's holocaust' (ibid.)? But which holocaust? And what is Derrida doing? 'What am I doing here?' (241b). He is 'playing with fire', asserts

Geoffrey Hartman.[59] Is Derrida burning? A few lines below, mention is made of Judas, the 'old Jewish name of Judas, which the traitor Iscariot had borne', and 'the Christian name of Jude [the name is the same in German]' (*G*, 242b), while in the other column, Derrida asks, and asks again, otherwise, 'what engages itself here? What is the stake at play in this column?' (241a).

What to make of these juxtapositions? I venture 'no explaint, no complanation'.[60] I merely wish to indicate that none of what I have cited – 'nothing in the text', in other words – is 'about' the Holocaust. Yet the holocaust, a holocaust (or holocausts), is literally and unavoidably named here. And much of what is said about it announces Derrida's more overt engagement with 'what is currently designated under this word'. In a more explicit section of *Cinders* entitled 'Animadversiones', Derrida himself will go on to reproduce the passages of the left column of *Glas* from which I have quoted. There, he juxtaposes them to additional iterations and appropriations (and de-propriations) of the 'motif' of ashes, fire and 'holocaust', and he will do so again, at once lifting and maintaining the ambiguity, the distance and the proximity, in *Dissemination*, *Glas*, *Post Card* and *Of Spirit*.

Reflections on the philosophy of Hitlerism

I do not believe that we as yet know how to think what Nazism is.

— Jacques Derrida[61]

And still, Derrida did not write anything that was explicitly dedicated to the Holocaust as such. No treatise like Adorno's *Dialectic of Enlightenment* or Lyotard's *Differend*, nothing approximating Arendt's *Origins of Totalitarianism* or *Eichmann in Jerusalem*, and nothing comparable to Agamben's *Remnants of Auschwitz*. Yet, beginning with Algeria and his disgraceful expulsion from school under the Vichy laws, his being stripped ('without the intervention of any Nazi') of citizenship, Derrida's peculiar insistence on – and paradoxical resistance to – the autobiographical has served on multiple occasions as a site and cipher of reflections on Nazism, anti-Semitism and the Holocaust.[62] At the same time, his reaction to the expulsion transcends the biographical, the subjective or individual, and is repeatedly alluded to as illustrative of an irreparable contamination, minimally, a juxtaposition and even a concatenation.

In a country where the number and the diversity of historical communities was as rich as in Jerusalem, West to East, this Jewish child could dream of a peaceful cultural, linguistic, and even national plural belonging only through the experience of nonbelonging: separations, rejections, ruptures, exclusions. If I did not forbid myself any lengthy first-person discourse (but is there 'living together' otherwise than among 'first persons'?), I would describe the contradictory movement that, at the time of the anti-Semitic zeal of the French authorities in Algeria during the war, pushed a little boy who was expelled from school and understood none of it to rebel, forever, against two ways of 'living together': at once against racist gregariousness, and therefore against anti-Semitic segregation, but also, more obscurely, and more, no doubt, against the conservative and self-protective confinement of a Jewish community that, seeking naturally, legitimately to defend itself, to constitute or reconstitute its whole [*ensemble*] under the ordeal of these traumas, was folding in upon itself, overbidding in the direction that I already then felt as a kind of exclusive, even fusional, communitarianism.[63]

Everything is as if 'two ways of living together' had themselves been associated, perhaps fused, at any rate, irreparably contaminated with and by each other. I dare not say that we have become familiar with the mechanism, which caused Gillian Rose's ire (among others).[64] And yet, as Rose herself insisted, thinking about what made the Holocaust possible, about 'abused and abusing, victim and perpetrator', guilt and good intentions, complicity and innocence, means having 'to think a far more dangerous thought'.[65] And it is one that goes well beyond Derrida's person or his philosophical or biographical positions. In fact, it goes well beyond any – guilty or triumphant – individual.

Under the ambiguous heading of autobiography or *otobiography* (biography, thanatography, etc.), Derrida was always reflecting on 'the worst of our times' (O, 7). Attending to the author, his life and his work, reading Nietzsche and his legacy, Derrida states explicitly that he does 'not aim to "clear" its "author" and neutralize or defuse either what might be troublesome … or what served as "language" for the most sinister rallying cries of National Socialism' (23). Thinking of his own participation, his complicity perhaps, in the teaching institution (the entire text being a persistent meditation on pedagogy and on 'academic freedom'), Derrida looks forward and backward (to Nietzsche and to the reception of deconstruction to which I have already alluded) and he affirms that 'one may wonder how and why what is so naively called a falsification was possible (one can't falsify just anything), how and why the "same" words and the "same" statements – if they are indeed the same – might several times be made to serve certain meanings and certain contexts that are said to be different, even incompatible. One may wonder', Derrida continues, 'why the only teaching institution or the only beginning of a teaching institution that ever succeeded in taking as its model the teaching of Nietzsche on teaching will have been a Nazi one' (24). Derrida insists on recalling 'the echo' Nietzsche's language 'received from the Nazi orchestration' at the same time as 'Nietzsche never wanted that or thought that' (28). Derrida's questioning remains in the proximity of these hesitations and oscillations, these oppositions and implications. For 'must there not be some powerful utterance-producing machine that programs the movements of the two opposing forces at once, and which couples, conjugates, or marries them in a given set, as life (does) death?' (29). Derrida also registers the objection: 'Careful!' he writes. 'Nietzsche's utterances are not the same as those of the Nazi ideologues, and not only because the latter grossly caricaturize the former to the point of apishness' (30). And yet. 'Yet it would still be necessary to account for the possibility of this mimetic inversion and perversion' (ibid.).

Everything is then as if, when it comes to Nazism, to the Holocaust, but also when it comes to their legacy (however terrifying, as Derrida insists), we may not be in a position to decide, minimally to extricate ourselves by way of our conscience or consciousness. This applies as well to the memorialization of the Holocaust and to deconstruction (or 'deconstructionism', that other caricature). We are not bound to decide, Derrida said, and said that he believed. 'We are not, I believe, bound to decide'.

> An interpretive decision does not have to draw a line between two intents or two political contents … This is the way it has always been – and always in a singular manner – for example, ever since what is called the end of philosophy, and beginning with the textual indicator named 'Hegel'. This is no accident. It is an effect of the destinational structure of the so-called post-Hegelian texts. There can always be a Hegelianism of the left and a Hegelianism of the right, a Heideggerianism of the left and a Heideggerianism of the right, a Nietzschenamism of the right and a Nietzscheanism of the left, and even, let us not overlook it, a Marxism of the right and a Marxism of the left. The one can always be the other, the double of the other. (32)

Can there be a Nazism of the left? A *liberal* Nazism? Can there be a deconstruction of the right? Can there be Holocaust memory, a memorialization of the right? A racist remembrance? A racist remembrance of racism? In the name of anti-racism? At the same time as 'we do not have to decide', Derrida tells us, we must confront these terrifying possibilities – more than possibilities – for they are no accident, and certainly not the biographical or autobiographical accident of a life, be this life double or not, innocent or not. This is not, nor can it ever be, therefore, about the individual author, the Nazi philosopher or (which should have led to some reflection too, beyond the clichés of 'self-hatred') the Jewish one. It is not restricted to Nietzsche. Nor is it about De Man or about Derrida, not simply or exclusively so. As we have already and all-too comfortably recognized,

> Nietzsche never wanted that or thought that, he would have vomited it up, or he didn't intend it in that manner, he didn't hear it with that ear. Even if this were possibly true, one would be justified in finding very little of interest in such a hypothesis ... I say this because, first of all, Nietzsche died as always *before* his name and therefore it is not a question of knowing what he would have thought, wanted, or done. (28–29)

Much as Nazism is an undeniable – if not inevitable – uptake of Nietzsche's language, but even if it was not; and even if Nazism 'were only a symptom of the accelerated decomposition of European culture and society as diagnosed, it still remains to be explained how reactive degeneration could exploit the same language, the same words, the same utterances, the same rallying cries as the active forces to which it stands opposed. Of course', Derrida adds for today, 'neither this phenomenon nor this specular ruse eluded Nietzsche' (29). It did not elude Derrida either. 'Beyond all regional considerations (historical, politico-economic, ideological, et cetera), Europe and not only Europe, this century and not only this century are at stake. And the stakes include the "present" in which we are, up to a certain point, and in which we take a position or take sides' (30).

Naming the Holocaust

Is the Holocaust today? Is today the Holocaust? It is imperative to recall once again that Derrida almost always discussed the Holocaust indirectly, without naming it, or alternatively by using the uncapitalized word *holocaust*. He also referred to the *brûle-tout* in those contexts and others. More importantly, and perhaps more often, Derrida also *refrained* from discussing the Holocaust, to assert its singularity or to call attention to it in any special way. Answering a question about Heidegger, Derrida said a few things that might help us read, if time permits, the passages I have quoted so far. He also makes clear that these same passages, and others we will go on to consider, are unavoidable. How not to speak, Derrida is saying once again, how not to speak about the Holocaust? In what ways and manners should one *not* speak of it or about it? Alternatively, could one adopt a moratorium of sorts and not speak of it? Not feel entitled, conscious and conscientious enough to speak of it? Can one *not* remember it? Yet, and at the same time, how not to speak of it? How to avoid speaking? The Jew, the German.

> I suppose, I hope you are not expecting me simply to say 'I condemn Auschwitz' or 'I condemn every silence on Auschwitz'. As regards this last phrase or its equivalents, I find a bit indecent, indeed, obscene, the mechanical nature of improvised trials instigated against all those whom one thinks one can accuse of not having named or thought 'Auschwitz' ... all this would be less grievous if one began by stating, rigorously, what we call 'Auschwitz' and what we think about it, if we think something. What is the referent here? Are we making a metonymical usage of this proper name? If we are, what governs this usage? Why this name rather than that of another camp, of other mass exterminations, etc. (and who has answered these questions seriously)? If not, why this forgetful and just as grievous restriction? If we admit – and this concession seems to me to be readable everywhere – that the thing remains unthinkable, that we still have no discourse equal to it, if we recognize that we have nothing to say about the real victims of Auschwitz, the same ones we nonetheless authorize ourselves to treat by metonymy or to name *via negativa*, then let's stop diagnosing the alleged silences, forcing avowals of the 'resistances' or the 'unthought' in everyone indiscriminately. Of course, silence on Auschwitz will never be justifiable; but neither is speaking about it in such an instrumental fashion and in order to say nothing, to say nothing about it that does not go without saying, trivially, serving primarily to give oneself a good conscience, so as not to be the last to accuse, to teach lessons, to take positions, or to grandstand.[66]

By all accounts, there are two names that particularly and, as it were, unavoidably resonate when considering Derrida's reflections on Nazism and on the Holocaust. Unequal in their manifest (and latent) inscriptions, they nonetheless accompany Derrida for much of his life and works: Martin Heidegger, whom he never sought to meet, and Paul Celan, whom he did meet after many years of being his unsuspecting colleague.[67] These are indeed names ('the politics of the proper name', we just saw, was the way Derrida encouraged us to think about Nietzsche and beyond), proper names, and though they could hardly function as metonyms, they transcend their individual bearers and implicate more than subjectivities. It is for this reason that they have been the occasions for some of the most detailed engagements with the questions that preoccupy me here. They also mark a certain fatality, what Derrida calls, in *Of Spirit*, 'the fatal necessity of a contamination' (*OS*, 10).

Already in 'Schibboleth', Derrida alerts us to the consistent individualism – the politics of proper names – that governs much of the debates surrounding Nazism and the Holocaust (the capitalization of these names). As we saw, Derrida explicitly identifies this necessity as exceeding authorship or individual intention. Besides, as with the *schibboleth*, the value of a word or name, the value of a gesture (of memory and of preservation, of mobilization for the good),

> may always, and tragically, be inverted. Tragically because this inversion overtakes the initiative of subjects, the goodwill of men, their mastery of language and politics. Watchword or password in a struggle against oppression, exclusion, fascism, and racism, it may also corrupt its differential value ... making of it a discriminatory limit, the grillwork of policing, of normalization, and of methodical subjugation.[68]

So, which side was Derrida on? On a number of occasions, he himself allowed that question as legitimate. I shall mention the instance dealing with the conflicts of the university, which in the context of Heidegger's trajectory seems strangely appropriate. Which side is Derrida on in all these conflicts? He might be, he says, '(1) to the right of the boundary or (2) to its left, or (3) more probably, as some might (rightly or wrongly) suppose, a tireless parasite moving in random agitation, passing over the boundary and back again'.[69] Yet, what is here implied goes, as I have tried to show, much beyond any subjectivity, beyond even 'the metaphysics of subjectivity' in which we remain, Derrida says, complicit. Why? Perhaps 'because one cannot demarcate oneself from biologism, from naturalism, from racism in its genetic form', without falling into their constraints; because these are the constraints of a programme that 'remains very strong, it reigns over the majority of discourses which, today and for a long time to come, state their opposition to racism, to totalitarianism, to nazism, to fascism, etc.' (*OS*, 39). This does not abolish or undo all differences, nor does it essentialize the subject. It does implicate current discourses such as 'democracy or "human rights"' (40), but that does not mean that Derrida fails to distinguish between 'Nazism and non-Nazism', as Wolin has it. Derrida is much more specific than that, much closer to history than that, the history of our present. 'We are talking about past, present, and future "events"', about 'a composition of forces and discourses which seem to have been waging merciless war on each other (for example from 1933 to our time)' (109). And it is now, 'after the disasters that have happened', for what 'remains to come after the disasters that happened', that we must confront the only choice there is. 'The only choice is the choice between the terrifying contaminations' assigned by the programme – the parasite and the virus – Derrida attends to, and which may or may not be transformed (40). This is not a universal but a geopolitical matter, Derrida goes on to clarify once again. 'Geopolitical, then: Europe, Russia, and America are named here, which still no doubt means just Europe' (45). Or perhaps it is just an example. But recall that 'on the basis of an example taken from a discourse which in general is not suspected of the worst, it is useful to recall that the reference to *spirit*, to the *freedom* of spirit, and to spirit as *European* spirit could and still can ally itself with the politics one would want to oppose to it' (121n). And who today would disagree? What has freedom not allied itself with, today? 'Where is the worse?' in other words? (ibid.). This is not a universal. 'We have here a program and a combinatory whose power remains abyssal. In all rigor it exculpates none of the discourses which can thus exchange their power. It leaves no place for any arbitrating authority. Nazism was not born in the desert' (109). This is Derrida's Holocaust, more precisely, his holocausts and, I am afraid, ours: the holocausts of Nazism, of course, but also of Marxism and of liberalism too.[70] There are untold holocausts and unnamed ones as well. Commenting on Celan, Derrida writes:

> Forgive me if I do not name, here, the holocaust, that is to say, literally, as I chose to call it elsewhere, the all-burning, except to say this: there is certainly today the date of that holocaust we know, the hell of our memory; but there is a holocaust for every date, and somewhere in the world at every hour. Every hour counts its holocaust. Every hour is unique, whether it recurs, and in the manner of a wheel that turns by itself, or whether, the last, it recurs no more, no more than the sister, its own, the same, its other revenant.[71]

This is more and less than 'Nazism and non-Nazism', and something else than modernity too, something broader and perhaps older. Ashes to ashes, Derrida seems to be saying at any rate, and saying to us still. Ashes to ashes, we all fall down.

Notes

1   Philippe Lacoue-Labarthe, *Poetry as Experience*, trans. Andrea Tarnowski (Stanford: Stanford University Press, 1999), 77.

2   Jacques Derrida, *Of Spirit: Heidegger and the Question*, trans. Geoffrey Bennington and Rachel Bowlby (Chicago: University of Chicago Press, 1989), 97 (hereafter cited in text as *OS*).

3   See the original, bilingual publication of Derrida 'Force of Law', translated by Mary Quaintance in the *Cardozo Law Review* 11 (1989–90), and see Jacques Derrida, *Force de Loi: Le 'Fondement mystique de l'autorité'* (Paris: Galilée, 1994).

4   Saul Friedlander, 'Introduction', in *Probing the Limits of Representation: Nazism and the 'Final Solution'*, ed. S. Friedlander (Cambridge, MA: Harvard University Press, 1992), 3.

5   On this 'incident' and more, see Marc Nichanian, *The Historiographic Perversion*, trans. Gil Anidjar (New York: Columbia University Press, 2009).

6   Jürgen Habermas, *The Philosophical Discourse of Modernity*, trans. Frederick Lawrence (Cambridge, MA: MIT Press, 1987), 182.

7   Isaac Nevo, 'What Price Deconstruction? Derrida on Heidegger and the Question of Nazism: A Critical Study', *Philosophia* 21, 3–4 (1992): 183–99; on Derrida and the architecture of Holocaust memory, see Karyn Ball, *Disciplining the Holocaust* (Albany: State University of New York Press, 2008), 45–93.

8   I take my title for this section from another strange inscription, a phrase that appears in Derrida's commentary on Edmond Jabès in *L'écriture et la différence* (Paris: Seuil, 1967), 110; the phrase did not make it into Alan Bass's otherwise formidable translation (J. Derrida, *Writing and Difference*, trans. A. Bass [New York: Routledge, 2005], 90).

9   Jacques Derrida, *The Post Card: From Socrates to Freud and Beyond*, trans. Alan Bass (Chicago: University of Chicago Press, 1987), 254.

10 Lauren Berlant, 'The Subject of True Feeling: Pain, Privacy, and Politics', in *Cultural Pluralism, Identity Politics, and the Law*, eds. Austin Sarat and Thomas R. Kearns (Ann Arbor: University of Michigan Press, 1999), 50.

11 Evelyn Barish, *The Double Life of Paul de Man* (New York: W. W. Norton, 2014), xiii; the book was immediately reviewed in a number of visible venues.

12 After Derrida, I use the verb 'solicit' in its obsolete sense, listed by the OED, 'To disturb, disquiet, trouble; to make anxious, fill with concern'. The verb is explicitly deployed by Derrida ('shaking in a way related to the whole [from *sollus*, in archaic Latin "the whole", and from *citare*, "to put in motion"]') in *Writing and Difference*, trans. Alan Bass (New York: Routledge, 2001), 5.

13 Naomi Mandel, *Against the Unspeakable: Complicity, the Holocaust, and Slavery in America* (Charlottesville: University of Virginia Press, 2006), 8.

14 Jacques Derrida, *Limited Inc.* (Evanston: Northwestern University Press, 1988).

15 Godwin's law is 'a facetious aphorism maintaining that as an online debate increases in length, it becomes inevitable that someone will eventually compare someone or something to Adolf Hitler or the Nazis' ('Godwin's Law, n.', *OED Online* [Oxford University Press, June 2014], accessed 9 August 2014).

16 Mandel, *Against the Unspeakable*, 213.

17 Ibid., 82.

18 Lauren Berlant, *The Female Complaint: The Unfinished Business of Sentimentality in American Culture* (Durham, NC: Duke University Press, 2008), 52.

19 Jean-François Lyotard, *Heidegger and 'the jews'*, trans. Andreas Michel and Mark Roberts (Minneapolis: University of Minnesota Press, 1990), 75.

20 Ball, *Disciplining the Holocaust*, 30.

21 Peter Novick, *The Holocaust in American Life* (New York: Houghton Mifflin, 1999); *The Americanization of the Holocaust*, ed. Hilene Flanzbaum (Baltimore: Johns Hopkins University Press, 1999); Norman Finkelstein, *The Holocaust Industry: Reflections on the Exploitation of Jewish Suffering* (New York: Verso, 2003); Gilbert Achcar, *The Arabs and the Holocaust: The Arab–Israeli War of Narratives*, trans. G. M. Goshgarian (London: Saqi Books, 2010).

22 See Gillian Rose, 'The Future of Auschwitz', in *Judaism and Modernity: Philosophical Essays* (Oxford: Blackwell, 1993), 34.

23 Jean-François Lyotard, *The Differend: Phrases in Dispute*, trans. George Van Den Abbeele (Minneapolis: University of Minnesota Press, 1988), 106.

24 Ibid.

25 Before the current fame of the acronym, ISIs were, in Althusser's lexicon, 'ideological state apparatuses' (Louis Althusser, *Lenin and Philosophy and Other Essays*, trans. Ben Brewster [New York: Monthly Review Press, 1971]).

26 Recall that what had shocked Habermas and others at the onset of the *Historikerstreit* was precisely the inclusion of communism as part of 'an attempt to make Auschwitz unexceptional' (J. Habermas, *The New Conservatism: Cultural Criticism and the Historian's Debate*, trans. Shierry Weber Nicholsen [Cambridge, MA: MIT Press, 1989], 211).

27 Timothy Snyder, *Bloodlands: Europe Between Hitler and Stalin* (New York: Basic Books, 2010). And consider that, writing in 1993, Saul Friedländer could still assert (quoting Arendt!) that 'immediate political efficiency notwithstanding, the reference to any other mass terror, including Stalinism, thenceforth took Nazism as its ultimate point of reference and comparison. As Hannah Arendt expressed it … The Nazi regime from a moral and not a social point of view was much more extreme than the Stalin regime at its worst' (S. Friedländer, *Memory, History, and the Extermination of the Jews of Europe* [Bloomington: Indiana University Press, 1993], 52–3).

28 Richard Brody, 'Why Does It Matter If Heidegger Was Anti-Semitic', *New Yorker*, March 27, 2014, accessed 17 March 2015, http://www.newyorker.com/culture/richard-brody/why-does-it-matter-if-heidegger-was-anti-semitic; emphasis added.

29 Robert Eaglestone, 'Derrida and the Holocaust: A Commentary on the Philosophy of Cinders', *Angelaki: Journal of the Theoretical Humanities* 7, 2 (August 2002): 28; and see Eaglestone, 'Derrida and the Legacies of the Holocaust', in *Derrida's Legacies: Literature and Philosophy*, eds Simon Glendinning and Robert Eaglestone (New York: Routledge, 2008), 66–75.

30 R. Wolin, 'Preface to the MIT Press Edition', in *The Heidegger Controversy: A Critical Reader*, ed. R. Wolin (Cambridge, MA: The MIT Press, 1993), xiii; I must admit that it is not clear to me what the referent of 'non-Nazism' might be, for what exactly would *not* be included? Nor is it clear who would even need to engage with Derrida if such were the degree of generalization ('everything is Nazism') or the extraordinary over-determination of the world by Nazism. At stake is not an absurdly general 'non-Nazism', therefore, but the much more specific, self-righteous and complacent, 'adversaries' of Nazism (and remember that communism no longer qualifies), beginning with liberalism.

31 Michal Ben-Naftali, 'An Interview with Professor Jacques Derrida', trans. Moshe Ron, accessed 17 March, 2015, www.yadvashem.org/odot_pdf/Microsoft%20 Word%20-%203851.pdf.

32 Ibid.

33 Geoffrey Bennington in Bennington and Derrida, *Jacques Derrida* (Chicago: University of Chicago Press, 1993), 124.

34 See Avital Ronell, 'The Differends of Man', *Diacritics* 19, 3/4 (Autumn–Winter, 1989): 62–7; Robert Eaglestone, 'Derrida and the Holocaust'; Steven Shakespeare, 'Thinking about *Fire*: Derrida and Judaism', *Literature & Theology* 12, 3 (September 1998): 242–55; David Michael Levin, 'Cinders, Traces, Shadows on the Page: The Holocaust in Derrida's Writing', *International Philosophical Quarterly* 43, 3 (September 2003): 269–88; Dorota Glowacka, 'A Date, a Place, a Name: Jacques Derrida's Holocaust Translations', *CR: The New Centennial Review* 7, 2 (Fall 2007): 111–39; Bruce Rosenstock, 'Derrida's Advent', *Contemporary French Civilization* 30, 1 (Winter–Spring 2006): 75–90.

35 'Deconstructionism', charged Deborah Lipstadt, 'created an atmosphere of permissiveness toward questioning the meaning of historical events and made it hard for its proponents to assert that there was anything "off limits" for this skeptical approach' (D. Lipstadt, *Denying the Holocaust: The Growing Assault on Truth and Memory* [New York: Plume, 1994], 18).

36 G. Bennington, 'Derridabase', in Bennington and Derrida, *Jacques Derrida*, 196.

37 Ronell, 'The Differends of Man', 63 n. 1.

38 Alain Finkielkraut, *The Imaginary Jew*, trans. Kevin O'Neill and David Suchoff (Lincoln, NB: University of Nebraska Press, 1994).

39 See e.g. 'Like the Sound of the Sea Deep within a Shell: Paul de Man's War', trans. Peggy Kamuf, *Critical Inquiry* 14, 3 (Spring 1988): 648; later describing his response to the extermination of the Jews of Europe, which he insisted was not comparable to his experience as an Algerian Jew, Derrida said that 'my compassion and my horrified indignation were and remain such as must move a universal conscience rather than that of a Jew affected in his own kin [*plutôt que celle d'un Juif touché dans les siens*]' (Derrida, 'Abraham, the Other', trans. Gil

Anidjar, in *Judeities: Questions for Jacques Derrida*, eds Bettina Bergo et al. [New York: Fordham University Press, 2007], 15; and see my 'Traité de Tous les Noms (What Is Called Naming)', *Epoché: A Journal for the History of Philosophy* 10, 2 (Spring 2006): 287–30).

40 Bennington in Bennington and Derrida, *Jacques Derrida*, 294; and see 'An Interview'.

41 Derrida, 'Schibboleth', in *Sovereignties in Question: The Poetics of Paul Celan*, eds. Thomas Dutoit and Outi Pasanen (New York: Fordham University Press, 2005), 50.

42 Derrida, *The Truth in Painting*, trans. Geoffrey Bennington and Ian McLeod (Chicago: University of Chicago Press, 1987), 263.

43 Ibid., 178.

44 Geoffrey H. Hartman, *The Fateful Question of Culture* (New York: Columbia University Press, 1997), 109–17; and see Levin, 'Cinders, Traces', 283, and Glowacka on 'the tantalizing obliqueness of Derrida's references to the Holocaust' ('A Date, a Place', 114).

45 Ball, *Disciplining the Holocaust*, 34–44.

46 Derrida, *Post Card*, 24.

47 Derrida, 'Typewriter Ribbon: Limited Ink (2)', trans. Peggy Kamuf, in Derrida, *Without Alibi*, ed. Peggy Kamuf (Stanford: Stanford University Press, 2002), 91.

48 Ibid.

49 Ibid., 92–3.

50 See e.g. Eaglestone, 'Derrida and the Holocaust', 32–3.

51 Levin, 'Cinders, Traces', 270.

52 Bruce Rosenstock, 'Derrida's Advent', *Contemporary French Civilization* 30, 1 (Winter–Spring 2006): 76.

53 Derrida, 'Typewriter Ribbon', 160.

54 Derrida, *Specters of Marx: The State of the Debt, the Work of Mourning and the New International*, trans. Peggy Kamuf (New York: Routledge, 1994), 10.

55 'The Jew, the German' is of course part of the title of another text by Derrida, namely, 'Interpretations at War: Kant, the Jew, the German', trans. Moshe Ron, in Derrida, *Acts of Religion*, 137–88.

56 Derrida, *Glas*, trans. John P. Leavey Jr. and Richard Rand (Lincoln, NB: University of Nebraska Press, 1986), 213a (hereafter cited in text as *G*).

57 Hegel, *Phenomenology of Spirit*, trans. Findlay, 419; the German reads 'die Gestaltung verzehrende Feuerströme'.

58 And compare: 'Holocaust of the Children … God himself had only the choice between two crematory ovens: with whom to begin? When? And the always imminent catastrophe' (Derrida, *Post Card*, 143).

59 Hartman, *The Fateful Question*, 112.

60 Gayatri Chakravorty Spivak pointedly coins the words, referring to 'explaints and complications – absolution by accusing knowledge' (G. C. Spivak, 'Psychoanalysis in Left Field and Fieldworking: Examples to Fit the Title', in *Speculations after Freud: Psychoanalysis, Philosophy and Culture*, eds. Sonu Shamdasani and Michael Münchow [New York: Routledge, 1994], 42).

61 Derrida, 'Otobiographies: The Teaching of Nietzsche and the Politics of the Proper Name', trans. Avital Ronell, in Derrida, *The Ear of the Other: Otobiography, Transference, Translation*, ed. Christie V. McDonald (New York: Schocken Books, 1985), 31 (hereafter cited in text as O).

62 Derrida, 'Circumfession', in Bennington and Derrida, *Jacques Derrida* (Chicago: University of Chicago Press, 1993), 288; and see the dense pages written by Sean Gaston in *The Impossible Mourning of Jacques Derrida* (New York: Continuum, 2006), 101–5.

63 Derrida, 'Avowing – the Impossible: "Returns", Repentance, and Reconciliation. A Lesson', trans. Gil Anidjar, in *Living Together: Jacques Derrida's Communities of Violence and Peace*, ed. Elisabeth Weber (New York: Fordham University Press, 2013), 27–8.

64 Gillian Rose, 'Of Derrida's Spirit', in Rose, *Judaism and Modernity: Philosophical Essays* (Oxford: Blackwell, 1993), 65–87.

65 For Rose, this dangerous thought is that 'it is morality itself which has corrupted us and which continues to corrupt us' (Rose, 'The Future of Auschwitz', in Rose, *Judaism and Modernity*, 34–5.

66 'Eating Well, Or the Calculation of the Subject', trans. Peter Connor and Avital Ronell, in *Points …, Interviews 1974–1994*, ed. Elisabeth Weber (Stanford: Stanford University Press, 1995), 286–7.

67 Benoît Peeters, *Derrida: A Biography*, trans. Andrew Brown (Cambridge: Polity, 2013), 191.

68 Derrida, 'Schibboleth', 30.

69 Derrida, *Eyes of the University: Right to Philosophy 2*, trans. Jan Plug and others (Stanford: Stanford University Press, 2004), 109.

70 See e.g. Sven Lindqvist, '*Exterminate All the Brutes*', trans. Joan Tate (New York: New Press, 1996); Mike Davis, *Late Victorian Holocausts: El Niño Famines and the Making of the Third World* (New York: Verso, 2001).

71 Derrida, 'Schibboleth', 46.

2

'There Shall Be No Mourning'

Simon Morgan Wortham

A sense of mourning: Rancière, Lyotard and the politics of forgetting

It has become all too common to view deconstruction as the predilection of the melancholic, one whose lovelorn preference for the Western canon and the European tradition only deepens in sentiment for being perhaps unrequited: a thoroughly mournful, even morbid practice given over to endless suspensions, obfuscations, prevarications or hesitations, rapt before some immemorial Other or, as Giorgio Agamben would have it, infinitely negotiating at the Law's doorstep, assuming an intractable impassability instead of asserting new means to cross the threshold.[1] Several of the critical voices currently enjoying ascendancy in continental philosophy today stake their positions at least in part on a declared dissatisfaction with a 'deconstructive' or 'post-structuralist' ethics-of-the-other position that is seen as responsible more widely for a certain blockage of emancipatory possibility in the political field. Such a position is frequently characterized as regressive, bound by the repetition of trauma and given to a sense of redemptive entitlement, to the extent that it remains preoccupied with the worst events of the European twentieth century.

This characterization of deconstruction has ramifications in both political and religious terms. While during the second half in particular of his lengthy philosophical career Derrida was called upon many times – and with a not insignificant degree of courage – to defend the right and possibility of, for example, a Pro-Palestine stance, and other positions of this kind, positions that for him remained incompatible with various forms of anti-Judaism or even anti-Israelism (a standpoint he felt was far from inconsistent with his philosophical writings), nowadays the 'ethics' associated with deconstruction and the forms of thought it is supposed to inherit is all too hastily assimilated to an unequivocally

'Judaic' religious disposition seen to be at diametrical odds with radical emancipatory causes of several kinds. This, then, represents a peculiar and perhaps
ironic turn in Derrida's fortunes: while the Derrida of the 1990s endured stiff
criticism for maintaining political attitudes about, let's say, the Middle East that
were seen in certain quarters as an affront to the historic plight of the Jews,
nowadays deconstruction is frequently dismissed as too closely aligned with
an ethico-theological sensibility caught up in just the type of attitudes that, less
than twenty years ago, it was held to transgress. (Needless to say, the image and
idea of the 'Jew', of what is 'Jewish' or of 'Jewishness', is in all of these scenarios
always to a significant extent something of a projection, a displacement, at the
very least a divided and troubled terrain of representations – no matter which
'side' one supposedly comes from, or speaks for – with political consequences
that are nonetheless very real.)

One could easily extend the terms of this brief survey of the contemporary
'theoretical' landscape, examining the different positions of thinkers given
to the same 'attitude' towards deconstruction and its supposed allies, rehearsing
the various scenes of critical dispute and multiplying examples along the way.
However, one instance of this kind of approach is to be found in the writings of
Jacques Rancière. For several years now this 'ethics-of-the-other' position that,
if one were to be inordinately hasty, recalls deconstruction or post-structuralist
thought more generally has been the subject of repeated critique by Rancière.
One of the places Rancière tends to ground this critique is Lyotard's interpretation of the Kantian sublime and his assessment of its 'modern' importance.
As is well known, many have sought to recuperate the idea of art's singular
resistance to appropriation, notably through reference to the Kant's notion of
sublimity. In *Aesthetics and its Discontents*[2] Rancière argues that what is at stake
in Lyotard's attempt to radicalize the sublime by emphasizing an 'irreducible
gap between the idea and the sensible' is the effort to define modern art as
that which testifies to 'the fact of the unpresentable', which in turn licenses the
founding of an 'ethical community' (*AD*, 20–1) on the basis of the aesthetic.
Such a 'community' is 'ethical', for Rancière, insofar as it is constructed upon
the supposed ruins of those discourses of collective, political emancipation to
which the aesthetic form of art was hitherto powerfully linked.[3] Rancière rejects
what he sees as the Lyotardian sublime's concern to place modern or 'avant-
garde' art at an absolute distance from the everyday world. For Rancière, such
detachment is not that of an alienation effect, replete with the 'promise-carrying
contradiction' (42) that paves the way for political emancipation. Instead, he
argues, sublimity of the Lyotardian stripe binds us to an absolute alterity which

can neither be reconciled nor overcome. The 'enigma' of the work formed by the world's contradictions is, for Rancière, thereby recast in terms of an impossible testimony to the power of the 'Other'. For Rancière, then, the 'ethical' task of such impossible witness testifies to the constitutive state of ruination that supposedly *is* modern art,[4] but also provides the (quasi-messianic) paradigm for keeping alive 'the memory of catastrophe' – twentieth-century 'catastrophe' in particular – without any capacity for developing new means of politics or 'becoming-life'.

Rancière's argument against Lyotard's Kantianism is that, to the extent that the sublime in Kant does not refer to an art work as such but rather to the experience of imagination's incapacity before reason,[5] it places us in the domain of morality and not aesthetics. The sublime reminds reason of its superiority over nature and indeed its 'legislative vocation in the supersensible order', as Rancière puts it, thus leading out from the realm of art into 'the ethical universe' (89).[6] Further, for Rancière, Lyotard twists Kant's thought such that imagination's shortcomings in the face of the sublime encourage not so much 'the autonomous law of the legislative mind' as 'subordination to the law of alterity' or heteronomy.[7] As such, the 'ethical' experience of the aesthetic sublime amounts to profound and insurmountable servitude to the 'Other' (93–4).

Rancière turns to Schiller's *Letters on the Aesthetic Education of Man* as, for him, the better example of inheritance in regard to Kantian aesthetics, insofar as Schiller reveals rather than effaces their emancipatory potential. Here, Rancière argues, it becomes clear that all aesthetic experience, whether it be of the sublime or the beautiful, suspends both the law of understanding that necessitates conceptual determination and the law of sensation that entails a desired object. If aesthetic experience *tout court* thereby 'suspends the power relations which usually structure the experience of the knowing, acting and desiring subject' (97), Rancière discerns in such experience freedom's promise rather than the condition of servitude. Be that as it may, since there is never simply harmonious 'agreement' of the faculties in aesthetic experience, but instead a break with any such agreement each time the aesthetic is involved, Rancière disputes the necessity of Lyotard's specific appeal to the sublime. Attraction and repulsion, agreement and disagreement, agitation and repose – for Rancière, such 'dissensual' tensions reside not merely in the sublime as a form of aesthetic experience profoundly distinct from that of the beautiful, but instead strike at the very heart of aesthetic experience as such. And as Rancière argues, it is just this dissensus that permits Schiller to attribute political capacity to the aesthetic state. For him, aesthetic experience fosters a common sense of the dissensual in that it powerfully undermines the class distinctions and hierarchies that hitherto tied art to the established order of the world, while at the same time exposing 'distant classes' to precisely the experience of their own 'distance' within the specific distribution of the sensible. Yet if, as Rancière argues, the aesthetic (that of the beautiful *as much as* the sublime) was always characterized by an internal movement of dissensus – as a movement that is replete with politics – then how is it possible for him to distinguish and isolate the sublime as that which encourages simply a politically conservative movement of separation, a more or less inert form of withdrawal, rather than politically charged distantiation? Just as engaged art – by desiring outreach or extension to the point of its own disappearance – propels itself towards new forms of life by dint of a movement for which aesthetic experience might be another name, so surely the sublime, to the extent that it must participate in this same dissensual structure of the aesthetic, cannot be entirely emptied of transformative political capacity?

Be that as it may, by the last chapter of *Aesthetics and its Discontents* the ethics of the 'Other' are read deeply into the contemporary situation of global politics. Here, since the absolute rights of the absolute victim – those powerlessly subjected to ethnic cleansing, religious persecution, sectarian warfare or other forms of extreme victimization – have become 'the absolute rights of those without rights', it has been deemed necessary for the rights of the 'other' to be transferred to and exercised (indeed, avenged) by the 'ethical' community, for example through humanitarian intervention, international peace-keeping forces, the war on terror, and so forth. For Rancière, such a situation radicalizes catastrophe or 'disaster' since, by dint of the 'affirmation of a state of exception' which in fact renders inoperative 'politics and right' in their classical forms, all we are left to hope for is some 'messianic' answer to despair. Yet forward-lookingness is relatively weak against the interminable memory of unrepresentable evil, of a catastrophic past extending itself seemingly endlessly into a desperate present (which is really all that calls up messianic 'hope'). It is through a reading of Lyotard's 1993 lecture for Amnesty International, 'The Other's Rights', that Rancière sees this situation captured perfectly. He argues that what opposes and seeks to violate this absolute right of the other is, in Lyotard's thought, the will to master the unmasterable, and to thereby attain self-mastery (a 'will' in Lyotard's work that, for Rancière, takes us far too directly from the Enlightenment to Revolution to Nazism). [8] Since what is at stake in this 'will' is a refusal to bear witness to the law of the 'Other', it is therefore to be resisted, from the 'ethical' perspective, by 'infinite justice wielded against infinite evil', in Rancière's ominous phrase (130) – a configuration of ethics that for him strongly suppresses the radical promise of emancipatory politics.

While Lyotard has of course written extensively and complexly on the sublime in a number of major texts, Rancière's condemnation of Lyotardian sublimity often revolves around just this short talk he gave as part of the Oxford Amnesty International Lectures in 1993.[9] This occurs not just in *Aesthetics and its Discontents* but also, for instance, in *The Politics of Aesthetics* and *Dissensus*. The reference is recursive, to say the least. While this decision to repeatedly ground much larger arguments on a comparatively minor work may strike some as odd, it is therefore worth revisiting this lecture in some detail in order to evaluate properly Rancière's criticisms.

From its opening paragraph, Lyotard's lecture evokes the 'other than human' which founds the possibility of human rights. Such rights, Lyotard argues, accrue only at the point at which 'the human is other than *a* human being', that is to say more than just basic or bare human life. As its primary historical instance, this 'other' or excess of the human is embodied in the notion of the citizen. Lyotard affirms that it is only on condition of being other-than-human that such a being may become 'an *other* human being' within the social realm of the community. 'Then "the others" can treat him as their fellow human being' (OR, 136). If what makes human beings alike is, then, 'the fact that every human being carries within him the figure of the other' (ibid.), this 'other' emerges as the other-than-human in the other human that I also am. As such, it arises not as some primeval origin, divine enigma or source of ancient debt. Instead, it is simply the foundational situation of citizenry in general, which – in a way that is surely not entirely remote from Rancière's thinking of dissensus – Lyotard formulates outside of notions of the absolute identity of the social bond.[10] (One implication of such citizenry as it occurs in Lyotard, of course, is that one never attains 'full' citizenship pure and simple, citizenship without remainder, since the figure of the citizen is also that of the '*other than*', meaning that human lives can never be unproblematically reduced to the citizen-form to which they nevertheless tend, but instead – to the extent that they partake of citizenry in some form – always risk its 'beyond'.)

What is the basis of this '*other than*' of the human? For Lyotard, the communicability which underpins human interlocution is characterized by a certain heterogeneity, in that human language entails forms of address which are necessarily dissymmetrical: I speak, you listen (and, alternately, vice versa). While animals can instinctively and sensorily 'merge into a community based on signals', the very circumstances of interlocution mean that human beings cannot

(138). This is a distinction that contemporary animal studies (in philosophy and elsewhere) would doubtless question, establishing as it does an instinctual and sensory identity for the 'animal' in contrast to the 'human'. Be that as it may, what in one sense founds human community (the other-than-human in me which makes me an-other human) also establishes the frontiers of communal identity, or in other words the limit of the community's integrity or coherence as such. It does so precisely to the extent that what founds the possibility of civil life is the heterogeneity and dissymmetry which grounds the operations of language or speech construed as a form of address to another. It is only with the reduction of the human being to bare life, or in other words the fall into complete non-citizenship, that the principle of heterogeneity established by human language is diminished. Or, rather, vice versa, as Lyotard puts it: 'only when the impossibility of interlocution' arises are we reduced 'to that meager resource' (ibid.). Consequently, just such a human '*we*' is therefore a product or condition of human interlocution, rather than the origin that founds its possibility. This is not to imply, since language and community do not derive from a prior human 'we' or an essential 'humanity', that the origin of the 'human' is non- or inhuman in the form of some divine or primordial Other to whom we are therefore impossibly indebted. Instead it simply affirms that the 'other' in me and in the other, which founds the possibility of human communicability and citizenry, is the necessary supplement to that possibility itself. It is not in any simple sense previous or external to but coterminous with the making of civil life.

For Lyotard, then, 'the citizen is the human individual whose right to address others is recognized by those others' (ibid.). The formulation of the human being as other-than-human/an-other-human, routed through the dissymmetry or heterogeneity of interlocution, is not equated with a law of the Other that is in any simple sense prior to or outside of the 'human', as its 'divine' or mystical origin. Instead, it is explicitly linked to the specific historical forms that civil society *will have taken*, entering in as a decisive yet non-integratable element. If the principle of the right to address the other, and of the other's recognition of this right, founds the historical possibility of human society in its modern sense, whether it be 'the Greek *politeia* or the modern *republic*' (ibid.), this possibility profoundly partakes of the future anterior, to the extent that in its very form or structure the 'model' cannot be spatially closed or temporally frozen since the heterogeneity which permits the interlocution of citizenry places a limit on the community's coherence, stability and identity (in other words, on what Rancière would perhaps call consensus), thus opening onto other possibilities, other futures, other forms of 'human' organization and interaction, for good or ill. Nonetheless, Lyotard asserts that while the social and geopolitical extension of civility may be promoted, restricted or otherwise managed by various means (of which there are many examples throughout history: 'an obligatory single language, an official language alongside which traditional languages are tolerated, compulsory multilingualism, effective multilingualism, and so on'), ultimately such strategies only determine how interlocution eventually extends, rather than being able to quell its extension more radically (140).

Amid model social forms, it is for Lyotard the 'republican principle' in particular which introduces 'civic interlocution' into the community, and which therefore maintains the principle of heterogeneity or alterity in the realm of human communication. Without it, he suggests, the 'demos' or 'demotic' in its pure form risks a fall into absolute consensuality. For Lyotard it is the 'nation' (presumably in its most 'nationalistic' form) that in modern terms most recalls such a situation. Here, alterity is excluded through a process of non-recognition in which the excluded is precisely not recognized as an other (Rancière would presumably have trouble disputing this analysis of exclusion since he frequently reminds us of it). Now, for Lyotard, the republican principle is avowedly 'contractual'. As such, the 'Other' it maintains within the social form that the community takes is not that of an ancient or divine law preceding human sociability and interlocution in absolute terms. Instead, it arises on the strength of a 'civil' agreement between humans concerning the right to speech and the radical dissymmetry of address – even if, amid the heterogeneity of civil 'time', such an 'Other' facilitates (and indeed puts at risk) that agreement as much as epitomizing it. I have the right to address you, and you me, a right established prior to any inkling that we may agree. Hence the heterogeneous time of the 'civil', which makes its agreement prior to the very possibility of agreement. Indeed, what binds 'us' is that *on principle* we may never be bound by anything other than the principle enshrined in the republican 'contact' – that of heterogeneous speech and dissymmetrical address, to which we will have unconditionally agreed without having agreed to it.

It is in light of these remarks that Lyotard evokes the 'forgotten', a term upon which Rancière dwells in order to mount his increasingly florid critique of Lyotardian thought as perhaps the most hyperbolic form of post-structuralism's discourse of the Other. Here, though, the term arises in the context of a fairly down-to-earth explanation of Amnesty's precise vocation, which Lyotard is careful not to inflate or overstate, describing it as 'minimal' and yet 'decisive' precisely within the limits of its own specificity:

Amnestos meant he who is forgotten. Amnesty does not demand that the judgment be revised or that the convicted man be rehabilitated. It simply asks that the institution that has condemned him to silence forget this decree and restore the victim to the community of speakers. (141)

While Lyotard does not say as much, logically speaking the restoration of interlocutory relations and rights might not just mean release without question. It might also take the form of a fair trial, proper rights and conditions in prison, insistence upon the legal accountability of the State, and so forth. To recall the forgotten in such contexts does not so much appeal to some primordial law of the Other, but first of all reaffirms the fundamental principle of the civil contract. 'The others rights', to reprise Lyotard's title, are in this sense not those of some absolutized Other, but refer instead to those rights which makes the 'civil' possible, possible among all of 'us' (rights which would seem especially important since, however it may be determined, the extension of the 'civil' cannot be curbed).

To the extent that remembering the forgotten is, here, the particular task of Amnesty as a human rights organization, such recollection is therefore less a matter of hyperbolic melancholy or paralysing obligation, testifying to itself in the enigmatic name of an absolute Other. Instead, perhaps more prosaically (or rather, more 'minimally' yet 'decisively'), Amnesty's task of vigilant non-forgetting is 'in accordance with the provisions of the public law of the republican democracies' (ibid.) – that is, law founded on the right to speech and the capacity of address. The law of the republic establishes duty as much as right, yet such duty is not the debt of the absolute *arche*, but occurs instead because the right of the human being as other-than-human/an-other-human is by definition not natural, and is therefore 'merited' or earned through civilization, or in other words through the education or instruction that the civil contract promises. Within this model of interlocutory civility, silence does not commemorate the 'Other' as the absolute resource of a pure enigma. It is simply the condition of possibility of address. For instance, for Lyotard it is only through recognizing the value of his own silence before the teacher's address – a silence which Lyotard equates with a certain productive 'distress' – that the pupil in his turn earns the right to speak (in a phrase that the Rancière of *The Ignorant Schoolmaster*[11] must have blanched at, Lyotard argues that 'the exaltation of interactivity as a pedagogic principle is pure demagogy' (142) – and no doubt it is this, as much as some erroneously detected trace of a commitment to ethical consensuality, that strongly fuels Rancière's attempt to dismiss Lyotard's politics, via a too hastily constructed confluence of the non-transformative and the non-egalitarian).

Whether the relationship of Rancière's thought to that of Lyotard is to be understood in terms of the 'distress' of the differend (or, put otherwise, the very dissymmetry of instruction and address that for Rancière would repeat the severance of emancipatory politics from an ethics of the other), or whether it is to be thought of in terms of the pained agitation occasioned by, let's say, *différance* (that is, of a differentiation which cannot fully repress deferral or, put differently, the limits of differentiation itself), one hesitates to see how its language games open on to the pure optimism of 'dissensus'.[12] Instead, the 'distress' I detect underlying Rancière's position is also that of a desire to stifle the sublime, to reduce it as constitutive of a pure impediment to emancipatory politics, a desire which knows it threatens to delegimitize other aspects of the very same project or analysis – by which I refer to the double gesture on Rancière's part of, on the one hand, a refutation of the sublime (as) blockage itself, and, on the other, the semi-repressed inclusion of the sublime within a 'Schillerian' aesthetics of emancipation.

Derrida mourning Lyotard

The central point of this lengthy preamble outlining Rancière's engagement with Lyotard is that claims about ethics, trauma and mourning – about memory, melancholy and blockage – made on behalf of a certain politics of emancipation are not necessarily constructed on very stable ground. We have seen how Lyotard's writings do not readily bear out Rancière's critique of him on just such terms. However, it is perhaps Derrida more than Lyotard who is most often the prime suspect where accusations about the melancholic disposition of a certain type of modern European philosophy are concerned – a 'melancholy' that must be resisted and overcome if new forms of political life are to be realized. Since, in the above, we have adopted a procedure of close reading of singular texts in order to weigh the validity of such criticisms (those which often circulate in rather loose and general ways, in the manner of scandal or rumour), let us do the same with Derrida. It might be fitting, indeed, to begin with those texts by Derrida that mourn Lyotard himself, since here if anywhere we might expect to find further evidence to support criticism of the Rancerian kind.

In *The Work of Mourning*, which gathers together an array of mourning writings by Derrida devoted to a host of thinkers including Barthes, de Man, Foucault, Althusser, Deleuze and Levinas, we find two texts on Lyotard.[13] One, barely a couple of pages long, published in *Libération* immediately after Lyotard's death, understandably includes little of substance on Lyotard's work, although tellingly speaks on more than one occasion of Lyotard's writings on childhood, and on childhood tears. (If space allowed, much could be said of this choice or decision on Derrida's part, not least since in 'The Other's Rights' the 'mute distress' which pertains to the situation of the *infantia* who is addressed by the Other as a form of instruction remains long after 'our native prematurity' (OR, 147), precisely since we owe to this very same childhood 'distress' the ability to speak and to question, as well as the capacity to be welcomed and acknowledged within civil life as 'other-than-human/an-other-human' – although such hospitality always comes at the price of potentially fundamental transformation of the scene upon which it relies.) The other text devoted to Lyotard in the volume, initially presented (with no title) at the International College of Philosophy in Paris almost a year after Lyotard's death, is lengthier, and approaches the question of mourning by concentrating with some rigour on Lyotard's own remarks on the subject. Here a certain phrase, found in a short essay by Lyotard included in a special issue of a French journal devoted to Derrida's work, recurs: 'There shall be no mourning'. How – if at all – are we to read such a phrase, asks Derrida? For whom – if anyone – is it meant? What exactly does it prohibit and – if anything – what might it nevertheless make possible?

It is not the manly rejection of excessive sentiment that is at stake here. Instead, the prospect of planned, organized mourning seems most under attack in this phrase, one that is also the very medium of a particular interaction between Derrida and Lyotard (found, as it originally is, in an essay that is in a certain way a reply to Derrida, and repeated here, over and again, in a text by Derrida devoted to Lyotard, and much concerned with their friendship).[14] For the *project* of mourning – mourning construed as a concerted 'work' or 'instituted commemoration' (*WM*, 217) – would negotiate the absolute obligation to the dead to which Derrida, in a footnote, alludes here only by way of a political pragmatism that is itself rebuffed by the phrase 'there shall be no mourning'.[15] In Lyotardian terms (as Derrida puts it), organized mourning risks converting the differend of the dead into the possibility of litigation, transforming what seems an unreckonable 'wrong' into calculable 'damages'.

Yet, for Derrida, the 'grammaticality' of the line, as much as its 'meaning', is of particular interest: 'there shall be no mourning' is less a constative statement than a normative or prescriptive phrase. In fact, it is less a normative phrase – in the sense that the former tends to control its own performativity in advance, formulating or effectuating by itself the legitimation of those obligations that it demands – than it is a prescriptive one. For the latter entails 'a further phrase

[that] is left to the addressee', as Derrida puts it: in the case of Lyotard's 'there shall be no mourning', the reader. In its very structure, then, the prescriptive phrase calls for the response of an addressee, therefore entailing an obligation (even if it may be absolute, in view of the dead) that is also a freedom of sorts, a freedom of the one who is obligated, as Lyotard himself observes. (Perhaps in a similar way, for the Sartre of 'Why Write?', that literature tasks the other with their freedom—perhaps, also, the freedom of the Lyotardian *infantia* addressed by the Other.) In a 'quasi-grammatical way', then, the phrase constitutes a form of address that demands reading, not in the sense of passive reception but in terms of active interpretation or response, albeit 'reading' that founders to some extent upon its own impossible desire for knowledge as to the motivation – that is to say, the destination or addressee – of such a phrase (219). For Derrida, nonetheless, this impossible experience, given to the reader by the phrase itself, is tantamount to that of mourning. Mourning thus reinhabits the phrase as the very mark of its readability: 'Readability bears this mourning ... This mourning provides the first chance and the terrible condition of all reading' (220). To the extent that Derrida mourns Lyotard by reading him, such mourning only occurs – can only occur – under the impossible jurisdiction of the phrase 'there shall be no mourning', an impossible injunction indeed that is quite at odds with mourning in its planned or organized forms, in the sense that its prescriptive 'no' disorganizes the very experience it at once prohibits and calls for, bans and necessitates.

If organized mourning aligns fundamentally with political pragmatism (in a footnote, Derrida writes that 'death obligates' in a form that is 'uncon-ditional', to the extent that, in contrast, 'one can always negotiate conditions with the living' – death, however, 'ruptures' this 'symmetry' [223–4]), then the phrase 'there shall be no mourning' opens at least the possibility of another politics. In their introduction to *The Work of Mourning*, Pascale-Anne Brault and Michael Naas observe that 'the genre of the funeral oration' (with which Derrida's various eulogies, letters of condolence, newspaper tributes, memorial essays and other mourning writings cannot help but engage) is 'more than a powerful genre within an already given social and political context; it consoli-dates the very power of that context, with all the promises and risks it entails' even up to the point where it may be said – alluding to such texts as Plato's *Menexenus* – that 'politics is related to, or founded on, mourning' (19). To the extent that the phrase 'there shall be no mourning' makes possible (and yet impossible) another mourning, outside of the organized forms mourning takes in its perhaps foundational relationship with conventional politics and political conventions (for example, those of the fraternal tradition), it entails neither a retreat from politics nor any possibility of maintaining the political status quo, but instead a new or rather unrecognized form of the 'political' beyond 'politics'. (For instance, beyond those forms of 'politics' we could easily decipher from Derrida's list of examples, including not just those negatively coded as 'laborious, guilt ridden and narcissistic, reactive and turned towards melancholy, if not envy' but even and perhaps especially those that, in the guise of a 'wake', border on 'celebration' (221).)

Derrida's essay relates, then, the 'quasi-grammaticality' of the phrase in question to dissymmetrical forms of address that remain initially resistant to the forms of consensuality or commonalty implied by a 'we' or an 'us', or indeed by any stable identity and self-identical expression of a 'you' or an 'I' upon which they may be founded. In this same context, the testamentary falters in its very possibility, even to the degree that 'what the most faithful inheritance demands is the absence of any testament', at any rate in its more conventional guises (ibid.). Derrida therefore seeks to honour this dissymmetry in the act of reading Lyotard, whereby terms like 'we', 'us', 'you' and 'me' (as well as *tu* and *vous*)[16] are not to be dispensed with but reconfigured – always at something of a guess – by the prescriptive phrase set down by Lyotard himself.[17] If, as Lyotard himself suggests, the only possibility of a 'we' may be a posthumous 'we', this might have to do with the impossible mourning beyond mourning ('there shall be no mourning') that, post-mortem, disorganizes all of the relations of intention and address[18] that give us the neat differentiations of 'you' and 'I'. And such dissymmetrical and disorganized interlocutionary relations may take place with a politics in view, to the extent that, as Derrida notes:

> He thus wrote what had to be written, and in the way it had to be written, for the identity of the destination to remain elusive, for the address to any particular addressee never to be, as we say, *proven*, not even by the one who signed it: neither publicly declared, nor obvious enough on its own, nor conclusively ascertained by means of a determining, theoretical judgment. In so doing, he asked publicly, in full light, and practically, but with reference to mourning, the question *of* the Enlightenment or the question *about* the Enlightenment, namely – in that Kantian space he tilled, furrowed, and sowed anew – the question of rational language and of its destination in the public space. (217)

Such would be a 'new' or an as yet – and perhaps permanently – 'unrecognizable' politics of the public sphere that in Lyotard's 'The Other's Rights' resonates powerfully with the evocation of the other-human/other-than-human that founds the fragile yet potentially transformative possibility of civic life (as a life beyond itself). For that matter, the radically dissymmetrical, perhaps untransactable conditions of the post-mortem 'relation' (as non-relation) to which Derrida alludes, via the phrase 'there shall be no mourning', only intensify the somewhat fraught interlocutionary situation of civil life that in fact foreshadows them. Importantly, as Derrida acknowledges toward the end of his essay for Lyotard, the untotalizable identities at play in such an interloctionary situation – 'you', 'I', 'we', 'us' – do not simply hazard a sort of deconstruction tending towards oblivion or radical paralysis, but instead run the risk of what Lyotard in *The Differend* terms the 'last phrase', the further phrase that is called for by the prescriptive one upon which we have so dwelt, as the very possibility of an obligated or tasked freedom.

However, as Derrida points out, Lyotard's writing furthermore demands that we consider this question of mourning in relation to that of the 'ordered' dead, those who die – or who are condemned to die – by another's order or hand. The 'beautiful death' (like that of Socrates, say) is the one that has meaning to the extent that it is conceived of as preferable by dint of an order given to an addressee ('you must die because ...'). Since such a death is effectively fulfilled and fulfilling in terms of its replete meaning, mourning as such may be dispensed with. It is almost as if such a death does not take place as death at all, as Derrida himself observes. The 'order' of such a death means that, in one sense, one dies in order not to die (rather than simply vanishing, to remain and transcend instead as pure and purely legible meaning). Auschwitz, meanwhile, is the exception to this order of the 'beautiful death', foremost because 'Auschwitz' is the name for a practice of the 'extinction of the name' whereby 'the victim is not the addressee of the order'. Thus, '"Auschwitz" cannot, except through an abuse of rhetoric, be turned into a "beautiful death," or a sacrificial holocaust' (236). For Derrida, nonetheless, on these terms 'Auschwitz' can no more be mourned than the 'beautiful death', or at any rate the word 'mourning' is conspicuous by its absence throughout Lyotard's discussion of these matters in *The Differend*:

> If there are no grounds for mourning, if there are no grounds for having to go through mourning these two ordered deaths, it is for diametrically opposed reasons. In the 'beautiful death,' it is because death has meaning: it brings to fulfillment a life full of meaning; this death gets over itself, overtakes or sublates itself, in this meaning. In the case of 'Auschwitz,' on the contrary, 'worse than death,' it is the extinction of the very name that forbids mourning, given that this murder of the name constitutes the very meaning of the order 'die.' (237)

The 'murder of the name' sees the death-order gather itself up to its full power. And yet the power of such an order – that which characterizes or defines it as such – is in another sense tied to the idea of an addressee ('it is you who must die …'). Just as, in the case of the 'beautiful death', the order in one sense fulfills itself but in another becomes self-confounding, because the order 'to die' is transcended by the immortality thereby obtained by the victim, so the death-order at 'Auschwitz' is quasi-suicidal in its practice of the 'extinction of names'. Be that as it may, in either case mourning is out of the question, not simply because there is no-one to be mourned (to say this would be an abuse of the logic we are pursuing here), but because a more conventional 'politics' of mourning is decommissioned in advance by the fact that neither 'death' has a negotiable meaning. The negotiation or reckoning of meaning is what comes to an end *by order* in both the 'beautiful death' and 'the extinction of the name'.

To the extent that it risks lapsing into a permanent state of organized mourning, of coming to 'signify the mourning of Auschwitz', Israel may mourn where 'mourning has no meaning' (237). In other words, it is as if 'Israel had wished to go through mourning' in the sense of 'establishing damages that can be repaired' or 'thinking that it can translate the wrong into damages and the differend into a litigation, which is and remains impossible', as Derrida puts it (ibid.). (Such a reckoning may well be impossible, but nonetheless another Derrida might recognize that it is still inevitable, although he might also insist that such a reckoning must always reckon with the impossible memory of its impossibility.) Derrida cites several passages from *The Differend* where Lyotard expresses these concerns about Israel. For Lyotard, Israel aimed to put to an end the silence to which the Jews had been condemned by Auschwitz, but by seeking the common idiom of international law and politics (as Lyotard puts it) Israel tried to establish a consensus about a 'wrong' that could never be measured or reckoned in consensual terms. (Indeed, Lyotard seems to hint at a connection between the establishment of such a consensus and that of Israel itself; although doubtless Derrida, for one, would question whether the resources of 'Israel', from its foundations up, would ever be exhausted by its affiliation with such a desire to convert a 'wrong' into a 'damages', whether it would have no other reserves.) From this, it is easy enough to distinguish Lyotard's position and thinking on these issues as in stark contrast to Rancière's dismissal of his writings as sponsoring an ethical consensus instituted upon an endless work of mourning and commemoration. Instead, Derrida's mourning essay for Lyotard not only acknowledges but enacts another mourning beyond that which Lyotard's prescriptive phrase proscribes, a mourning it calls for only under the sign of a certain prohibition – a mourning which does not readily partake of the forms of political limitation that Rancière associates with 'ethical' mourning *per se*.

'As for mourning, there shall be none. There shall be *none* of it'

The phrase above, shared between Lyotard and Derrida in the latter's mourning essay for the former, is powerful indeed. But perhaps after all it is neither Derrida nor Lyotard who is really responsible for ethical melancholy, the repetition of trauma and a sense of mourning that keeps us enchained, but instead Emanuel Levinas, to whom the work of both seems to owe so much? Since, above, we have been concentrating on mourning texts, let's now turn to some of those written by Levinas, pertinently enough soon after the end of the Second World War, in order to begin evaluating such a notion. In Derrida's funeral oration for Levinas, found in *The Work of Mourning*, it is said that for Levinas the survivor survives 'without fault and without debt' but instead through an 'entrusted responsibility' (204). What could this mean? Are we once more in the midst of the task of freedom, or of an irresponsibilizing responsibility? Could such a position, if it were possible – one of a 'responsi-bility' or a 'trust' that might somehow elude crushing indebtedness or blame –genuinely escape reinscription within the terms of a Rancière-type critique? Is it possible to read Levinas's own mourning writing in the way Derrida suggests, even to the point of detecting some resonance with the phrase shared between Lyotard and Derrida: 'As for mourning, there shall be none. There shall be *none* of it'?

In 1949, four years after the end of the Second World War, Emmanuel Levinas wrote a short essay in memory of Léon Brunschvicg, who in the year before the war's ending had died an elderly man, lying low in Aix-les-Bains. [19] From 1942 onwards, Brunschvicg had, as Levinas observes, been denied the opportunity to 'take part in any activity' by the Vichy regime, although this had afforded him the chance to review the notebooks in which, since the 1890s, he had written daily diary entries, to be read by his friend Élie Halévy, the French philosopher and historian (many of them were returned to him shortly after Halévy's death in 1937). Concentrating on Brunschvicg's return to these diaries, against the backdrop of both war and old age, Levinas's essay fosters the conceit of a dialogue between the elderly and youthful 'self' of a Jewish scholar whose identity and history – both personal and public – were much tied to the European idea or project. In particular, on rereading the notebooks afresh, the idealistic youth – initially strange to the older man of experience –gradually becomes more familiar as another version or representation of 'me', despite all of life's subsequent 'failures and compromises' (DLB, 41), as if even at this late stage in European history a prewar 'self' can not only be recalled but still identified with in some fashion.

Born in 1869, Brunschvicg was an idealist philosopher known for his studies of Descartes and Spinoza, although he is also remembered for his work on Pascal, including the standard edition in French for which he was responsible. During the interwar years, Levinas had attended Brunschvicg's courses at the Sorbonne, which, so some of Levinas's correspondence suggests, were found not to be entirely satisfactory or compelling, philosophically speaking. The subsequent connection between the two, comparatively slight though it was, probably arose from Brunschvicg's interest in Husserlian phenomenology (Brunschvicg had been instrumental in organizing Husserl's lectures on the *Cartesian Mediations* at the Sorbonne). However, Brunschvicg is remembered here not just as a philosopher of the Sorbonne, but as a Jewish intellectual at the time of the Dreyfus Affair who, however much he later despaired in the face of the horrors of the Second World War, must be recalled as one who fought on the side of the victors in the political scandal that divided France at the turn of the century and who also stood for the victorious side in 1918. [20] In this, in fact, his Judaism is not singularly paramount, says Levinas (although neither can it be split decisively away from the European that he also 'is', for reasons Levinas later elaborates). As such, to remember Brunschvicg is to recollect 'a whole generation' of whom it can be said that what was most important was not the possibility of injustice in a supposedly civilized age, but 'the triumph recorded by justice' itself. 'This memory marked them' insists Levinas (43). More than his philosophy, it is this feature of Brunschvicg's 'life' that Levinas considers most noteworthy.

In many ways, then, the passing of a man like Brunschvicg provides the occasion for Levinas to question or complicate the synonymous idea of the passing of an age. Brunschvicg is associated with virtues and ideas that many felt must perish – indeed, had already succumbed – with the advent of two world wars. Levinas does not shy away from the image of Brunschvicg as a European Jew born in the last century who is also a man of European culture and civilization, but instead affirms the continuing importance of those same attributes that may be recalled in his name. Without hesitation, he celebrates Brunschvicg as a man of reason and of the university, drawing connections between the scholarly disposition, the refusal of vulgar thought and the taste for justice in terms of a 'civil status' that Brunschvicg both participates in and epitomizes (ibid.). This 'civil status', remarks Levinas, came down to the fact that, through a commitment to proof rather than propaganda, men of Brunschvicg's generation had 'proved the existence of justice' (ibid.). Indeed, Brunschvicg is recommended as an example to those among the postwar 'Jewish youth' who understandably felt immense disenchantment with the whole proposition of Europe and the West (of which Levinas was also strongly critical at various points in his philosophical career), and who only see a future beyond its borders, in a 'simple life on a soil that is worked and defended with self-sacrifice and heroism' (39).[21] Levinas counsels that the virtues which helped to found and secure Israel must not be presumed to consume without remainder the resources of a 'renewed Judaism'. The 'basic toughness and straight-forwardness' of the farmer-soldier of the Israeli state should not be allowed to exhaust the meaning or significance of the Jewish diaspora.[22] Instead, the critical attributes of a lively and learned intelligence must survive, including the sense of irony which, through reference to Brunschvicg's own youthful reflections in his diary entries from the early 1890s, Levinas takes to complicate too-simplistic notions of the relation of thought – or faith – to action. If, in contrast to the attitudes found among young farmer-soldiers of postwar Israel, Brunschvicg's juvenilia should be regarded as born of an era of comparative peace and happiness, Levinas nevertheless salutes peace as 'man's vocation', in rather the same way that recollection of the Dreyfus Affair prompts not the memory of injury and wrongdoing so much as the happy remembrance of victory and justice. As far as this particular essay is concerned, then, the idea of peace is not absolutely blighted by the experience of unjust war, any more than the appeal of justice is quelled by offences against it, however heinous they may be. On the contrary, renewal – including 'Jewish' renewal – comes as much from the memory that injustice did not prevail, as from the harsh lessons of its experience. [23] In this respect, then, the crisis of modernity sensed in the aftermath of war cannot merely be reduced to the deficiencies and defects of prewar attitudes and ideas (which were so often referenced precisely to legitimate such a sense of crisis) since there is also something in the prewar mind-set that remains of value for postwar life. Indeed, one implication of Levinas's writing on Brunschvicg is that the very nature or meaning of any such 'crisis' depends crucially upon how one responds to it now and in the future, so that from this perspective it looks far from simply an implacable or immutable catastrophic inheritance (of the kind Rancière associates with the emergence of the ethics-of-the-other position).

Brunschvicg was born into an age of 'material security' in which 'every revolution was already over', Levinas tells us, and in which equilibrium therefore reigned among Europe's great powers. The ideological meaning of nation-states such as Germany and Russia had not yet intensified in the political form witnessed in the twentieth century. The possibility of forms of self-expression and enquiry not limited to directly 'political' responses to historical and social conditions potentialized certain types of distance or detachment in which phrases 'light but rich in possibilities' might not simply degenerate into 'maxims', as Levinas puts it (42). This is evoked as 'civilized speech', wholly divorced from 'speechifying'. For that matter, it is for Levinas far from reducible to merely the immediate 'concerns' of the author or speaker himself. In other words, such speech is open, responsive, hospitable to other meanings and possibilities; it trembles with the possibility of 'thought' not limited to merely a self-assertive or self-gratifying intention, constituting instead a certain type of 'resistance' in language which excites thinking (ibid.). Such resistant language is traced back by Levinas to Brunschvicg's 'French training' at the École Normale Supérieure – indeed 'to everything that is most nobly French about the traditions of that School' (ibid.). Here, as Brunschvicg himself writes in 1942, if expression 'betrays the thought that it should have served', still thought is tasked with subduing 'the rebellious slave' that nonetheless excites it.[24] As a 'man' as much as a philosopher, Brunschvicg's very 'life' may well be characterized, and perhaps dominated, by this idea of a 'thought' that cannot bring to book or place in order the forms of self-expression it requires – though such an incapacity is less a limitation or failing than a virtue, a strength, indeed an origin of sorts. (It is for this very same reason, perhaps, that Levinas is unwilling to reduce such a lifetime to mere 'biography' [39]). The latter would be inadequate in the sense that the more complex relations of thought to language recalled via Brunschvicg necessarily problematize the very conditions of biographical writing, and also therefore because on this same basis such a lifetime cannot be reduced to a single, personal biography. Henceforth, Brunschvicg's life cannot help but become exemplary or indicative, in ways that Levinas deliberately puts to use throughout his essay.) The notion of a language resistant to and yet inspiring of thought, one that hesitates at the limits of its own self-expression (as opposed to the idea of a more immediate and direct relation of thought or faith to action) is of course being promoted here as an inheritance that is also a necessary supplement to the attitudes of a contemporaneous 'Jewish youth'. Cross-fertilized by the European and the Judaic, rather than emanating from their decisive separation, this inheritance is once more connected with a memory not just dominated by catastrophe or disaster, but enriched by possibility itself.

If, for the likes of Rancière, Levinas might represent a certain origin of the ethical position to be lamented in philosophy, one that Rancière depicts as perpetually paralysed by the sense of an oppressively traumatic history which those who desire emancipation must escape at all costs, it is therefore important to remember the Levinas who writes 'The Diary of Léon Brunschvicg'. For in this text, we are not just trapped by the past, although neither is the future dependent upon simple flight from it. On two counts, then, this Levinas problematizes Rancière's discourse, eluding his reductive image of the 'ethical' as just a state of permanent and inescapable mourning and at the same time weakening the premise or rationale of its emancipatory alternative – in other words, its line of flight. For Levinas, unfettered by a propagandist will-to-power Brunschvicg epitomizes a desire for justice that is neither retributive, slavish, nor located in what Levinas terms 'the horrible prestige of the Sacred'. Furthermore, not 'the slightest trace of a specifically Jewish reaction' can be detected in the 1942 notebook entries, writes Levinas, although Brunschvicg 'was a member of the Central Committee of the Israeli Alliance from well before the war and never tried to forget his origins'. His desire for justice is founded instead upon the 'moral conscience' that cements his 'civil status' (43). Thus, Levinas's Brunschvicg hardly resembles the Rancièrian subject of an ethics of the Other (although he does look something more like Lyotard's civil-human). As Levinas observes, one may well decry – and no doubt justly – the 'profoundly respectable form of successful assimilation' of men like Brunschvicg for whom Judaism is still a defining characteristic, but nonetheless the latter's assimilation is not to be put down to 'betrayal' but instead proceeds from 'adherence to a universal ideal' that surpasses any 'particularism'.[25] (While Levinas does not dwell upon the idea that certain forms of Jewish 'particularism' might be resistant to this 'universal ideal' – a resistance that would, here, not be his own – it should also be recalled that in this essay resistance does not so much set a limit upon what it resists, but rather *excites* it.)

In a way that once again eludes Rancière's characterization of what we might term a post-Levinasian ethical position, Brunschvicg is avowedly non-sentimental. Mistrust of sentiment and avoidance of platitude are essential in responding with intelligence to grief. Such intelligence must resist rigid forms of thought or 'static ideas' that stifle its creativity (as having futural capacity), and in this must maintain its aptitude for irony. Levinas recalls the 1937 Descartes Congress during which 'new philosophical tendencies' such as existentialist and Marxist thought (avant-garde Catholicism, too) 'were already being affirmed' so as to address topics that were self-consciously contemporary: 'Anguish, death, care' (44). One participant, Gabriel Marcel, bitterly attacked thinkers like Brunschvicg for their 'intellectualism' or lack of 'inner life', which Marcel associated in turn with a lack of care for God and death on their part. According to Levinas, Brunschvicg's bone-dry retort was that he, Léon Brunschvicg, was indeed much less preoccupied by his own death than Marcel was with his. (The fact that Levinas takes pleasure in this remark might also be linked to his concern, in the 1934 'Phenomenology' for instance, for the Heideggerian attitude towards death as the 'proper' of being, something he would connect not only with the climate of Heideggerian thought but also with the philosophy of Hitlerism.) In a flash of irony, the coldness and detachment attributed to men of Brunschvicg's stripe is refigured as a necessary bulwark against the ultimately narcissistic, self-regarding and self-gratifying hyperbole of the impassioned counterpart. Brunschvicg's 'inner life', insists Levinas, is not dominated by 'mysticism' or 'religious anxiety' of the kind that prevails upon a Christian existentialist like Marcel, but proceeds from the deep-felt values of 'reason and enlightenment' (44), such that any idea of God (even a Jewish God) he may have had would arise from the 'coincidence of rational activity and moral conscience' (this would therefore be the God of Descartes rather than Pascal, as Levinas himself observes). [26] Such thinking commits itself to one immediate concern only, that of justice, which, if it is to be demanded at all – that is, demanded justly – must be demanded immediately. Levinas associates such a demand, then, not with 'the mystical experiences and horrors of the Sacred' (of the type that linked 'the supposed religious revival of our contemporaries' (45) to political objectives of different kinds – in other words, various forms of political ontology or theology), but instead with a type of 'atheism' (the sceptical element of which establishes the true conditions of possibility of faith, as Derrida has asserted in Levinas's wake, so that such atheism can here be referenced by Levinas as bringing us 'much closer to the One God' than the theologico-political revival to which he alludes). [27]

Levinas concludes his essay by stating that, while 'our generation could not derive from the experience of Hitler what Brunschvicg's generation derived from the Dreyfus Affair', nevertheless its experience, however traumatic, demonstrates once more the possibility of justice; although Levinas quickly asserts that he has no desire to see this demonstration repeated – in other words, he harbours no wish that history (the history of immense suffering) be replayed. Such a reaction is not merely dominated by trauma. Nonetheless, history is not to be forgotten through the more direct gesture of pure flight. Levinas hopes that the 'new spiritual and sometimes geographical horizons' of 'today's Jewish youth' do not blind them to what is precious in the past. Although he does not say as much, it seems clear that such 'gold-dust' might be prized as something that may aid future resistance against the repetition of an otherwise disregarded history. (As such, the past is to be remembered not only so as to endlessly preserve or reprise trauma, but also to resource a difficult freedom, to protectively equip it against any recurrence of the horrors from which it emerged.)

In another essay by Levinas from the same period, published just two years later in 1951, Brunschvicg crops up once more. 'Being a Westerner' starts out by acknowledging the widespread sense of loss and despair at the end of two world wars, whereby faith in reason, science, progress and 'human dignity' seem to have given way to thanatology, new forms of mysticism, the will to power and a taste for the irrational.[28] However, Levinas speculates that reason's fall from grace has less to do with the twentieth century's 'moments of anguish and ecstasy' (the test of which one might presume it had failed) than with its withdrawal into itself 'by virtue of its very nobility' (BW, 46). In other words, Levinas seems to imply, it is a mistake to see in the aftermath of two such terrible wars proof of reason's innate shortcomings; if anything, such crises attest to a need for reason to be newly mobilized. If Léon Brunschvicg's name may be associated with a sense of the 'absolute society' or enclosed tradition of reason – 'Galileo, Descartes, Kepler, Huyghens, Newton, Cantor, Einstein' – the intellectual output of which is considered by him to be coterminous with its best moral and religious sensibilities, nevertheless for Levinas, Brunschvicg's work continues to speak to us from beyond the grave, with, it is hoped:

> the salutary effect of giving a bad intellectual conscience to those who have forgotten, using the pretext of youth, what has after all, for three centuries, now gauged the exact gap between thought and childishness. (ibid.)

Brunschvicg's example demonstrates what must not be forgotten, namely, reason's call, the irreducibility of an address to the other that forms the indispensable supplement (and question) of its inner consistency. Reason must therefore open itself to the other of itself, in this case stirring in those who languish and revel in their 'childishness' the 'bad intellectual conscience' of which they are guilty. If for Lyotard the distress of the *infantia* represents the very condition of possibility of civil locution and society, in Levinas we find the sense (which one may indeed refract out of a certain Lyotard) that such infantile experience obtains its true meaning and significance only through the passage to adulthood: that is, in the proper acquisition of what Levinas terms 'civil status' (albeit, for Lyotard, such 'status' is always marked by a certain divisibility, rendered other-than-itself by the 'right' or demand of speech, thus being shared unstably with the 'other' that one also always 'is'). In this respect, it is interesting that another lecture included in *Difficult Freedom*, where the two texts under discussion are collected (along with other essays on Judaism), was given the title 'A Religion for Adults'.[29] Here, in a way that is reminiscent of the discourse of 'Being a Westerner', Judaism is assigned the avowedly educative task of decharming the world, as Levinas puts it, 'contesting the notion that religions apparently evolved out of enthusiasm and the Sacred' (RA, 14). (We might note here a stark contrast with the Žižekian claim that it is Christianity rather than Judaism that demystifies the Sacred, notably since this Christian 'preference' is strongly allied to the transformative politics to which Žižek frequently alludes.) This 'decharming' is in the interests of 'freedom', in Levinas's terms ('freedom' being with equated here with 'conscience').[30] Judaism is for adults in the sense that in Judaism one must attain the 'age of doubt', as Levinas puts it, in order to resist false pieties. Indeed, it is this that ties Judaism to the West, since the 'Western spirit', or 'philosophy' in other terms, is perhaps 'in the last analysis the position of a humanity that accepts the risk of atheism' (16).[31] As the essay proceeds, this position – one of a godly atheism, one might say, or of spiritual conscience – is linked by Levinas to the possibility of ethics and justice. It is in this context that Levinas speaks of the Other. But the 'freedom' to which Levinas alludes, and to which much of his philosophical career demonstrated powerful commitment (over and above, for instance, the binding sense of past and destiny he elsewhere associates with the pagan concept of fate that helps define Hitlerian 'particularism') is 'not in the least bit pathological, or strained or heartrending'.[32] It 'relegates the values to do with roots and institutes other forms of fidelity and responsibility. Man, after all, is not a tree' – 'freer forms' are required if 'all those heavy and sedentary things' ('the dark voices of hereditary' or the call of the 'village') are to be surpassed in the interests of precisely those 'other forms of fidelity and responsibility', and, in particular, in favour of 'a freedom with regard to history in the name of morality' (22–3). (All of this, one might note, seems quite at odds with Rancière's characterization of the emergence of an ethics-of-the-other position in terms of some quasi-mystical, paralysing sense of obligation and retrogression.)

In 'Being a Westerner', then, Brunschvicg's books are celebrated as bulwarks against voguish irrationalism, primitivism, mysticism or (as Levinas puts it) 'mythology and war', and against the widespread rumour of a 'crisis of the scientific spirit'. In fact, his books are presented as a (pedagogic) instrument with which to curtail such adolescent behaviour and thus facilitate the onset of maturity (BW, 47–8). Just as 'thought' must strive to master the 'rebellious' language that excites it, so we might say that the 'childishness' which reason must curtail is also that which asks of its supposed inner consistency that it speak to the other. (If I am attempting a partial synthesis here of thinkers as different as Lyotard and Levinas, it is in the interests of reinforcing my general point that these figures of an ethics-of-the-other, to recall Rancière's discourse, do not just promote perpetual retrogression or mourning of loss, but instead encourage futural thinking about 'civil status', let's say, in which the idea of the 'other' as revered primordial origin must be treated with some suspicion.)

In 'Being a Westerner', then, reason in general must not be static, but mobile, creative, open, future-oriented, hospitable.[33] It must explore new ideas as much as guard valuable ones. In particular, however, the 'thought' of the West (as its very 'spiritual life') differentiates itself from forms of religion based on the notion of salvation.[34] It must free itself from the desire for salvation that Levinas believes embodies a powerful form of egoism. For Brunschvicg, such 'self-love' as is witnessed in the striving for salvation implies in turn a certain detachment from God (that is to say, in Levinas's interpretation, a departure from the disin-terested moral and religious values consonant with enlightenment and reason that, once stripped of theologico-political drive or will-to-power, ensure man's dignity and, as it were, his spirituality) (47–8).[35] For Levinas, Judaism has the potential resources to combat the 'childishness' of which he speaks because, in favouring 'inner morality' over 'outer dogmatism', it eschews the 'supernatural', or the 'impure element of magic and sorcery and that drunkenness of the Sacred and of war that prolong the animal within the civilized' (48–9). Whatever one might have to say, today, about the evocation of animality here, what is clear is that Levinas speaks against *not for* an entire ensemble of ideas with which Rancière suggests the ethics-of-the-other position is associated. The sacred or the mystical (or a feeling of redemptive entitlement) is no more indulged than a sense of war is oppressively retained as merely a species of traumatic repetition. Rather, these ideas are well understood to belong more properly to the opposing side, as it were. For Levinas – supposedly the ethical thinker *par excellence* – in the wake of World War Two, and all that it stood for, such ideas are therefore to be resisted *not* embraced by Europe and Judaism alike. Brunschvicg's is 'a profound text', 'not because it involves the extrinsic witness of history, but because it denounces the very ambiguity of exaltation' (49).[36] Here, perhaps, we might detect a powerful echo of the phrase: 'As for mourning, there shall be none. There shall be *none* of it'.

Of course, Levinas's entire thought cannot be reduced to his writings on Brunschvicg, nor explained by them. But if his postwar writing is concerned with mourning, it also consists of a desire for freedom (in however difficult a sense) – freedom from traumatic memory, or put differently the desire for memory as a possible source of freedom. Levinas's writing after the Brunschvicg texts is far from just a philosophical working-through of these attitudes. As Caygill demonstrates, it often navigates a difficult and sometimes distressing path between the philosophical and the political, notably in relation to Levinas's somewhat agonized relationship to Israel. At times when Levinas is more 'philosophically' critical of the state-form, the idea of citizenship is allied to the problem of assimilation, a criticism to which Lyotard's notion of civil life as expressed by the other-than-human/other human offers a possible rejoinder. Of course, there is also the Levinas that Derrida remembers, the one we have already glimpsed in 'A Religion for Adults', for whom it was clear that 'the holy land' of Israel is 'but nakedness and desert, a heap of wood and stone' next to 'a person who has been affronted'.[37] (The events in Gaza during the summer of 2014, the time of writing of the present essay, make these words tremble.) However, so close to the experience of war, what the Brunschvicg writings do suggest is that the attitudes formed from such a desire were not devoted to some sense of an absolutely unsurpassable catastrophe to be endlessly replayed, but were based instead upon a certain resistance to mourning within mourning that we have been insisting upon all along. Subjecting the texts we have read to closer scrutiny may well not diminish the gap that exists between the 'agents' and the 'objects' of such critique as we find in Rancière – perhaps, on the contrary – but it might shed a different light not just upon the nature of the dispute in question, but the objectives and desires behind it.

Notes

1   See Giorgio Agamben, *Homer Sacer: Sovereign Power and Bare Life* (Stanford: Stanford University Press, 1998), 54.

2   Jacques Rancière, *Aesthetics and its Discontents*, trans. Steven Corcoran (Cambridge: Polity, 2012) (hereafter cited in text as *AD*).

3   As we will see, Rancière makes such arguments, with varying degrees of nuance, across a number of his texts. They often centre on Lyotard, where critical intensity tends to heighten. Indeed, Rancière is clearly fond of reprising his critique of the Lyotardian sublime, finding subtle ways to reiterate acrimonious dissatisfaction. See for instance the Foreword to *The Politics of Aesthetics: The Distribution of the Sensible*, trans. Gabriel Rockhill (London and New York: Continuum, 2004), and those sections of the chapter on 'Artistic Regimes and the Shortcomings of the Notion of Modernity' in which the comments included in the Foreword are further worked out (see esp. 29). See also, for example, *Dissensus: On Politics and*

Aesthetics, trans. Steven Corcoran (London and New York: Continuum, 2010), esp. 59–60, 72–4, 182. Here, across a series of different essays Rancière's rancor gathers itself, as will be seen, through repetitive focus on Lyotard's 1993 lecture for Amnesty International, 'The Other's Rights'. This is a text we will therefore go on to read closely.

4   To be more specific regarding Lyotard, in *Aesthetics and its Discontents* Rancière argues as we shall see that Lyotard contrasts the 'positivistic nihilism of aesthetics as a discourse which, under the name of culture, delights in the ruined ideals of a civilization' with just this 'negative task' of bearing impossible witness to the 'unpresentable' (*AD*, 89).

5   Although Rancière argues otherwise, Lyotard of course knows this. For instance, in *Heidegger and 'the jews'*, trans. Andreas Michel and Mark S. Roberts (Minneapolis: University of Minnesota Press, 1990), 45, he writes: 'Art is an artifact; it constructs its representation. Art cannot be sublime; it can "make" sublime ….' While, on this basis, there would be much to say about his characterization of Lyotard's 'mistaken' thinking about the sublime, if nothing else it points to Rancière's haste in wanting to present a reductive image of the Lyotardian project.

6   In *The Future of the Image*, Rancière describes the 'ethical turn' with which he is concerned in *Aesthetics and its Discontents* in terms of 'a Platonic ethical framework that does not involve the notion of art, but where what is judged is simply *images*, where what is examined is simply their relationship to their origin (are they worthy of what they represent?) and their destination (what effects do they produce on those who receive them?)'. See Rancière, *The Future of the Image*, trans. Gregory Elliott (London and New York: Verso, 2007), 111. See, though, my note 5 above.

7   In the final essay included in *Aesthetics and its Discontents*, 'The Ethical Turn of Aesthetics and Politics', Rancière argues that through his reading of the Kantian sublime Lyotard twists ethics into the very law of aesthetics, whereas in Kant it opens a pathway out of the realm of art, so that in the process aesthetic freedom and Kantian moral autonomy are together overturned by and twisted into the (ethical) monster of art's heteronomy, its subjection to the law of the 'Other'. See esp. 127–8. In similar vein, in *The Future of the Image*, when discussing Lyotard, Rancière writes: 'The problem of "sublime art" is thus posed in simple terms: one cannot have sublimity both in the form of the commandment prohibiting the image and in the form of an image witnessing the prohibition. To resolve the problem, the sublime character of the commandment prohibiting the image must be identified with the principle of a non-representative art. But in order to do that, Kant's extra-artistic sublime has to be identified with a sublime that is defined within art. This is what Lyotard does when he identifies Kant's moral sublime with the poetic sublime analyzed by Burke' (132). Again, see my note 5 above.

8   In the last chapter of *The Future of the Image*, Rancière argues that the paradox
     of Lyotard's sublime is that it seeks to disrupt the machinery of dialectical
     thought by drawing on the conceptual resources of its philosophical 'master':
     'In short, the concept of art summoned to disrupt the Hegelian machine is none
     other than the Hegelian concept of the sublime' (133). Whether or not this is
     true, Rancière rereads Hegel to argue that, for the latter, the sublime does not
     simply entail a symbolic art that cannot find an adequate material form for its
     idea, and which is therefore prior to representation; more complexly, with the
     decline of representative art and the Romantic separation of form and content,
     the sublime makes possible 'a new symbolic moment' which is (at) the *end* of
     art, one that insists through a strongly polemical gesture on Hegel's part that
     after 'the dissolution of the determinate relationship between idea and material
     presentation' (136), as Rancière puts it, art is simply over, once and for all. For
     Rancière, Lyotard's disastrous move is therefore to reappropriate this 'end' in terms
     of an interminable (ethical) debt to the 'Other'.

9   Jean-François Lyotard, 'The Other's Rights', in *On Human Rights*, eds. Stephen
     Shute and Susan Hurley (New York: Basic Books, 1993), 135–47 (hereafter cited in
     text as OR).

10   Lyotard therefore continues: 'The likeness that they have in common follows from
     the difference of each from each' (OR, 136).

11   Jacques Rancière, *The Ignorant Schoolmaster: Five Lessons in Intellectual
     Emancipation*, trans. Kristin Ross (Stanford: Stanford University Press, 1991).
     The premise of this book is that the scene of teaching is characterized by an equal
     intelligence shared by teacher and student alike and thus that the beginnings of
     education are to be found in such 'equality'.

12   Fittingly, if ironically, the term is also used by Lyotard (even if its meaning is not
     identical with that of Rancière), for instance at the very close of *Peregrinations:
     Law, Form, Event* (New York: Columbia University Press, 1988), where Lyotard
     writes that 'the only consensus' we should concern ourselves with pursuing is 'one
     that would encourage ... heterogeneity or "dissensus"' (OR, 45).

13   Jacques Derrida, *The Work of Mourning*, eds Pascale-Anne Brault and Michael
     Naas (Chicago and London: University of Chicago Press, 2001) (hereafter cited in
     text as *WM*).

14   The text in question is a short piece by Lyotard entitled 'Translator's Notes'
     (Derrida concentrates on the section on 'Mourning') that was published in a 1990
     special issue on Derrida of *Revue philosophique de la France et de l'étranger*, edited
     by Catherine Malabou.

15   As we will see, in *The Work of Mourning* Derrida writes that 'death obligates' in a
     form that is 'unconditional' to the extent that, in contrast, 'one can always negotiate
     conditions with the living'. Death, however, 'ruptures' this 'symmetry' (*WM*, 223–4).

16 Derrida notes that, perhaps alone among their peers, he and Lyotard eschewed the
    'tu' and instead retained the 'vous' as a therefore anomalous form of interchange,
    a 'secret code' with 'transgressive value', a practice of 'exception' or 'contravention',
    a 'grammatical contraband' that, as such, 'left open its destinal singularity'
    (*WM*, 226–8).

17 In the essay, Derrida gives reasons why he may speculate that the phrase in fact
    addresses him, though of course this falls well short of an assertion or proof.

18 Not to mention the forms and borders of internality and externality that,
    post-mortem, introjection and incorporation struggle to maintain or negotiate.

19 Emmanuel Levinas, 'The Diary of Léon Brunschvicg', in *Difficult Freedom: Essays
    on Judaism*, trans. Seán Hand (London: Athlone, 1990), 39–45 (hereafter cited in
    text as DLB).

20 In *Levinas and the Political* (London and New York: Routledge, 2002), Howard
    Caygill draws attention to the importance assumed by the Dreyfus Affair not only
    in Levinas's thinking of the relationship between ethics and politics, but in terms
    of his broader politics as oriented towards a radical republicanism. Caygill also
    treats the Dreyfus Affair as the occasion to distinguish Levinas's response to its
    anti-Semitism in relation to that brand of Zionism that ultimately proceeded from
    coverage of the affair by the likes of Theodor Herzl, who propounded the need for
    radical Jewish separatism.

21 Taking just one subsequent text in *Difficult Freedom*, 'Place and Utopia', 99–102,
    for instance, Levinas shows himself more sharply critical of the Christian
    participation in Europe, in contrast to the achievements he discerns in the
    Jewish contribution to it. Here, Levinas is much more sceptical about Christian
    utopianism than, say, Žižek, arguing that its rejection of the world can foster
    otherworldly tendencies that often obstruct worldly change, or alternatively
    that may encourage partisan dwelling which answers what in 'A Religion for
    Adults' Levinas terms the sedentary call of the 'village'. (For more on this contrast
    between Levinas and Žižek, see my book, *Modern Thought in Pain: Philosophy,
    Politics, Psychoanalysis* [Edinburgh: Edinburgh University Press, 2014].)

22 The connection between labour and freedom has frequently been a concern of
    French and leftist Hegelians, although the more famous example is of course
    found above the gates of the Nazi death camps. The postwar Levinas is critical of
    such valorizations of work, particularly in regard to Zionism, to the extent that
    for him they promote not creative endeavour but a sense of effort and fatigue that
    does not equate easily with the enjoyment of freedom and futurity. Nonetheless,
    Caygill asserts that, in his writings on Brunschvicg, Levinas (despite his fierce
    criticisms of Zionism) is concerned neither simply to oppose the European or
    'assimilated' Jew to the Israeli farmer-soldier, nor to indicate a simple preference
    of one over the other, but instead to think through the complex resources of what

it may mean to be Jewish or to reinvent Jewishness after the war, by looking at historical contributions beyond but not merely outside of the state of Israel.

23 Of course in *Totality and Infinity* and other texts Levinas shows himself to be far from naïve concerning the continuing possibility of war.

24 Cited in Levinas, 'The Diary of Léon Brunschvicg', 42.

25 Levinas was critical both of assimilation and Zionist separatism (although his writings on the Israeli state are sometimes more critical than others); needless to say, however, he is at all times keen to avoid a biologistic or racial conception of the Judaic, and is indeed reluctant to concede any simple or fixed sense of Jewish identity or place in the world. The rejection of 'particularism', here, links to Levinas's critique of paganism, its concept of fate and its relationship to Hitlerism.

26 The specific character of Gabriel Marcel's Christian existentialism left him feeling at odds with a thinker like Sartre; like Ernst Jünger although in a rather different way, he was known for obsessing over technological dehumanization in particular. For a fuller reading of Jünger see my book, *Modern Thought in Pain*.

27 In 'A Religion for Adults', also found in *Difficult Freedom* (11–23), Levinas writes, as we shall see, of a monotheism which 'surpasses and incorporates atheism' (as much as, for Levinas, it would also oppose the paganism he associates with Hitlerism); but which 'is impossible unless you attain the age of doubt, solitude and revolt'. Thus, such 'atheism is worth more than the piety bestowed on mythical gods' (16).

28 In *Difficult Freedom*, 46–9 (hereafter cited in text as BW).

29 In *Difficult Freedom*, 11–23 (hereafter cited in text as RA).

30 Such a connection, made in the context of this particular text by Levinas, obviously does not fully exhaust his idea of freedom or do justice to its development, a much fuller and more complex account of which can be found running throughout Caygill's *Levinas and the Political*. In broad terms, Caygill offers a cogent demonstration of Levinas's philosophically hard-fought commitment to the notion of freedom, especially during the earlier part of his career (albeit that responsibility takes centre-stage over freedom later on, at any rate as the context in which freedom needs to be rethought). For Caygill Levinas's interest in freedom stems initially from the Bergsonian notion of creative spontaneity (although this was revised by the sense of a difficult freedom after the Second World War), rather than from a liberalistic identification with autonomy. But it is also a view of freedom that eschews the pagan concept of fate which may itself be used to contrast the cultic particularism of Hitlerian philosophy with the universalist resources of Western civilization (albeit a 'particularism' that sought universal expansion for itself). Caygill shows how Levinas's concern with freedom powerfully affected his relationship to both Heideggerian and Husserlian thought. All of this may be placed in contrast to Rancière's notion of the advent of an

ethics-of-the-other position as dominated by the sense of paralysing obligation not creative, or even difficult, freedom.

31 Of course, throughout his career Levinas is also far from uncritical of the Western tradition, as significantly a *philosophical* tradition, when considered as a backdrop to the advent of Nazism.

32 See note 20 above.

33 To the extent that, for Levinas, the law is a bulwark against the dogmatism of the Sacred or mysticism, it is funded by the 'inner life' of conscience and morality as, precisely, far from dogmatic or simply repetitive.

34 In *Levinas and the Political*, Caygill shows how Levinas's notion of a redeeming repentance, where it exists in some of his earlier writings, is not so much tied to the memory of an inescapable fate as inspired by the Bergsonian idea of creative spontaneity and absolute freedom in relation to the world (albeit one that Levinas later sought to refine from the standpoint of heteronomy). In 'Reflections on Hitlerism', however (the text on which Caygill concentrates in this regard), it is also true that enlightenment and reason seek to forfeit the drama of redemption and repentance, although this departure is also what licenses certain anti-liberal dramatic narratives of repentance and redemption that, in Caygill's terms, seek to exploit the deficit of liberal rationalism. Nonetheless, on this basis redemptive thought would be a supplement rather than merely an oppressive origin for future social forms (even, Levinas suggests, those deriving from Marxism).

35 In 'A Religion for Adults' Levinas writes: 'The way that leads to God therefore leads *ipso facto* – and not in addition – to man', and this same 'way' leads to man's 'self-education' (RA, 18).

36 Brunschvicg is evoked in similar vein in other essays included in *Difficult Freedom*. For instance, in 'A Voice on Israel' (123–6) also from 1951, he is cited as teaching us about the 'trace of wretchedness within the fervor of feelings' that are here associated with 'love' of, or in other words refusal to relinquish, war (125); while in 'Exclusive Rights' (239–41) Levinas reprises Brunschvicg's motto: 'To mistrust every thing and love every man' (239), which in the context we have been exploring surely reads as the veneration of conscience and morality (as not merely personal attributes) over propagandist or cultic politics.

37 The reference here is to Levinas's preface to Marlène Zarader's *Heidegger et les paroles de l'origine* (Paris: Vrin, 1986), 12–13; the citation occurs in *WM*, 202.

3

Transference Love in the Age of 'isms'

Herman Rapaport

Books are not life, only its ashes.

— Marguerite Yourcenar

Of '-isms'

When Anglo-American academics begin thinking in terms of 'isms', they often imagine that a body of thought is some sort of social actor that has agency in the public sphere and therefore may be considered a threat, if only because an agency is imagined to be motivated by some sort of wish, will or desire. The model that gives credence to this assumption is to be drawn from political philosophy in which 'isms', some much more extreme than others, are perceived as doctrines predicated on controversial beliefs that when put into practice are considered dangerous. Such 'isms' are of concern not only because they maintain doctrines that are explicitly antagonistic to certain people and groups, but because these doctrines can be motivated by the sort of *collective desire* and will that can drive people to behave fanatically in the name of an ideal. In other words, what can make an 'ism' worrisome is the fact that doctrinaire thinking leads to – and even requires – praxis which may well depart significantly from the status quo and institute the sort of changes that will be socially and politically transformative. After all, one can't have communism or fascism – to take the most extreme cases – without a thorough-going revolution that radically changes the order of things. Or, to take a more twenty-first century 'ism', environmentalism, one can't have an ecological vision and not practice it. If one believes that climate change is going to be disastrous, then ethically one is a hypocrite if one doesn't engage in a politics of legislating meaningful changes in order to combat global warming. In that sense, 'isms' can be said to want (that is, require) something of us, which is to say, an 'ism' could be identified as a demand.

We know that 'isms' interpolate us if only because 'isms' require us to decide whether we are willing to be allied with them or not. 'Jihadism' interpolates all American citizens, just to reference the United States, insofar as one is talking about a violent ideology that doesn't leave room for neutrality. One either desires *jihad* or not. However, politically inactive 'isms' may well not require a yea or nay. Art critics in the 1980s used to take stands against 'formalism', because formalist analysis was perceived to be socially regressive in that it didn't beat the drum for social justice. But today no one cares particularly about formal analysis as an 'ism', largely because it has become so marginal in relation to content analysis. So on this issue most people remain fairly agnostic, given that there is no perceived threat. Of course, 'isms', whether threatening or not, do implicitly raise the question of our allegiances to beliefs and reveal something about our desires in terms of adherence, commitments and connectedness. Also 'isms' classify academics into sub-specialties, and one's desire to be part of an 'ism' or not speaks to how one wants to be known. This speaks to both one's intellectual commitments – the beliefs, methods and concerns that one has – and one's allegiance to a group of people, however formal or informal, who have been active in developing a movement in order to promote a certain intellectual agenda. Those who disparage such adherence speak of their colleagues in terms of 'jumping on the band wagon', as if identifying with an 'ism' were merely opportunistic and flippant, which, no doubt, can be the case, something that raises the question whether adherence can be considered authentic or not. Moreover, whereas one may desire to self-identify with whatever 'ism' one chooses, getting the recognition of those who are publically guiding a movement is usually quite difficult, since recognition implies legitimation, which translates into one's being trusted to uphold views and group identity, if not to be given the authority to assume a role as someone whose ideas are to have an influential effect by way of repetition, adoption, extension and contestation.

As Benoît Peeters' recent biography of Jacques Derrida shows, young French intellectuals in the 1960s who were undertaking university degrees at places such as the École Normale Supérieure were being encouraged (perhaps 'forced' would be the more accurate term) to become a part of some group or other that would crystallize around a seminar or set of seminars.[1] Louis Althusser's lectures on 'reading *Capital*' attracted adherents such as Jacques Rancière and Etienne Balibar, who would become officially representative of a certain Althusserian-*ism*. Similarly, Jacques Lacan's lectures at the École Normale attracted Alain Badiou, Jacques-Alain Miller and others who promoted a Lacanian-*ism*. Such small 'isms' in the making were often allied with or represented by journals that advanced the impression culture was a confluence or conflict of 'isms' and that to become important as a thinker one had to advance an intellectual movement. Jacques Derrida, like everyone else, was encouraged to sign up with one group or another, something that apparently he was reluctant to do.

Problematic, of course, was that once one committed to an intellectual orientation, one was subject to criticism or worse. According to Balibar, young intellectuals were subjected to a sort of intellectual terrorism. 'There were camps, strategic alliances, manoeuvres of encirclement and exclusion … The diplomacy of evasion: silence, you don't quote …'.[2] Derrida himself 'felt all the more condemned to silence because the discourse of the Althusserians was accompanied by a sort of 'intellectual terrorism' or at least 'theoretical intimidation'. People were immediately suspicious of phenemonological, transcendental and ontological sorts of questioning because these were 'considered suspicious, backward, idealistic, even reactionary'. Yet, even if, as Balibar reported, 'it didn't bother *us* that Derrida wasn't a Marxist …',[3] Derrida would be vehemently rejected by many French intellectuals on the grounds that he wasn't an adherent to Marx*ism*, which is notable given that Derrida not only got along with the Althusserians but worked under Althusser's explicit supervision and became a devoted life-long friend to Althusser.

What may strike one as odd is that despite the exclusivity of French intellectual coteries, they were quite open to non-members, even outliers. Hence, although we generally think of the serial *Cahiers pour l'Analyse* as the mouthpiece for a self-selecting group of Lacanian/Althusserian thinkers, its major figures, Alain Badiou and Jacques-Alain-Miller, weren't as dominant as the recent English translation of selected texts from the *Cahiers* suggests.[4] In fact, a diverse number of theorists contributed to its pages, including: Michel Foucault, who distanced himself from both Freud and Marx by way of studying the history of madness in institutional terms; Claude Levi-Strauss, representative of a certain form of structuralism already in dispute; *and* Jacques Derrida, an outlier of interest to the Lacanians at the time. Indeed, the very critique of Levi-Strauss that Derrida published in *Cahiers* was to be included in *Of Grammatology* (1967).

During the second half of the 1960s, Derrida affiliated himself with the more literary *Tel Quel* group (including Phillippe Sollers and Julia Kristeva), which was less influenced by Lacan, but open to theoretical writings that were focusing on aspects of linguistics in order to radically reinvent Hegel, Marx and Freud as kindred thinkers. Along with Roland Barthes and Foucault, Derrida's name appeared prominently in large print on the cover of the highly influential *Théorie d'ensemble* of 1968 ahead of the names of the Tel Quel regulars. However, circa 1970, when members close to the journal embraced Maoism and refocused their thinking much more along political lines, Derrida came under fire for not being Marxist-materialist enough to stand out as representative of a movement with all its twists and turns.[5] Suddenly the toleration of the Tel Quellers took a back seat to the orthodoxies of embracing Mao*ism* such that not only the pressure to subscribe to an 'ism' was palpable, but the punishment (condemnation, excommunication) for non-adherence was in evidence, as well.

In the later 1970s, Derrida affiliated himself with the Group de Recherches sur l'Enseignement Philosophique (or GREPH), which he helped found in order to publically denounce the French government's rationale for gutting the philosophy requirement in secondary education, something that he saw would have a knock-on effect for universities. GREPH, however, was a political action group or collective, not an 'ism', and its first proposition was that 'Pour le GREPH – il n'y a pas *la* philosophie'.[6] In the 1980s, Derrida played a leading role on the board of the Collège Internationale de Philosophie at the urging of various people and even was put in the role of being a chief architect of the school.[7] However, the school wasn't an 'ism' but open to all manner of different intellectual approaches. In contrast to Lacan's Ecole Freudienne, it was never Derrida's intention for the Collège Internationale de Philosophie to uphold and carry on his teachings or even his influence by way of being established as some sort of school of deconstruction, though he did favour 'the most irruptive provocations' of the various disciplines by speakers, whether they had academic qualifications or not.[8] That spoke to a tendency to be open to the marginalized and the unaligned, that is, people unassociated with schools (even degrees) or 'isms'. This, of course, also spoke to a strong desire for intellectual freedom which, of course, is anathema to an academia of 'isms'.

Although in time Derrida would be called the 'father of deconstruction', if not the founder of an 'ism' called deconstruction*ism*, it has to be said that at no time in his life did Derrida express any desire in founding a school or movement in the name of his own teachings, which means that unlike Lacan, who developed a procedure for what he called 'the Pass' in order to become a certified, schooled Lacanian analyst, Derrida was quite unwilling to embrace a doctrinaire formalization of his insights that students would have to master in order to become disciples.[9]

Sceptics would immediately point out, and rightly so, that one can't overlook the fact that if deconstruction was not to become a formal school, it nevertheless had some of the appearances of an 'ism'. For example, when the first colloquium on Derrida at Cérisy produced a 700-page book entitled *Les fins de l'homme* in 1981, it was clear that Derrida was the centre of a loosely affiliated group of admiring adherents that over time would become more defined.[10] Indeed, if Derrida appeared comfortable in the intellectual company of Cixous, Kofman, Agacinski, Lacoue-Labarthe, Lyotard and Nancy (all of them outliers, more or less) it would become clear over time that he would also give pride of place to various of his translators, conference organizers and redactors by means of publically avowing friendship with them. This is not to say, however, that Derrida treated his fellow travellers as subordinates in the way that Lacan treated the contributors of the serial *Scilicet* whose names were suppressed in order that the truth of Lacan's teachings not be overshadowed by the individuality or person of the contributor. To the contrary, in the case of the collaborative book *Jacques Derrida*, Geoffrey Bennington (the translator of Derrida's *La vérité en peinture*) is given pride of place as explicator of Derrida, given that Bennington's text comprises the main body of each page, whereas Derrida's essay 'Circumfession' is a running footnote in small print on the bottom margin, hence inverting the usual protocol of putting the secondary reader in a subordinate position as introducer or marginal commentator.[11] By inverting the structure of priority, Bennington was highlighted as an independent thinker, not the promoter of some form of 'ism'.

This doesn't mean Derrida could escape crude 'ism-ication'. His influence was far too great not to be reified in places such as England and the United States where detractors wanted to box him into the framework of a school, doctrine or 'ism' for the sake of making war upon him. Already quite early on (long before the Cérisy conferences on Derrida) academics in Britain and America insisted that deconstruction *had* to be thought of as a school with a footing in both so-called 'post-structuralism', and what by the late 1970s had been known as the 'Yale School'. Of course, today it's very hard to imagine that Harold Bloom, Geoffrey Hartman, Paul de Man, J. Hillis Miller and Jacques Derrida could possibly make up a school or 'ism', which Derrida well knew. But here again the pressure to think in terms of movements and 'isms' as a basis for understanding the possibility, emergence and invention of new ideas was necessary in order to place and institutionalize thought, if only for the sake of disputation in the interests of maintaining what Americans now call 'core values'.

Projection

If Derrida desired something, it wasn't to be the leader of an 'ism'. And yet at some point in the late 1980s he did have to back down and acknowledge the word 'deconstructionism', however alien it was to him. This occurred most conspicuously in 'Some Statements and Truisms about Neologisms, Newisms, Postisms, Parasitisms and Other Small Seismisms' written for a conference on the 'States of Theory' (1987) in which the word 'states' did double duty for the notion of there being conditions of theory as well as states in which theory occurs, for example, the United States. In that context, the 'isms' are united in their statehood as instituted entities that are, nevertheless, in conflict, something that makes up their condition.

Is there ever a 'state' of theory? What there is, Derrida argues, is an 'open and nonunified field' that is characterized by forces. These are libidinal (desiring), political–institutional and historical–socioeconomic forces bound up with interests in power. 'Forces never go without their representations, their specular images, the phenomena of refraction and diffraction, the reflection or reappropriation of distinct or opposite forces, the identification with the other or the opponent, etc. – so many structures which divide each identifiable force, de-identify it, displace it in its very proliferation.'[12] Here, of course, desires to identify or dis-identify are themselves in conflict and flux, which means that the states of theory are *states of desire*. No doubt, one could elaborate by recalling Deleuze and Guattari's desiring machines, Kristeva's *l'automate trans-corporal, désagrégation du corps*, or Barthes' plaisir du texte ('criticism always deals with the texts of pleasure').[13]

Derrida's resistance to adhering to an 'ism' of any sort is reflected not only in his rejection of theory as divisible into states, but in his rejection of the common-place account of 'isms' with which I began, namely, the view (1) that 'isms' are self-enclosed systems of beliefs that deviate from social and cultural norms (this is the logocentric, rationalist fallacy), (2) that 'isms' function like social actors (this is the anthropomorphic fallacy of political philosophy), (3) that 'isms' are antagonistic by definition (this is the *Kampfplatz* fallacy of Medieval *disputatio*) and (4) that 'isms' are dangerous because they elicit and even require fanatical adherence to the promotion of radical change (revolution), as conservatives fear. In particular, Derrida was certainly opposed to the reactionary belief that in essence 'isms' are necessarily to be seen as bad political actors engaging in civil and cultural subversion, if only because 'deconstructionism' was vilified in the press on precisely such assumptions. That is not to say that Derrida didn't perceive violent conflict when it comes to the interrelation of different bodies of thought; rather, what he rejected is the idea that different bodies of thought are self-organizing in a way that rationalizes antagonism in terms of clearly delineated pitched battles among opposing forces. Whereas Anglo-American academicians often imagine (or in fact desire) a more or less fixed state in which differences of opinion and perspective are clearly delineated for the sake of contestation but also of co-existence, Derrida argues that there is no such rational battlefield or *Kampfplatz*, as he terms it. What there is, rather, is a desire for *Kampf*, or *polemos*, a default *lust* for war. Furthermore, the *desire* for a certain pacifism, namely, the anodyne idea that academia is a tolerant society in which differences of opinion are encouraged in order to ensure people can civilly test if not challenge one another's ideas, presupposes a wish for an enlightenment rationalization (e.g. classification) of difference (conceptual as well as interpersonal) that is unrealistic with respect to the social psychology of how people actually behave: aggressively, opportunistically, irrationally and with severe prejudice.[14]

Whereas it is the nature of 'isms' to think in a way that is off the beaten track, it is Derrida's conviction that this thinking is never entirely identifiable within some overall table of classification. For an 'ism' should first and foremost be considered in terms of a 'force of movement', a desire to jump out ahead of other conceptual positions in order to 're-inscribe' them within itself. That is, if we must entertain the notion of 'isms', we should understand them dynamically in terms of a breaking forth, leap or jumping ahead. 'In this field of plural forces, where even counting is no longer possible, there are only theoretical jetties.'[15] Derrida's stress upon the striking metaphor of the jetty speaks to a projection, leap (*jété*, as in ballet) or pushing out ahead that is akin to a drive, which is to say, a *desire* to put oneself in the place of a vanguard, of a forward position that in time may, in military terms, gather reinforcements, or bring up the line. To project, which is the aim of any 'ism', is to break through, to aggressively advance, wilfully to insert oneself or something into an unfamiliar region (say, to apply an idea to a remote field of study). As Derrida tells us, the jetty is the bulwark (the 'break water') that divides the waters into zones, the one placid behind the jetty and hospitable to boats and the other violent and inhospitable to seafaring ships. If jetties (that is, 'isms') are defensive structures that cut off disruptive currents and provide barriers against turbulent inundation, they are also open fortifications that only partially organize a turbulent environment.

Applying this to Marxism, Derrida writes:

> If one wanted to identify what is called or what calls itself Marxism ... one
> could not identify it without immediately perceiving the traits of the elements

integrated by that Marxism...concepts, themes, questions, words, sentences which belong to that which this Marxist discourse opposes today [:] structuralism, psycho-analysis, neo- or poststructuralism ... This work assumes the integration of motives which come from the very places they themselves consider to be the places of an opposing theory.[16]

What interests Derrida are 'the modes of ... integration' and the distortions and transformations they reveal. Of course, not only the 'ism' known as 'Marxism' is at issue, for

> One might naturally use other examples: the incorporation of some Marxist philosophemes into French structuralism, of structuralism into poststructuralism, of psychoanalytic theories into all of the above. And you can imagine to what kinds of monsters these combinatory operations must give birth ...[17]

This contaminating plurality of forces – the turbulent impulse or desire to appropriate and re-appropriate – contributes to a taxonomic disorder, sometimes reasoned, sometimes absurdly mixed up. What one can say is that instead of an 'ism' having a particular state, it's subjected to various states in fast motion. 'The very structure of the jetty, of all jetties [is an] introjective multiplicity [that] corresponds neither to a linear and temporal order of succession, nor to the order of a juxtaposing simultaneity.'[18] Of concern are the *desired* introjections of outside forces into what lies behind the jetty, say, the academic administrative types of organization that have stabilizing effects. What are 'isms' as seen from behind the jetty but authoritative lists of books to be read, authors to be emulated, ideas to be memorized? In fact, such stability is just a localization behind the jetty, for there are zones where there will be convergences and instabilities, too. Consider Dadaism, Surrealism, Neo-Dadaism and Fluxus. Are they the same or different? Can one clearly distinguish between existentialism and phenomenology, between historicism and new historicism, communism and Marxism? No doubt, academics would have us believe that a university is a unified *Kampfplatz* of ideas within a sphere of what Derrida calls competitive plurality, but, in fact, there is a

> multiplicity as a law of the field, a clause of nonclosure which would not only never allow itself to be ordered and inscribed, situated in the general Kampfplatz, but would also make possible and inevitable synecdochic and metonymic competitions: not as their normal condition of possibility, their ratio essendi or ratio cognoscendi, but as a means of disseminal alterity or alteration, which would make impossible the pure identity, the pure identification of what it simultaneously makes possible – which would thus delimit and

destabilize the state of the establishment to which it gives rise in order for this state or establishment to take place.[19]

Derrida adds that what allows competitive plurality has 'no stable or theorizable place' and that '*it is this non-place that the appearance of the effects of deconstruction can be situated*', a deconstruction that Derrida will be careful to distinguish from 'deconstruction*ism*'.[20] In this context, the jetty is the incipit, the occasion for creating such a de-constitution of place that enables one to escape the situatedness of bodies of thought as doctrines, conceptual networks, defensive strategies, articles of faith, differentiated histories and codified oppositions. Of course, this would suit Derrida whose entire career reveals a desire to escape the prison house of 'isms'.

Extremism

Institutionally (scholastically, pedagogically) one can talk about a mode of thought such as Hegelianism as a closed off moribund 'ism', a systematized set of positions and logical procedures that could make up a chapter on the history of Western thought. But what makes a text such as Hegel's *Phenomenology of Spirit* live on and survive its institutional entombment as an 'ism' is the fact that it has come down to us in a fairly unreadable form, if by readable one means immediately comprehensible. A similar case can be made for certain treatises by Kant, who, despite having been systematized by commentators, is unreadable enough to escape a definitive reduction to any one account. None of this speaks to Hegel's or Kant's attempts to escape being reduced to some 'ism'; rather, it speaks to an inherent resistance in their thinking to conceptual closure, however self-conscious or not. When Sherry Turkle, in the 1970s, pointed out that perhaps Lacan's greatest gift was that 'he was good to think with', as opposed to fairly understandable or even comprehensible, she was pointing out that there is great merit in work that isn't fully resolved and doesn't self-complete; moreover, she was noticing that reading works by major thinkers involves the incomprehensibility within comprehension and that therefore one can always say such figures have and haven't been read.[21]

Derrida himself famously complained that he felt people were writing about him without having read him. He even accused as major a commentator as Gayatri Chakravorty Spivak of such a practice in response to her criticism of *Specters of Marx*.[22] However, what Derrida left out, for polemical reasons, is that reading and non-reading are invaginated. Paul de Man, in *Blindness and Insight*, had noticed in his analysis of Maurice Blanchot that the non-reading (the incomprehensibility that is so foundational to any major text) negates, mediates and sublates the reading. If a text appears finite and filled with signification, it is also open-ended and quite capable of 'not saying'. De Man asks, 'How are we to understand a reading-process which, in Blanchot's words, is located before or beyond the act of understanding?' In fact, texts 'suspend the very act of comprehension' that they elicit.[23] This, of course, flies in the face of 'isms' that assume transparency and expert comprehension. Moreover, the suspension that de Man cites concerns an 'inaccessible space' that is at once evident (perceptible) and withdrawn (concealed). It is, in Blanchot's words, a 'rebel space ... perhaps immutable, perhaps ever restless, the contained violence in the face of which we always feel in excess'.[24] This is the space of unreadability, or what de Man famously called the blind spot. Recalling the jetty metaphor, this unreadability or blind spot is where turbulence instantiates itself on the leading edge of the break water.

What the institutionalization of 'isms' generally leaves aside is the fact that the inaccessible excess and *rebellion* that animates the writings or speeches from which an 'ism' is derived cannot be divorced from the 'ism' itself. In other words, this turbulence, excess and rebellion usually relates to an extremism that by definition constitutes 'isms'. Think of the stability of the 'ism' as the inner side of the jetty behind which safe harbour is created and the instability or *extremism* of the 'ism' as the turbulent waters that lie on the side of the jetty that looks out to open sea. On the one side, everything is settled categorically, while, on the other side, everything is divergent, unstable, in process, as yet to come about. The word deconstruction obviously points to this unstable dimension so extreme in its rejection of all stabilities that have come before, which is why so many academics, wedded to categorical stabilities or fields of inquiry, have greeted it with such abhorrence. For such academics, extremism has to be delegitimized, compromised, even trivialized in the name of a normative objectivity that Martin Heidegger in the 1920s once called 'sloth tailor-made for instructors'.[25] Such sloth is the essence of the normal and its requirement to preserve itself by expelling anything that could be identified as extreme. As Heidegger but also Blanchot indicated: extreme never has its source in a group, but in an individual, and as that which constitutes an inaccessible, rebellious space. In his lecture course, 'Fantom of the Other' (1985), Derrida called this rebel space 'the idiom of idiom', that is, a zone of individual expression that isn't translatable, comprehensible, knowable, though its unique signature never escapes us.

In the self-conscious encounter of this idiom of idiom, a reader necessarily assumes the burden of this inaccessible, incomprehensible space of revolt. As Blanchot puts it, the reader 'relieves the book of its author'.[26] To be 'radicalized' by the work of an author means that one has assumed this inaccessibility, that one has relieved the author of this *passion* for one's own sake *as a desiring subject*. Not only does one take up that passion with zeal, but one engages with it in terms of a certain transference love: the establishment of an imaginary bond by way of the sharing (partage) of the rebel space, a bond constitutive of all those who share in the 'ism' that the writer has brought about, whether absurdism, realism, surrealism, futurism, lettrism, etc. No doubt one can always project a particular content onto the rebel space; however, essentially constitutive of that space universally is extremism: the desire to leap, take things further, break out, transcend, deconstitute, construct otherwise, and so on. When people speak of taking up radical positions or of following a radical line of thinking, it is to the *extreme* that they are appealing. To speak of a 'Derridean' or 'Lacanian' or 'Heideggerian' mode of thinking is to appeal to the radical, the extreme, the rebel space, perhaps with fear and loathing, perhaps with devotion and love.

If this extremism is inherently revolutionary, destabilizing, upsetting, problematic and much else besides, according to Blanchot it is also beyond comprehension, which means that it can't be satisfactorily accounted for. In terms of 'isms' such as surrealism, cubism, minimalism, postmodernism or language-ism the strong attractor has always had to do with going too far as the driving force that cannot be entirely rationalized and understood, though it can be felt and even transferred (adopted, assimilated, assumed, etc.) and hence incorporated within us. Indeed, it is only when an 'ism's' popularity has long passed that this extremism begins to appear preposterous, absurd, ridiculous or, more simply, out of date. Consider, for example, what now appear to be mere antics of Dada at the Cabaret Voltaire.

That said, consider that from the perspective of transference love it is also the case that our attachment to the extreme, when it occurs, is in all cases an attachment to 'the good'. Even when Milton's Satan says 'evil be thou my good' in *Paradise Lost*, it is to the good to which his extremism is attached. Even Heidegger's appalling anti-Semitism, given the comments he made in his *Schwarze Hefte*, were advanced in the name of the good: with what to him amounted to a saving of the world. Indeed, no one signs up with an 'ism' for any other reason than that they think they are serving a higher good: aesthetically, critically, culturally, socially, pedagogically and so on. In no matter what cause (fascism, veganism, feminism, Republicanism, liberalism, communism,

Evangelicanism, Buddhism, etc.) one will find a link between a certain form of extremism and the good. In fact, as Freud noticed, it's because the good and the extreme are bedfellows that transference love is possible.

Transference love

Derrida explicitly desired and imagined his own mission – which is to say, the mission of deconstruction – to be functioning *in the service of the good*, which is why so many of the later seminars, in particular, were focused on ethical issues (pardon, forgiveness, hospitality, etc.). Yet, ever since his emergence as a major thinker, Derrida had been accused by Meyer Abrams and numerous others of being a bad influence on us, something that brings us around more centrally to issues of transference love, the subject of Lacan's *Seminar 8: The Transference (1960–61)*, substantially devoted to an analysis of Plato's *The Symposium*.

Central to Lacan's concern is the *agalma* (the good) that Alcibiades sees in Socrates. Lacan's overall thesis is that it's an illusion (or misrecognition) that the analysand should perceive the *agalma* in the analyst, as if it were some wondrous thing. In fact, proper transference, as opposed to transference love, requires the analyst to occupy the place of his or her own that must be offered as vacant to the desire of the analysand so that the analysand can realize himself or herself as the desire of the Other. With respect to Plato's dialogue, Lacan is particularly interested in Alcibiades' testimonial in praise of Socrates, Alcibiades being a man of immense extremes. According to Alcibiades, 'What he [Socrates] reminds me of more than anything is one of those little sileni that you see on the statuaries' stalls ... modelled with pipes and flutes in their hands ... [that] when you open them down the middle there are little figures of the gods inside.' These gods, of course, are the *agalma*. 'I don't know whether anybody else has ever opened him up when he's been being serious, and seen the little images inside, but I saw them once, and they looked so godlike, so golden, so beautiful, and so utterly amazing that there was nothing for it but to do exactly what he told me.' This falling into line – this obedience – is transference love on Alcibiades' part. Of considerable significance is mention of 'when he's being serious', because this refers to Socrates' speech, which Alcibiades associates with the pipes and flutes of the selini, an incredibly seductive speech (elsewhere equated with the singing of the Sirens) inside of which are these golden images that Alcibiades identifies with what he calls 'this philosophical frenzy, this sacred rage' (218a). It's as if, Acibiades confesses by means of a zoological comparison, 'I've been bitten by something much more poisonous than a snake; in fact, mine is the most painful kind of bite there is. I've been bitten in the heart, or the mind, or whatever you like to call it, by Socrates' philosophy, which clings like an adder to any young and gifted mind it can get hold of, and does exactly what it likes with it' (218a). Earlier, Alcibiades admits: 'But when we listen to you [Socrates] … we're absolutely staggered and bewitched.' What is one to conclude but that the *agalma* (associated by Alcibiades with the ethical good – right action, wisdom) is to be identified with *the extreme*. Indeed, by his own admission it is with this extremism that Alcibiades has fallen in love, not so much out of some sort of rational choice, but on account of being stalked, pursued and/or attacked (bitten) by something highly aggressive and dangerous, like a snake. This is why Alcibiades, himself a man of considerable frenzied political extremism (this is underscored by Lacan), can say by way of transference love to Socrates: 'You're the only lover I've ever had who's been really worthy of me' (218c). In other words, he's saying they share the same extremism, the same rebel space, to put it in Blanchot's context. As Lacan tells us, 'it is by measuring something as going beyond the danger level that we can judge what love is'.[27]

If Alcibiades and Socrates share something in common – the aggressive, the dangerous, the extreme – it is the case that Alcibiades knows, and even says as much, that in Socrates he has not just met his match, but his superior. Lacan tells us that everyone knows that by definition fundamental to love is the uniqueness of the object, the fact that there is nothing equivalent, which means that there is something radical about the beloved that spurs the lover to frenzied action. In association with the seleni, Lacan speaks of *agalmata* (he is referring to Pausanias) which references a sanctuary in which sorceresses are to be found who hold something back. So that even if Alcibiades speaks of opening Socrates up, he's merely boasting, because the *agalma* are, to some extent, hidden, withdrawn and inaccessible – a rebel place of sorcery and spell casting. Hence the beloved is one who *en retrait* appears to be casting a spell over the lover, which speaks to the beloved's extreme powers. Recall that metaphorically it is by Socrates cloaked in the form of a poisonous snake that Alcibiades is bitten.

Lacan argues that if the *agalma* is an object in the psychoanalytical sense, it is a 'part object', an object that escapes totalization and escapes the perfection that it indicates. This has the effect of the object functioning as the thing (Lacan's famous 'object a'– cause of desire) from which the subject remains suspended [*le sujet reste suspendu*]. This thing, which is less than perfect, is the object of the lover's doubt. Lacan's psychoanalytical example is taken from Freud who noticed that it is the hysteric's tendency to doubt the *agalma* that is associated with her analyst, a man, in the role of healer and saviour – as 'subject supposed to know'. Indeed, it is the hysteric's tendency to suspect this analyst of being an impostor, which she tries to demonstrate through sexual seduction, given that this offers proof that the analyst is disreputable and vile – that if there is excess, it is an excess that is unethical and depraved. This is the seamy side of transference love wherein the analysand loves the analyst as saviour as long as the analysis isn't psychologically threatening. In fact, we see this seamy side of transference love in the lecture hall as well, for example, in the charge that Lacan was a Char-Lacan (charlatan), something that a French journal once announced on its cover. The doctor's *agalma* is said to be merely an imposture, his admirable rebel space a fraud.

Derrida, whose writings were dedicated to the good of philosophy – its study, analysis, promotion, elaboration – was scandalized when as public intellectual he was being called an impostor by various analytical philosophers within and outside of Cambridge University when the matter of conferring an honorary degree upon him came up for discussion in 1992.[28] The consensus among the analytical philosophers and others who were advising Cambridge not to confer an honorary degree upon Derrida was that his work was fraudulent, something that from the Lacanian perspective amounts to 'the discourse of the hysteric' whereby the hysteric tries to defile the good by bringing it down to the hysteric's own unethical level. In fact, Derrida's hysterical detractors had committed the very intellectual fraudulence that they had imputed to their enemy. This may recall Lacan's observation that in the *Symposium* Alcibiades attempts to knock Socrates 'off his perch', which Socrates anticipates and successfully defends against.

In what is said to have been Derrida's last interview, with Jean Birnbaum, Derrida tells us, somewhat gloomily, that no one has as yet read him, aside from perhaps a couple of dozen people, writer-poets, for example. 'In the end it is later on that all this [the serious, adequate work on Derrida] has a chance of appearing; but also, on the other hand, and thus simultaneously, I have the feeling that two weeks or a month after my death *there will be nothing left*. Nothing except what has been copyrighted and deposited in libraries.'[29] The objects will fall away because the creator will have disappeared. And yet, it is the poets, fellow creators, who will lovingly 'read' him in the way he had intended his work to be read. But what is this way? Unfortunately, Birnbaum didn't ask.

What the interviewer misses is Derrida speaking from the perspective of transference love. Derrida says that there are those who know how to read him because they love him (they recognize the *agalma*), and there are those who won't care that he ever existed and won't ever bother to read him. That ends the response to the question that began 'You have invented a form of writing ...' that Derrida answered beginning with

> If I had invented my writing, I would have done so as a *perpetual revolution*. For it is necessary in each situation to create an appropriate mode of exposition, to invent the law of the singular event, *to take into account the presumed or desired addressee*; and, at the same time, to make as if this writing will determine the reader, who will learn to read (to 'live') something he or she was not accustomed to receiving from anywhere else.[30]

This something is the *agalma*, the unique object that lacks concrete objectification and as such fits in what Lacan calls 'the field of the fantasy' where objects are both over and under-estimated at the same time.[31] Indeed, as object of fantasy, its estimation depends on the one who claims it for himself or herself. It is this object, however subject to over and under-estimation, that gives consistency to love, even though this object in terms *of its revolutionary behaviour isn't comprehensible as a whole*. When the object is posited as the good, it is always, in the case of an admired thinker, an *extremism in perpetual revolution* on the way to the good in its ever more perfect dimensions, even if one doesn't always grasp how this is occurring, given the difficulty (the extremism) of the philosopher's thought, its twists and turns, its obscure vocabularies, its multiplicities/divisions ('as a law of the field'), and so on. This coincides with what Derrida says *he desired* as intended for a 'desired addressee' whom the writing determines such that the reader will learn to read/live (they are equated) by means of the *agalma*, something that the reader cannot get from anywhere else, as it is unequivocal and *given* only in what Derrida calls 'my writing', that is, his *body* of work. ('This is my body, take it and eat' was among the texts Derrida glossed in lectures on the Eucharist in the seminar 'Eating the Other' [1990]). This *agalma* (this object which is, after all, a *part* of him) is what Derrida says he intended to give, a *part-object* (a *pas tout*) of the invention, a 'not all' that gives consistency to writings that in seminar and book form were clearly only segments of an infinite conversation. 'Each book is a pedagogy aimed at forming its reader' and 'one hopes that [the reader] will be *reborn* differently, determined otherwise, as a result ....'[32] *To change and resurrect (to redeem) the reader, this was the author's desire.*

Having admitted that much, Derrida suddenly turns pessimistic. The reader cannot be known, the writings are traces not for anyone in particular but for everyone in general:

> you invent and create silhouettes, but in the end it no longer belongs to you. Spoken or written all these gestures leave us and began to act independently

of us. Like machines or, better, like marionettes … At the moment I leave 'my' book (to be published) … I become appearing-disappearing, like that unedu-cable specter who will have never learned how to live.

There is no *agalma*. It's all an illusion. All one has, really, are part-objects left behind like scraps, and whether they have any significance or not is up to an other. 'I leave a piece of paper behind, I go away, I die: it is impossible to escape this structure, it is the unchanging form of my life.' One 'expropriates oneself without knowing exactly who is being entrusted with what is left behind'.[33] Is it the lovers or the haters who are entrusted? Those who desire these writings? Or those who don't care? If *agalma* is at issue, will anyone notice it in the defiles of the signifier? Was there ever anything good about this invention known as 'my writing' that will encourage people to preserve and study it 'after my death'? That is, will this writing inspire love, devotion and companionship? Will it inspire people to finally 'read' Derrida, the word 'read' having been left in obscurity? This rounds out Derrida's fantasy (his over and under-estimation of the object-*agalma* [*objet a*]) that his writings will and won't have a future, that possibly his teachings will be immediately forgotten at the same time that the future harbours his most ideal readers who will think and thank.

Derrida's fantasy (really, his *fantasm*) speaks to the concern that whatever 'good object' a public intellectual is trying to give to society by means of his or her hard work, that object may, in fact, be ignored, perhaps because it had been demoted to merely a trick or fraud whose purpose is mere dupery for the sake of self-aggrandizement. Speaking of 'faire déchoir Socrate'[34] Lacan says that what love (the admiration of the *agalma*) dissimulates is actually the shameful desire to diminish the other, to knock the beloved off his or her perch in order to expose an imposture of the good as false-seeming. Transference love, Lacan tells us, is incapable of avoiding this destructive desire to degrade the other, which involves, to some extent, even the degrading of love to an 'ism' (libertine-ism, romanticism, eroticism). Why? Because *agalma* is, however perceptible and highly prized, intangible, *unreadable* and incomprehensible, and, as Socrates demonstrated, *rebellious* in not necessarily conforming to the ways of the world. In short, *it is agalma as 'rebel space' that is problematic and that people cannot abide, which leads them to extremes.*

Lacan was well aware that one could just as easily have been speaking of the *agalma* of Jesus Christ (its rebelliousness in relation to Jewish law, its other worldliness, its infinite compassion, etc.) in terms of transference love. Indeed, the social hysteria that led to cries of imposture and crucifixion should be self-explanatory to us at this point. Moreover, if we can speak of Christianity as an 'ism' – for example, as a Catholicism or Protestantism – we would be looking at the condensation of all the problems we have been exploring so far. Mention of the figure of Christ speaks to what is a Messianic dimension that Derrida wasn't keen on foreclosing with respect to philosophizing. We see these religious overtones most usually in academia in terms of not just the Messianism of new ways of thinking (i.e. 'theory') but in the speed with which ideas are reduced to heresies ('Ayranism' could be a religious model for an 'ism') and figures knocked off their perches as impostors. In that sense, 'deconstruction*ism*' or 'deconstruction*ist*' are actually slurs used to expose the imposture of the good.

But I think Derrida also understood that, despite this, these terms also had the potential of any 'ism' to become a sort of social body, perhaps even akin to a sect or church (with Jean-Luc Nancy, Hélène Cixous and some others as apostles), characterized by a certain transference love for the good that Derrida wanted to disseminate (radical deconstruction). What Derrida's personal resistances to belonging and analysis of the jetty indicate, however, is that despite this wish to convey the good in a body of work to a body of people, he was, nevertheless, wary of putting himself in the role of intellectual savoir for all the reasons that the vicissitudes of transference love entail. And yet, recall *A Portrait of Jacques Derrida as a Young Jewish Saint* in which Derrida is enlisted into this very role by one of his dearest and most eloquent followers, Cixous. Was she countersigning Derrida's secret desire? 'He is the divided, the one who – it took me so long to fathom this mystery – strikes the mountains twice yes, yes, twice, the one who makes the heart of belief tremble, the philosophical divider, the one who knows that one cannot say I believe without doubting, without crossing out I and believe and doubt … Jacques on a superhuman scale. Vanquished and vanquisher.'[35]

Lacan, of course, knew about this business of dividing as well as about the followers. He had been betrayed enough times, certainly, to be wary of transference love. In his very first remark on French television, in the role of public intellectual and French national treasure (*agalma*), Lacan cut to the quick when he pronounced:

> I always speak the truth. Not the whole truth, because there is no way, to say it all. Saying it all is literally impossible: words fail. Yet it is through this very impossibility that the truth holds onto the real … The aberration consists in this idea of speaking so as to be understood by idiots. An idea that is ordinarily so foreign to me that it could only have been suggested to me. Through friendship. Beware.[36]

Notes

1   Benoît Peeters, *Derrida: A Biography* (Cambridge: Polity Press, 2012).

2   Ibid., 151.

3   Ibid., 150.

4   See Peter Hallward and Knox Peden, eds., *Concept and Form: Key Texts from the Cahiers pour l'Analyse* (London: Verso, 2012).

5   See Jacques Derrida, *Positions*, trans. Alan Bass (Chicago: University of Chicago Press, 1981). This book contains interviews that reveal aspects of Derrida's incompatibility with Tel Quel thinking.

6   GREPH, *Qui a peur de la philosophie* (Paris: Flammarion, 1977), 5. This book is nearly 500 pages long and among its contributors were Sylviane Agacinski, Alain Delormes, Sarah Kofman, Michèle Le Dœuff, Jean Luc Nancy, Bernard Pautrat and Michael Ryan.

7   Peeters, *Derrida: A Biography*, 21. 'It was there [as a young person in Algeria] … that I began to recognize … this ill, this malaise, the ill-being that, throughout my life, rendered me inapt for "communitarian" experience, incapable of enjoying any kind of membership in a group.'

8   Ibid., 347. The quote is by Derrida as reported by Peeters.

9   Lacan, for his part, was self-aware enough to ironize the possibility that he personally could ever be a Lacanian, hence securing for himself a freedom that operated at will outside the confines of his own doctrines. Lacan, therefore, was quite successful at not getting himself trapped within the confines of his own strictures by performatively eluding his own doctrines to the point that he could violate and practice his own teachings at will. As to the 'ism' that is Lacanian*ism*, it had the characteristic French liberal trait of being founded on the principle of being open to all. Anyone could attend Lacan's seminar and, without any special induction or training, affiliate with Lacan's school, though those who wanted to be recognized as official insiders were required to undergo a process of formal admission and recognition. No doubt, that spoke to Lacan's desire to have devoted followers who would uphold his teachings and thereby carry on his work. In contrast, it was never Derrida's intention for anyone to carry the burden of being his apostles.

10   Jean-Luc Nancy and Philippe Lacoue-Labarthe, eds., *Les fins de l'homme* (Paris: Galilée, 1981).

11   Geoffrey Bennington and Jacques Derrida, *Jacques Derrida*, trans. Geoffrey Bennington (Chicago: University of Chicago Press, 1993).

12   Jacques Derrida, 'Some Statements and Truisms about Neo-Logisms, Newisms, Postisms, Parasitisms, and Other Small Seismisms', in *The States of 'Theory'*, ed. David Carroll (New York: Columbia University Press, 1990), 65.

13 Julia Kristeva, 'Le Sujet en procès', *Polylogue* (Paris: Seuil, 1977), 83; Roland Barthes, *The Pleasure of the Text*, trans. Richard Howard (New York: Farrar, Straus and Giroux, 1975), 21. *Le plaisir du texte* (Paris: Seuil, 1973), 35.

14 See my *The Theory Mess: Deconstruction in Eclipse* (New York: Columbia University Press, 2001).

15 Derrida, 'Some Statements and Truisms', 65.

16 Ibid., 66.

17 Ibid.

18 Ibid., 69.

19 Ibid., 72.

20 Ibid.

21 Sherry Turkle, *Psychoanalytic Politics* (New York: Basic Books, 1978), 19.

22 Jacques Derrida, 'Marx & Sons', in *Ghostly Demarcations*, ed. Michael Sprinker (London: Verso, 1999), 245.

23 Paul de Man, *Blindness and Insight*, 2nd rev. ed. (Minneapolis: University of Minnesota Press, 1983), 63.

24 Maurice Blanchot, *The Space of Literature*, trans. Ann Smock (Lincoln, NB: Nebraska University Press, 1989), 192. *L'espace littéraire* (Paris: Gallimard, 1955), 255.

25 Martin Heidegger, *Logic: The Question of Truth*, trans. Thomas Sheehan (Bloomington: Indiana University Press, 2010), 10.

26 Maurice Blanchot, *The Space of Literature*, 193. *L'espace littéraire*, 256.

27 'C'est donc à la mesure de ce qui dépasse la cote d'alerte que nous pouvons juger de ce que c'est que l'amour'. The translation is by Cormac Gallagher, *The Seminar of Jacques Lacan, Book VIII, Transference (1960–61)*, 48. Available on www.lacaninireland.com. Accessed 1 March 2015.

28 See Jacques Derrida, 'Honoris Causa: "This is also extremely funny"', in *Points …, Interviews 1974–1994* (Stanford: Stanford University Press, 1995).

29 Jacques Derrida, *Learning to Live Finally: The Last Interview* (Brooklyn, NY: Melvillehouse, 2007), 34.

30 Ibid., 31.

31 Lacan's well known matheme for the field of the fantasy is $\$<>a$, in which the angled brackets stand for over- and under-estimation of the object. Buyer's remorse would be a commonplace example of the field of the fantasy.

32 Derrida, *Learning to Live Finally*, 31.

33 Ibid., 31, 32.

34 Lacan, *Le Transfert: Seminaire VIII*, ed. Jacques-Alain Miller (Paris: Seuil, 1991), 209.

35 Hélène Cixous, *Portrait of Jacques Derrida as a Young Jewish Saint*, trans. B. Bie Brahic (New York: Columbia University Press, 2004), 123.

36 Jacques Lacan, *Television*, ed. J.-A. Miller (New York: Norton, 1990), 3.

4

Kindling; or, Suicide by Fire

Elissa Marder

Thus, when an 'original' speaks about its language by speaking its language, it prepares a kind of suicide by translation, as one says suicide by gas or suicide by fire. Suicide by fire, rather, for it lets itself be destroyed almost without remainder, without apparent remainder inside the corpus.

— Jacques Derrida[1]

I don't see Heidegger burning a manuscript ...
When it's a matter of burning, the question of the difference between doing and saying is more burning than ever.

— Jacques Derrida[2]

The symbol? A great holocaustic fire, a burn-everything into which we would throw finally, along with our entire memory, our names, the letters, photos, small objects, keys, fetishes, etc. And if nothing remains

— Jacques Derrida[3]

Burning letters

Before any reading of the letters in *Envois*, there will have been fire (*PC*, 325–6). Fire is not a figure among others. Fire is Derrida's name in *The Post Card* for what happens to language within the body of writing so that reading will have been given a chance.

The text begins with burning letters. Reading *The Post Card* begins with reading burning letters.[4] And if, as the text announces from its first words, burning is a condition of possibility for reading the *Envois* rather than an incidental incendiary accident, it is because, as Derrida will insist, the postal principle (the principle whereby a letter always can (not) arrive at destination) must also take into account that which, within any language, cannot be put into circulation. To the extent that any writing worthy of the name writing gives language a body by composing unique arrangements of words made up of singular letters that cannot be substituted, exchanged, transposed or translated into any other form (and such arrangements often go by the name 'literature'), all reading involves playing with fire. Like the encounter between a tongue of flame and the tinder that it touches, reading lingers on the materiality of the letters in the word before it is coaxed into meaning as its letters become consumed by signification.

Reading burns letters the way a flame divides into manifold tongues as it consumes the body of what it touches. This erotic and destructive inflammatory encounter inaugurates the event of reading as something we would have been tempted to call *obliterature* (had that word not already acquired a more vulgar meaning in the lexicon of the urban dictionary) and so we offer instead something like 'incinerate-iteration'. Reading, Derrida suggests throughout *The Post Card*, only happens when letters are set on fire. The *Envois* are love letters because they burn.

Fire, flames, tinder, embers, cinders and ash link the work on mourning (on the crypt and the incalculable remainder) in *Glas* and *Fors* to the pyrotechnic erotic encounter between philosophy and psychoanalysis in *The Post Card* and announce the later writings on the translation, poetry and the secret.

The *Envois* opens and closes with fire. A ring of fire circumscribes the entire text. The text begins after the end, in the smoldering aftermath of an incineration.

> As for the 'Envois' themselves, I do not know if their reading is bearable. You might consider them, if you really wish to, as the remainders of a recently destroyed correspondence. Destroyed by fire or by that which figuratively takes its place, more certain of leaving nothing out of the reach of what I like to call tongue of fire, not even the cinders if cinders there are [*s'il y a là cendre*]. Save [*fors*] a chance. (4)

> *Quant aux Envois eux-mêmes, je ne sais pas si la lecture en est soutenable. Vous pourriez les considérer, si le coeur vous en dit, comme les restes d'une correspondance récemment détruite. Par le feu ou par ce qui d'une figure en tient lieu, plus sûr de ne rien laisser hors d'atteinte pour ce que j'aime appeler langue de feu, pas même la cendre s'il y a là cendre. Fors – une chance.*[5]

From the beginning, the language of Derrida's text (which, as we shall see, is explicitly concerned with what, in the body of language, is untranslatable) is eradicated, in translation, by the erasure of the body in his language. The English translation literally removes the words 'heart' and the 'love' from the text. Where Derrida writes '*si le coeur vous en dit*' (literally: 'if the heart speaks to you about it'), the English says 'if you really wish to'. Where the French gives '*pour ce que j'aime appeler langue de feu*' (literally: 'for that which I love to call tongue of fire'), the English says 'what I like to call tongue of fire'. The 'heart' is excised; 'love' becomes downgraded to 'like'.

Tongue of fire

But even in French, Derrida's text already anticipates (and even calls for) the effects of the translation to come. Whenever he invokes the idiom 'tongue of fire' ('*langue de feu*') he is always already writing about how translation teases out what is untranslatable within the body of language by exposing it to the fire of translation. Like all forms of reading, translation burns the body of the text it touches. This is why, whenever he writes about the relation between translation and the untranslatable, he invokes fire and tongues of flame. In 'What is a "Relevant" Translation', he describes how translation consumes and consummates the unique body of the other in the caress of a burning tongue:

> I believe I can say that if I love the word, it is only in the body of its idiomatic singularity, that is, where a passion for translation comes to lick it as a flame or an amorous tongue might: approaching as closely as possible while refusing at the last moment to threaten or to reduce, to consume or consummate, leaving the body of the other intact but not without causing the other to appear – on the very brink of this refusal or withdrawal – and after having aroused or excited a desire for the idiom for the unique body of the other, in the flame's flicker or through a tongue's caress.[6]

If fire is a figure for both reading and translation, it is because the 'tongue of fire' alights on the untranslatable matter in every language (the idiomatic singularity of the word) that renders all languages foreign to themselves. This is another way of saying that for Derrida translation is not primarily a relation between languages, but rather something that happens in language and to all languages. Translation touches the secret heart of that which in language does not belong to it: its internal other, its non-mattering matter. Translation exposes the material matter of language to the process of signification and, in so doing, destroys it. Burning (in passion and in immolation) is what happens to untranslatable matter in any encounter with the other. Writing harbours secrets in the body of language; it gives a space to literature and a chance for the relation to the wholly other that we call love.

The *Envois* closes with the following request made by the lover to his beloved:

> Tomorrow I will write you again, in our foreign language. I won't retain a word of it and in September, without my even having seen you again, you will burn [ ] you will burn it, you, it has to be you (*PC*, 256)

Love letters are written in a 'foreign language'. If this language is foreign, it is because its matter is estranged from language itself. Reading sparks letters and kindles them into meaning; they become consummated and consumed by meaning. Letters of love must burn in order to be read, and they burn in being read. Only by being burned do they have a chance of survival. Survival, that is, *in* the body of the other, *as* the body of the other:

> Our only chance for *survival*, now, but in what sense, would be to burn everything, in order to get back to our original desire. (171)

Learning by heart

But there are many ways to burn letters. Early on in the *Envois*, the lover's demand that the other 'burn everything' is linked to copying, incorporating, mourning and learning by heart.

> But in fact, yes, you had understood my order or my prayer, the demand of the first letter: 'burn everything', understood it so well that you told me you copied over ('I am burning, stupid impression of being faithful, nevertheless kept several simulacra, etc', isn't that it?), in your writing, and in pencil, the words of that first letter (not the others). Another way of saying that you had reread it, no? which is *what one begins by doing* when one reads, even for the first time. Repetition, memory, etc. I love you by heart, there, between parentheses or quotation marks, such is the origin of the post card. ... Keep what you burn, such is the demand. Mourn what I send to you, myself, in order to have me under your skin. No longer *before* you, like someone from whose gaze you could turn away, rejecting his advances, your object, but within you, speaking to you and kissing you without interruption even before you have the chance to breathe and to turn around. To have the other within oneself, right up close but stronger than oneself and his tongue in your ear before being able

to say a word while looking at yourself in the depths of the rearview mirror
.... (59–60)

This is one of the few passages in the *Envois* in which we are exposed to the words of the addressee of the letters: the beloved other. He (and the speaker is indubitably a 'he') quotes her written response to his written request to 'burn everything' by reporting her avowal of having faithfully burned, after having (re)copied, his letter in her own handwriting. Her quoted words are buried in parentheses: ('I am burning, stupid impression of being faithful, nevertheless kept several simulacra, etc.', isn't that it?). As the text goes on to say, reading (even reading for the first time) always involves burning, copying (as in 'learning by heart') the words of the other. His text copies her words that copy his letter: he answers, 'yes, you had understood my order or my prayer, the demand of the first letter' to her reported response ('I am burning, stupid impression of being faithful, nevertheless kept several simulacra, etc.') to his original demand that she 'burn everything'. The passage ends with his avowal of this linguistic erotic desire: 'to have the other within oneself, right up close but stronger than oneself and his tongue in your ear'.

Love letters burn with this desire: to keep the words of the other within oneself, in secret. Fire is the element that links the motif of the secret (as the body of the letter that does not suffer translation, circulation, transposition) to all of the principles of destination and adestination that regulate the postal principle. It is fire that allows the *Envois* to function as love letters as well as public postcards. The very gambit of *The Post Card* turns on the fact that it is, by necessity and design, both a book of secrets and a comprehensive interrogation of the postal principle (from Plato to Freud and beyond) according to which the philosophical tradition (and all of the institutions, including psychoanalysis, that are ancillary to that tradition) determines everything that is bound up with destination, transmission, transference, transferal and (male) inheritance.

A foretaste of the secret

Fire introduces an irreducibly secret element into the very possibility of transfers and transferences upon which the postal principle relies. By relating burning to secrets, *The Post Card* also asks about what remains of literature in an age of tele-technology. Literature is another name for any writing that keeps its secret even when circulated in public: it burns its own letters in public.

> The secret of the postcard burns – the hands and the tongues – it cannot be kept, q.e.d. It remains secret, what it is, but what must immediately circulate, like the most hermetic and most fascinating of anonymous – and open – letters. (188)

As that which guards the secret of the letter by burning it, fire inhabits the postal principle from within. It resists the blinding transparency of public space in which everything is exposed to light. This is why Derrida is attracted to the image of burning his own (public) image in public: '[w]hen I have nothing to do in a public place, I photograph myself and with few exceptions burn myself' (37).

Because fire consumes and destroys everything it touches, it troubles the difference between life and death. Fire makes no distinctions between expressions of love and the work of mourning. Fire is both alive and dead: like all living creatures, it needs to eat the other in order to survive. As the very principle of *tekhne*, art or artifice, it lives otherwise than biologically.

In a missive dated simply May 1979, the author writes:

> I 'worked' this morning but you know now what I mean by that: mourning – for me, for us in me.

The 'work' of mourning described here is inextricable from everything that we have been saying about the way the other secretly burns me from within.

On the following page, in another letter also dated May 1979, we read the following:

> The Wolfman died 7 May. A little bit of me is gone. Had I told you that I am also Ernst, Heinele, Sigmund, Sophie and HAlberstAdt (the latter, the reproducing son-in-law, the genitor of Ernst, was, don't forget a phOtOgrApher)? (194)

'A little bit of me is gone', Derrida writes, in passing, about the passing of Freud's famous patient Wolfman. The phrase 'a little bit of me is gone' is both an expression of mourning and a description of its labour. If a bit of Derrida dies with the Wolfman, it is no less true that a bit of the Wolfman lives on in Derrida's corpus.[7] Derrida's text (*Fors*) about Nicolas Abraham and Maria Torok's case history about the Wolfman's magic secret words was, after all, the basis for his own mourning work. During the Wolfman's 'life', in *Fors* Derrida had written about how the Wolfman had kept his (unmourned and undead) others secretly alive within him. So secretly, in fact, that he didn't even know they were there. What happens, Derrida appears to ask here, to the letters of the living undead (the beloved encrypted others) when their host dies? Following the work of Abraham and Torok, in Derrida's writings, the Wolfman (whose secret loves remain hidden ('incorporated') within him in the form of bits of secret words or burning letters) is a figure for the most secret of secrets. As the very incarnation of letters that do not (and cannot) pass, he is also a figure of burning letters:

[ ] question concerning the Wolfman: does an 'incorporated' letter arrive at its destination? And can one give to someone other than oneself, if to give, *the* giving must also be introjected? Have we ever given ourselves to each other? If we have given ourselves *something* we have given ourselves nothing. This is why more and more I believe in the necessity of burning everything, of keeping nothing of what has *passed* (been given) between us: our only chance. (195)

Ashes

Immediately after mentioning the death of the Wolfman, Derrida goes on to invoke the lineage of psychoanalysis's first family and to inscribe himself into it through an identification with its dead: Ernst, Heinele, Sigmund, Sophie and HAlberstAdt. This evocative list implicitly places Sophie (Freud's beloved daughter, whose death in 1920 coincides with the publication of *Beyond the Pleasure Principle* and whose body was cremated) at the centre of a ring of fire. Sophie (daughter to Sigmund Freud, mother to Ernst and Heinele, wife to Halberstadt) is the burning feminine figure whose cremated body and (mourned/unmourned) death secretly alters and seals the course of psychoanalytic thinking and the possibility of its transmission.

When fire dies, there are ashes. Ashes are what remain of the bodies that have been consumed by fire. When Sophie dies, from flu, far away from her parents, her body is turned into ashes. Sophie's ashes are scattered throughout *The Post Card*. In 'To Speculate – On Freud', Derrida writes extensively about how her death haunts the institution of psychoanalysis and troubles the story Freud tells himself about its transmission and survival. But in the *Envois*, Sophie's body returns, like a burning letter, in the form of a photograph and as ashes, as a reminder of what has not been mourned and as a remainder of what does not pass.

On 9 May 1979, he writes:

I'm flipping through my albums. For all the time I've been talking about her, and that she has been obsessing me like your double, I had never seen Sophie. Here she is, with her father, I'm trying to describe her in the way that I see her (through Freud's eyes, of course). [ ] what a couple! Inseparable. Moreover, they are reunited in the same photograph, he full face, looking out toward the world, she, a bit lower, in profile, turned toward him (tender and protected). (189–90)

In a letter dated End of June 1979, he writes:

> Imagine the old man who remains with his will, which has just come back to him, in his hands (Freud said that the most monstrous thing is to see one's own children die, this is the thing of his that I have best understood – and you, of mine, the least well perhaps, unless it is the opposite – and this is why I found it monstrous that after his daughter's death he could have said '*la séance continue*'), the old man who remains the last to read himself, late at night. (199)

In the penultimate pages of the *Envois*, in a letter dated 28 August 1979, when musing about how the names of the apostles have passed like letters ('epistles') into his family line, he conjures up his dead sibling Paul, whose death remains unexplained and unread, like a dead letter.

> I follow the order: Paul in the first place (the little brother dead before me, a year before, I think, and they have never wanted to know or to say of what: 'He fell badly,' I heard once, yes, yes, I swear. He was only a few months old.) Then Jacques, of course, then Pierre and Jean. (254)

In the same letter, presumably trying to assure his beloved that the postcards will have guarded their secrets, despite (because?) of having been circulated in public, he writes:

> Especially where I speak truly they will only see fire. On this subject, you know that Freud's Sophie was cremated. (255)

After (love) letters burn, they leave ashes. Ashes follow all the 'posts' of the postal principle; they are its secret remains and the remains of its secrets.[8]

In a letter dated 31 May 1979 (the final day in the mourning month of May), the lover imagines the following scene:

> I'd like to die. In the mountains, a lake, long before you. This is what I dream of, and this postal sorting nauseates me. Before my death I would give orders. If you aren't there, my body is to be pulled out of the lake and burned, my ashes are to be sent to you, the urn well-protected ("fragile") but not registered, in order to tempt fate. This would be an *envoi* of/from me *un envoi de moi* which would no longer come from me (or an *envoi* come from me, who would have ordered it, but no longer an *envoi* of/from me, as you like). And then you would enjoy mixing my ashes with what you eat (morning coffee, brioche, tea at 5 o'clock, etc.). After a certain dose, you would start to go numb, to fall in love

with yourself, I would watch you slowing advance toward death, you would approach me within you with a serenity that we have no idea of, absolute recon-ciliation. And you would give orders ... While waiting for you I'm going to sleep, you're always there, my sweet love. (196)

The scene in which the lover expresses this desire to die is described as a 'dream'. The dream (which is not literally a dream) is apparently a response to the 'nausea' that accompanies 'postal sorting'. The dreamer imagines he is dying so that he can give his cremated body to his lover as if it were an absolutely secret letter, addressed only to her. Posting his ashes to her, he wants to give himself to her uniquely and as *nothing*, as nothing that is, but only as the incalculable remains of the body that has been consumed by fire. He then imagines that she will incorporate him, bit by bit, eating the ashes of the very body that the fire has consumed. Like a burning letter, his body will enter her body, like a letter that does not pass. The remains of his burned letters intermingle with the ashes of his burned body, as he becomes nothing but a dead letter. All of this is, of course, a fantasy of the ultimate love letter: a letter so uniquely addressed to the other that it never enters circulation and hence remains untouched by the postal principle. In keeping with this fantasy, he imagines that she commits suicide by eating him. It is a suicide by fire: all his dead letters enter her body un-translated. She dies from letting the words enter her without making them part of her. She kills herself with the words of the other. But this dream of a letter so secret – so uniquely addressed – that it escapes from the determinations of the postal system is, of course, only a fiction. Or rather, the foreign language called literature, if by literature we understand the form that undelivered letters take, as they become tinder in the moment of burning.

PS

Perhaps it is Melville (and not Poe) who secretly watches over the letters as they are prepared for the fire in the *Envois*:

Dead letters! does it not sound like dead men? Conceive a man by nature prone to a pallid hopelessness, can any business seem more fitted to heighten it than that of continually handling these dead letters, and assorting them for the flames? For by the cart-load they are annually burned. Sometimes from out of the folded paper the pale clerk takes a ring: – the finger it was meant for, perhaps, moulders in the grave; a bank-note sent in swiftest charity: – he whom it would relieve, nor eats nor hungers any more; pardon for those who died despairing; hope for those who died unhoping; good tidings for those who died stifled by unrelieved calamities.[9]

Notes

1   Jacques Derrida, 'If There is Cause to Translate I', in *Eyes of the University: Right to Philosophy 2* (Stanford: Stanford University Press, 2004), 19. Originally published in *Semiotic Inquiry* 4.2 (1984): 91–154.

2   Jacques Derrida, '*Istrice 2: Ick bünn all hier*', in *Points ..., Interviews, 1974-1994*, ed. Elisabeth Weber (Stanford: Stanford University Press, 1995), 326.

3   Jacques Derrida, 'Envois', in *The Post Card: From Plato to Freud and Beyond*, trans. Alan Bass (Chicago and London: The University of Chicago Press, 1987), 40 (hereafter cited in text as *PC*).

4   See David Wills' book *Matchbook: Essays in Deconstruction* (Stanford: Stanford University Press, 2005) for a very fine set of readings of the *Envois*. He concludes the chapter called 'Matchbook' by pointing out that '[t]he reader is not often called upon to burn a book', 68.

5   Jacques Derrida, *La carte postale: de Socrate à Freud et au-delà* (Paris: Flammarion, 1980), 7. All further French quotation of this text will refer to this edition.

6   Jacques Derrida, 'What is a "Relevant" Translation?', trans. Lawrence Venuti, in *The Translation Studies Reader: Second Edition*, ed. Lawrence Venuti (New York and London: Routledge, 2004), 424.

7   For a more extensive treatment of Derrida's work on mourning and its relation to Freud's patient Wolfman, see my book: *The Mother in the Age of Mechanical Reproduction: Psychoanalysis, Photography, Deconstruction* (New York: Fordham University Press, 2012). In particular, see the following chapters: 'Mourning, Magic and Telepathy'; 'The Sexual Animal and the Primal Scene of Birth'; and 'Bit: Mourning Remains in Derrida and Cixous'.

8   In *Feu la cendre* [*Cinders*] published in 1987 (seven years after *La Carte postale*), Derrida reprints portions of the postcards from the *Envois* and, in so doing, poses the question of what remains of any reading and any writing. Jacques Derrida, *Cinders*, ed. and trans. Ned Lukacher (Lincoln, NB: University of Nebraska Press, 1991).

9   Herman Melville, 'Bartleby, the Scrivener', in *Billy Budd, Sailor and Selected Tales* (Oxford: Oxford University Press, 2009), 41.

5

Fort Spa:
In at the Deep End with Derrida and Ferenczi

Lynn Turner

Now, it is here that the very possibility of a speculation that would be neither philosophical nor scientific in the classical sense (the devil for science and philosophy), nevertheless could open onto another science, as it does to another fiction ....

— Jacques Derrida[1]

... when the psychic system fails, the organism begins to think.

— Sándor Ferenczi[2]

Deconstruction, Psychoanalysis, Philosophy: this contact zone remains a journey into hot water, waters further heated by the addition of a fourth ingredient – Feminism. This chapter specifically engages the return of the body and the biological within contemporary material feminism in light of Derrida's early insistence on the soma and psyche as that which is mutually informed.[3]

Without a significant barrier decisively separating them, the commensality of soma and psyche is yet 'marred' or perhaps conditioned in Derrida by the work of repression that is also the scene of writing. The return of the repressed in the deconstructive transformation of psychoanalysis, however, cannot be guaranteed: the death drive already at home within the archive puts paid to that.[4] Strongly identified with the body as the scene of representation, it has taken a long time for feminist theory to shake loose the influence of Jacques Lacan's *Ecrits*. These 'writings' were formerly assumed to authorize a non-essentialist version of the body by virtue of its fading before the signifier, with the concomitant assumption that this – and only this – shift into signification gave room for a political future of emancipation.[5] Loosening this legacy allows us to entertain the notion of the body as something beyond a disengaged support for the inscription of the psyche. For the sake of brevity this chapter will only nod towards the Deleuzian turn in feminism of the 1990s and its important alternate emphasis on what a body can do, since this work tended to misapprehend Derrida as closer to Lacan and thus in continuation with the dialectical tradition.[6] Departing from that tradition, 'Fort Spa' solicits another kind of speculation in view of another kind of body.[7] Mixing deconstruction, psychoanalysis, philosophy and feminism, this chapter welcomes a return not simply to 'the body' as if there were only one, but to biology as a scene of dynamism. Rather than the infernal trap that would spring the most patriarchal of destinies upon women without hesitation, as found in the explicit appeal to the teleology of nature in Sigmund Freud's essay on 'Femininity', biology becomes something for us to think with.[8] 'Fort Spa' keeps the performative 'SF' of Donna Haraway in mind: trained as a biologist, her work frequently solicits the supplement of a 'speculative fabulation' or 'speculative feminism' that might dispel the tendency of origin stories from condensing into patri-*arkhe*.[9] Adding in 'So Far' to the title of her paper headed by this acronym was not merely poetic frivolity but a pointer to the contingency and the incompleteness of SF. 'Fort Spa' gives specific attention to Elizabeth A. Wilson, one of a new generation of feminists who are also readers of Derrida, and zones in on her recuperation of a dynamic biology in the more marginal archives of psychoanalysis such as the works of Sándor Ferenczi.[10] While Wilson emphasizes Ferenczi's radicality in proposing what he names 'bioanalysis' thus stepping beyond the psyche as a closed system, this chapter asks after the antiquated models of sexual difference that may yet hinder his speculation. With Derrida's suggestive reading of the legacy of psychoanalysis in 'To Speculate-on "Freud"' in mind, we can dive in.

SF

A common abbreviation of the genre 'science fiction', 'SF' also promiscuously speaks to other terms. Derrida's doubling of 'Beyond the Pleasure Principle' travels under the title of 'To Speculate-on "Freud"'. SF might thus claim Speculation on 'Freud'. Treading cautiously in the troubled steps of Freud, Derrida remarks on Freud's resistance to philosophy, on his hesitation regarding possible debts that psychoanalysis might incur, and in particular on what might be smuggled in under the name of 'speculation' (such as the dialectical tradition). Philosophy is of 'no concern', apparently.[11] If it was, and if it did have something to say about pleasure, Freud would 'readily express [his] gratitude'.[12] As things stand, Freud feels free to speculate upon a ground cleared from the influence of such a dominant discipline and thus without debt. For Derrida, Freud's auto-acquittal serves the purpose of allowing for the inauguration of the free-standing house of 'Freud': psychoanalysis properly begins with the name of Sigmund Freud, SF. SF betting on SF. Interweaving the emergence of the field and the legacy of its progenitor – taking shape beneath the 'same roof', 'Beyond the Pleasure Principle' becomes autobiography by another name (TS, 293). 'Auto-biologos-graphy' we might say, given Freud's later concession that '… the uncertainty of [his] speculation has been greatly increased by the necessity for borrowing from the science of biology. Biology is truly a land of unlimited possibilities'.[13] Alternatively, perhaps that other name is SF, or the constitutive 'becoming literary of the literal' that Derrida advocated in 'Freud and the Scene of Writing' (FS, 230). If the 'greater pleasure was attached to the second act', as Freud remarks regarding his nephew's infamous game, that second act or return is both the rewarding logic of *re*presentation for which, in Derrida's reading, *fort-da* is the minimal unit, and the dangerous revival of the inorganic (TS, 317). For the uncanny life of psychoanalysis is such that the devil of the death drive can never be driven out and thus this autobiographical gesture is also auto-thanatographical (393). The ensuing two-step of what Derrida casts as 'life death', without diacritical instruction or necessarily a successive pattern of *fort* then *da*, troubles the securing of any new position. If 'beyond' there be, it is of a wholly other order.[14] Indeed Derrida refers to Freud's text not as a thesis and not as antithesis, nor yet a synthesis, but rather as an *athesis* (259). The gambit of speculation falls short.

SF is also Sándor Ferenczi. Like the Freud of *Totem and Taboo*, Ferenczi also draws on fabulation to embed his theory in a legend: the closing pages of *Thalassa* name the speculations of SF precisely as a 'fairy tale'.[15] Yet SF lives in fear of SF. For nine years, Ferenczi 'confesses' through a rhetoric inescapably evocative of the uncanny, the material eventually published under the title *Thalassa: A Theory of Genitality* lay 'buried in [his] desk' until he 'g[ave] birth' to it (*T*, 5). During this time, when *Thalassa* was buried alive, Freud published 'Beyond the Pleasure Principle'.[16] In one of a series of articles re-examining the less-well-travelled archives of psychoanalysis, Elizabeth A. Wilson notes the agonized relation between Ferenczi and Freud detailed in their corre-spondence, as their work overlapped but also significantly parted ways.[17] For Wilson's interest this discrepancy rests on the status of the biological – the terrain that she wishes to reactivate. In light of Derrida's emphasis on filiation in psychoanalysis we can see that Ferenczi's position as a much junior colleague, and thus an ostensible legatee, made his departure from the canon – from the house of SF – all the more alarming. Anxiety regarding this departure hampers Ferenczi's own attempt to step 'beyond': beyond Freud his intellectual master, beyond the pleasure principle, indeed beyond the 'PP' as Derrida's capacious abbreviation has it. As silently as the death drive, this 'PP', in Derrida's hands, also slips in the 'postal principle'. Again any speculative security of the concept comes under the intrinsic threat of getting lost in the post. Today the private correspondence between SF and SF is publically available for anyone to read: for anyone radically unforeseen to become the addressee, for example Elizabeth A. Wilson.[18]

Alongside drawing out the dynamism that Wilson finds in the Ferenczian body, and one that dares embrace the name 'bioanalysis' (rather than psycho-analysis), this chapter turns to two related topics (*T*, 19). One is the version of the death drive surfacing in *Thalassa* in the guise of a death *dive*, that is to say the SF desire to return to life in water. This return invokes both ontogenesis, in terms of individual explusion from amniotic fluid, and phylogenesis, in terms of the seas and the evolutionary remembrance of swimming amongst other species. The other is the still pressing, still vexacious matter of sexual difference, or in a more Derridean light, sexual differences. Given Wilson's strong situation of Ferenczi within her project of 'Gut *Feminism*' readers might expect more of a forthright engagement with the sexual.[19] It may be that by significantly shifting attention to the stomach, or the 'brain in the gut' as she calls it in her 2004 book *Psychosomatic*, for the purpose of dramatically rethinking what happens and where it happens when we are depressed, sexually differentiated Oedipal complexes have ceased to organize Wilson's focus.[20] It may be that the stomach is participant in sexuality in ways that are yet to be set forth (she invokes the contractions of peristalsis and antiperistalsis that Ferenczi traces phylogeneti-cally to the 'same digestive tube') (GF, 79; *T*, 86). It may also be – to continue this speculation – that she avoids the unpleasure of trawling back through frequently frustrating material in the psychoanalytic canon, material that endures amongst Ferenczi's problematically radical thought. Bridging her insistence on the gut she quotes Ferenczi's highly suggestive reframing of 'the genital' in the opening pages of *Thalassa*, yet without speculating upon its possible consequences for sexuality. This genital

> ... would then no longer be the unique and incomparable magic wand which
> conjures eroticisms from all the organs of the body; on the contrary, genital

amphimixis would merely be one particular instance out of the many in which such fusion of eroticisms takes place (GF, 81; *T*, 12).[21]

Whether Ferenczi himself follows through on disbanding this 'magic wand', as this selective quotation implies, is another question.

Damp squibs

Excavating the 'Freudian Crypt' with Todd Dufresne would be enough to put off many readers – particularly feminist ones – from supposing that there may be any room for manoeuvre in SF. Admittedly, Dufresne entertains short shrift with the Freudian legend tout court, advising that we let it die rather than symptomatically induce psychoanalytic persistence in mimesis of the PP through the stimulating effect of criticism (albeit in the form of a book length disquisition on the subject). In acknowledgement of Derrida's situation of Freud's writing as that which itself carries out his ostensible topic, Dufresne says no too to deconstruction by missing the possibility that repetition can always be an alteration; that gone can really mean gone; that traces can always be erased or wiped away. Dufresne's derision sparks at the junctures proximate to those which Wilson finds enabling. In reference to SF, Dufresne only finds 'ridiculous' passages, even 'especially ridiculous' ones that narrate a too familiar battle of the sexes retrofitting the seemingly inevitable domination of women into our phylogenetic makeup: biology – 'Biological Frenzy' no less – appears as origin and destiny in one (*TF*, 34; 57; 61). When Dufresne reads of this frenzy in psychoanalysis it is only ever recourse to 'blatant biologism' (xv; *passim*). Nevertheless, I find the trace of a different argument.

In contrast to Freud and Josef Breuer's development of the concept of conversion hysteria as that which was played out upon the bodies of female patients in their *Studies on Hysteria*, *Thalassa* clinically begins with male sexual dysfunction.[22] Comparing the functioning of premature ejaculation with that of men who virtually refuse to ejaculate, Ferenczi comes to the speculative conclusion that even in 'normal ejaculation' a 'synergetic harmony of anal and urethral innervations is essential' (*T*, 7). That is to say, rather than the cumulative achievement of phallic sexuality, Ferenczi supposes that ejaculation is always helped or hindered by the tendencies to expel or to retain. This physical rhythm of what we might call the PP as *fort* and *da* is effectively tutored by the urethra or anal sphincter respectively.

Ferenczi calls the group work of this organic ensemble 'amphimixis', a term otherwise medically used in reference to the merging of gametes in sexual reproduction. Not only do the genitals, urinary and excretory organs work in communication with each other, but, as the earlier quotation from Ferenczi suggests, this is merely one instance out of 'many'. Beginning with phallic fallibility, Ferenczi appears to disperse the apparently singular end point of the phallic phase by sharing it out amongst other organs and rendering this dispersal comparable to many other bodily contexts. This group work is both physical and cathected. For Wilson, this departure from a utilitarian biology that might assign each organ an individual task habituated to 'their utility for the preservation of life' allows not just for a dynamic understanding of the body but also for the SF body to engage in the 'expression of wishes' and even 'complicated thought' (GF, 76). From here she leaves the letter of *Thalassa* to turn toward the belly of the bulimic as participant rather than puppet in the thought processes of depression. In line with Ferenczi this participation does not award a consciousness to any alternative organ but suggests the phylogenetic sedimentation of what he calls a 'biological unconscious' throughout the body, rendering that body amenable to analysis (77).

Given the affirmation of this dynamic, material, bodily, biological capacity, detached from exclusively preserving life that we find in Wilson, it is remarkable how single-minded the thought of this SF body becomes in the subsequent pages of *Thalassa*, subjected to what Ferenczi calls the 'thalassal trend'.

Lost at sea

In her account of the dynamic possibilities of the SF body in *Thalassa*, Wilson accentuates the disseminative effect of amphimixis on the erstwhile magic wand to produce a reading significantly less conservative from the more apparent one given by the text. She virtually obliges Ferenczi to follow through on his own intuition. Or rather, as I would like to think, it is as if the explicit engagement with Derrida that she brought to her first book *Neural Geographies* has already been activated in the pages of 'Gut Feminism', yet silently, without the signposts of argument as such.[23] Derrida's work only warrants a handful of acknowledgements in *Psychosomatic*, but they are telling in light of what she might have spelled out in 'Gut Feminism'. Early in that book Wilson reassures the reader that the 'circuit of nerves-penis-cortex-psyche' found in Freud's writing on neurasthenia need not equate to 'self-contained elements arranged in determinable relations of cause and effect.[24] While her argument zones in on the question of how trauma and specifically mourning registers not just at the level of the psyche but in 'serotonergic pathways', the theoretical flashpoint turns on decentring the penis as a supposedly discrete agent. The structure she advances in her distinctive reading of Freud

> could be called a relational or distributed network only when certain ontological conditions have been met. ... a logic of distribution is critically valuable only as it approximates a Derridean notion of dissemination or *différance* – that is a distribution or relationality that is constitutive of its component elements.[25]

As with the biology emerging in 'Gut Feminism' any sense of the utilitarian or instrumentation of individual organs dissipates. Following Wilson's implication, if not her argument, regarding *Thalassa*, another kind of SF body must come forth.

Returning to the pages of *Thalassa*, however, we find less distribution of the erotic than synthesis. SF remains loyal to SF when it comes to 'genital primacy' in sexuality. Indeed the first indication of amphimixis in *Thalassa* ties it in to a teleological formation in which two or more erotisms synthesize into a 'higher unity' (*T*, 9). While opening up the terrain of the biological, SF nevertheless concedes to 'harmonis[ation]' with canonical sexual theory (11). Indeed the pleasure principle is legible as the motivational circuit of compensation as to why organs such as urethra and anus should communicate. In what Ferenczi calls 'pregenital amphimixis' the would-be liberal pee pee learns restraint from the pleasures of retention, the retentive bowel learns to expel 'by borrowing the urethral pleasure in voiding' (12). In such an exchange no pleasures are lost, no tensions remain, equilibrium is maintained. Except, when SF casually mentions the clitoris it is to locate a proper displacement of pleasure to the vagina rather than entertain any amphimictic constellation (14; 24). The traffic in pleasure in this case filters it away from the clitoris, famously rendered as the analogue of the male organ by Freud, and toward the vagina, which again he famously claimed as 'the female organ proper' in spite of its 'virtual non-existen[ce]' for 'several years'.[26] A slightly more complex if no less vexed story emerges in the third chapter of *Thalassa*, which wrestles with proper feminine sexuality again in line with SF authority.

Reading SF in a very forgiving light we might understand the clitoris as so profoundly generous that it shares its pleasures not only with the vagina but with 'other parts of the body ... in particular the nipple and the surrounding area' (*T*, 24). While SF describes this displacement in comparison to hysteria,

Wilson would remind us that the soma of SF hysteria renders the body as participant in displaced affects: it is not simply hijacked by a foreign agent. The body is widely eroticized because it can be rather than is obliged to be. However, unlike the organization evoked by Gayatri Spivak in which '[t]he clitoris escapes reproductive framing' and might therefore speak to an economy of pleasure alone unbound to function, SF is blind to that possibility and tightly binds this vector of escape.[27] Amphimixis shows up. However the ends of reproduction are served by expelling expulsion from feminine rhythms. In SF, the vagina may borrow 'considerable amounts' of erotism from elsewhere – peristalsis from oral ingestion and retention from the anus, but this is all in the service of retaining semen and 'sheltering' the vulnerable penis in coitus (*T*, 24). 'There/there (*da/da*)' her rhythms might mutter. The urethra is virtually as forsaken as the clitoris in this story. Yet the SF endorsement of the desire to return to life in water remains to be taken into account. This is only configured for the woman by virtue of introducing a more categorical split between the psycho- and the bio-analytic: she retains 'at any rate in the psychic sphere' a masculine wish to return to the womb achievable through identification with the 'penis-possessing male' as well as his symbolic equivalent – the 'child that she harbors within her own body' who has apparently successfully made that trip (and negated any feminine material or symbol) (24–5). Amphimixis again makes an appearance in a further convolution. Her 'female penis' as former but not 'pre-' genital prior to the proper adoption of feminine passivity was itself consolidated through amphimixis – we can only assume along the same *fort/da* pulsions at play in the masculine model since symmetry is being invoked – only to retract or 'regress' into her 'whole body' and 'whole ego' (25).

The success story of genital amphimixis turns out to be the speculation of the penis and the phallus (since body and symbol are both invoked). Coitus becomes the stage upon which to bet on its safe return. With a singularly SF flourish, this return is bound to the phallogocentric economy of representation – an economy that Luce Irigaray specifically addresses and offsets with the concave speculum of her *Speculum Of the Other Woman*.[28] In her analysis speculation hones a regime of the visual and/as the erasure of sexual difference:

> If woman had desires other than 'penis-envy', this would call into question the unity, the uniqueness, the simplicity of the mirror charged with sending man's image back to him – albeit inverted. Call into question its flatness. The specularization, and speculation, of the purpose of (his) desire could no longer be two-dimensional.[29]

In *Thalassa*, man's anxieties over the safety of his 'most precious organ' during coitus are mollified by his 'introjection' of 'the organ of the woman' (we are not told which one) (*T*, 17).[30] With such a capture in place the terrifying sexual other is annulled while his organ does not really go anywhere, or undergo any change, in which it might 'get lost' (ibid.). Having ventured the safety of the environment however, Ferenczi returns to the amphimixic labours of ejaculation and the fortification of that secretion. Again identification steps in, now unifying the whole of the – masculine – organism with firstly his genital, secondly his female partner (*Thalassa* swims in heteronormative waters) and thirdly his emission (*T*, 18). This deposit must be secured. SF banks on the uterus: where else would be free of discord, free of enervating stimuli? Free of difference? While the organism and the organ achieve 'hallucinatory' or partial identification with this return, the best is saved for the third term. In SF 'the sexual secretion' alone achieves reunion '*in reality* to the womb of the mother' (ibid., italics original). Whereas he suggests that *all* (human) beings desire to return to the peace of intrauterine life, and *all* mammalian life desires to return to life in water, only one entity manages to '*in reality*' regain this state.[31] Insemination is homeward bound. With so many steps set up to secure safe passage, including the specular elimination of the sexual other such that she only reflects 'the same', as Irigaray would say, Ferenczi neither steps beyond Freud nor into the warm thalassal seas that are ostensibly the object of desire.

This over-valuation and fierce protection of seminal fluid is all the more ironic given the success of its arrival, assuming, with SF, that this is so. Reuniting with the uterus would serve only to set this game little gamete in a sea of searching for the ovum, since however jubilant in its homecoming the sperm may be, the reproducibility that is supposed to motivate this return is pointless without amphimixis in the strict sense.[32] The ovum evades any identification, any speculation at all. We do not even know if *this* germ plasm is prized at all. If the tale of a violent and oppositional sexual difference, whether Oedipally or phylogenetically inscribed, afforded by Sigmund Freud and Sándor Ferenczi were to be our only story we would stop forthwith. The SF solution effectively produces the intrauterine environment as one entity, as liquid behaving like a solid, as *da*, when it might otherwise enjoy the differentiated consistency of a spa. 'Spa' here speaks to what we might, after Irigaray, call a poetics of fluids that, in light of both Irigaray and Derrida, refuse speculative recuperation.[33] That is to say, fluids can always wash and be washed away. Fluids do not seal a single point of origin, as Astrida Neimanis insists '*We are all* [always and already] *bodies of water*.'[34] Water remains our condition of possibility, our mutable common

'ground'. This poetics might also sustain a more hospitable address to biology –
an address that is a long way from the biological essentialism of which Irigaray
has frequently and mistakenly been accused.[35]

Sea food

From *Psychosomatic*'s insistence on the Enteric Nervous System (the stomach)
as supplement to the Central Nervous System (the brain) to the retrieval
of Melanie Klein in 'Underbelly', Wilson has been occupied with the gut.
It is all the more intriguing then, that what escapes her attention in SF is
the brief address to a primal mode of ingestion that effectively prevents the
imagined environment desired in *Thalassa* from holding watertight. Ingestion
emerges in the pages that most directly acknowledge 'Beyond the Pleasure
Principle'. It follows on from Ferenczi's evocation of the 'poetic fantasy' in
Plato's *Symposium* as the scene of a catastrophic division of matter into two
halves 'leaving it with an impulsion to reunite wherein organic life had its
earliest inception' (*T*, 61). It follows on too from the confession that Ferenczi's
earlier account of coitus may be 'inadequate and unsatisfying' precisely at the
level of fertilization, albeit unsatisfying in terms of his fear that reproductive
practicality (a flat biology of the need to reproduce the species) will trump
thalassal regression (the bioanalysis of the desire to return to an earlier state)
(*T*, 60). Claiming further differentiation than Freud, Ferenczi suggests two
catastrophes – the first prompts a division between inorganic and organic,
the second introduces that of sexual difference. SF tries again invoking the
'fanciful' ideas of Wilhelm Bölsche, who speculated that '[w]ith the firstlings
of life there was no opposition between eating and love; eating was a purely
logical condition of love'.[36] In the race to the land before the pleasure principle,
Ferenczi hypothesizes an 'even more archaic cataclysm' – more archaic
than coitus – that obliged 'unicellular organisms … to eat each other up,
in such a manner that no one of the participants in the struggle succeeded in
annihilating its opponent' (*T*, 62). Finessing Bölsche's incorporation of Ernst
Haeckel's 'gastraea' or primitive stomach produced through the invagination
of the zygote of multicellular organisms, Ferenczi conjures this mutually
beneficial commensality as a prelude to the production of sexually differentiated cells – germ cells, though what pressures this production he does not
say.[37] This 'more archaic' cataclysm that obliges entities to eat each other does
so without murder, miraculously enough for an origin story. Yet it is framed as

the anticipation of sexual reproduction and one whose struggle, as accounted for in *Thalassa*, is far less agreeable.

More curiously, eating figures again in the book's final chapter. After passages that offer greater consonance with the athetic non-oppositional relation of life and death on which Derrida speculates –

> What if … death and dying were not anything absolute, if germs of life and regressive tendencies lay hidden even within inorganic matter … we should have to drop once and for all the question of the beginning and end of life, and conceive the whole inorganic and organic world as a perpetual oscillating between the will to live and the will to die in which an absolute hegemony on the part of either of life or of death is never attained. (*T*, 94–5)

– and immediately preceding the summation of SF in his fairy tale, Ferenczi blurts out: '[A]ppetite comes with eating!'(99). This – whatever this is – is immediately retracted for fear of the 'unacceptability' of 'piling hypothesis upon hypothesis', even as the pleasures of which the proverb speaks confirms the PP, while exceeding the pee pee. It is unclear whether SF refers to the ingestion of food, or whether the proverb is meant only to operate metaphorically and eating serves as a figure for any pleasure. Whether eating could sustain a distinction between the literal and the figural, however, is something that both Derrida and Wilson put into doubt.

Breach

'Underbelly' parallels the project of 'Gut Feminism' in that Wilson rehearses the denigration of the body in second wave feminism only to find a surprisingly subtle rejoinder in the work of Melanie Klein (one of Ferenczi's 'most famous analysands', as she remarks, and as such breaches the house of SF herself).[38] Gayle Rubin's influential work on the 'sex/gender' distinction serves Wilson with a classic anthropological division between simple hunger and complex cuisine.[39] Through Klein, Wilson finds it possible and desirable to argue for the belly's complexity and participation in psychic life. Again this speaks to a kind of bioanalysis in which the material frequently merely assumed to support a complex structure such as phantasy is implicated with it instead. Wilson position's the belly in Klein as 'psychically alive' to the infant, full of good and bad objects introjected from the first (U, 204). Klein writes:

> … the child receives his main satisfaction through his mouth, which therefore becomes the main channel through which the child takes in not only his food,

but also in his phantasy, the whole world outside him. Not only the mouth, but to a certain degree the whole body with all its senses and functions, performs this 'taking in' process ... the child breathes in, takes in through his eyes, his ears, through touch and so on.[40]

Klein continues to activate the breast as the first object of introjection, but her 'not only' has already opened a path. While Wilson maintains her focus upon the oral-entomological transit as home to numerous objects (both phantastic and pharmaceutical), albeit in a manner that is crucially 'impurely, relationally constituted,' Derrida revises this path (U, 204).

In the enigmatic closing paragraphs of 'Freud and the Scene of Writing' Derrida gestures to 'what might be called a new *psychoanalytic graphology*' and suggests that 'Klein perhaps opens the way' (FS, 231; emphasis as original). Derrida's phrasing is evocative given his preceding discussion on breaching as a 'ciphered spacing,' as that event of writing that upsets classical models of inside and outside, time and space, before and beyond (203). While few scholars have so much as noticed this reference to Klein, compare the following citation from his interview on 'Eating Well':

> For everything that happens at the edge of the orifices (of orality, but also of the ear, the eye – and all the 'senses' in general) the metonymy of 'eating well' (*bien manger*) would always be the rule.[41]

Though they are not named in this interview, Derrida's metonymy of eating well and its relation to introjection are developed in relation to the work of Nicolas Abraham and Maria Torok.[42] A certain kind of genealogy of the notion of introjection shapes the house of SF, passing between Ferenczi, Freud, Klein, Karl Abraham, Abraham, Torok and Derrida.[43] In a figural peristalsis, introjection undergoes a tighter and looser grip on its subjects and on itself. Even though Derrida ostensibly supplied a 'Foreword' to Abraham and Torok's book *The Wolf Man's Magic Word* and one that magnified the uncanny architecture of their 'crypt' from the outset of its idiosyncratic title, '*Fors*', his work radicalizes the path of introjection.[44] Soliciting all the senses in general, Derrida detaches psychic ingestion from the mouth, insists on the metonymical quality of eating and drops the teleological anticipation of speech as the zone of the human (habitual to psychoanalysis and philosophy). While SF interjects '[A]ppetite comes with eating!' and common sense might attribute his meaning to the purely figural, Derrida quite seriously asks 'What is eating?', shattering its supposedly simple expression of a basic need and posing it as always and already enmeshed in the 'becoming-literary of the literal'.[45] Introjection is not the action of an intending subject that can appropriate the other like a tool. Psychoanalytic graphology speaks to bioanalysis insofar as the body is breached. Regression cannot compel the same phantasy, only repetition that can expunge in the same gesture. This can only be sustained by bringing the trace to the fore.

Notes

1   Jacques Derrida, 'To Speculate-on "Freud"', in *The Post Card: From Socrates to Freud and Beyond*, trans. Alan Bass (Chicago: Chicago University Press, 1987), 288 (hereafter cited in text as TS).

2   Sándor Ferenczi, *The Clinical Diary of Sándor Ferenczi*, trans. Nicola Jackson (Cambridge, MA: Harvard University Press, 1995), 6.

3   For 'material feminism' see eds. Stacy Alaimo and Susan Hekman, *Material Feminisms* (Indianapolis: Indiana University Press, 2007). Jacques Derrida, 'Freud and the Scene of Writing', in *Writing and Difference*, trans. Alan Bass (London: Routledge Kegan Paul, 1978), 196–231 (hereafter cited in text as FS).

4   Jacques Derrida, *Archive Fever: A Freudian Impression*, trans. Eric Prenowitz (Chicago: Chicago University Press, 1998).

5   Jacques Lacan, *Ecrits: A Selection*, trans. Alan Sheridan (New York and London: Routledge, 2001). For examples of this moment in feminist theory see, Kaja Silverman, *The Subject of Semiotics* (Oxford: Oxford University Press, 1984); Jacqueline Rose, *Sexuality in the Field of Vision* (London: Verso, 1986).

6   See for example, Rosi Braidotti, *Nomadic Subjects: Embodiment and Sexual Difference in Contemporary Feminist Theory* (New York: Columbia University Press, 1994).

7   Though it is beyond the remit of this chapter, speculation has returned with some vigor in recent years under the name 'Speculative Realism'. For a critique of this return see Johnny Golding, 'Ecce Homo Sexual: Ontology and Eros in the Age of Incompleteness and Entanglement', *Parallax* 20.3 (2014): 217–30.

8   Freud writes:

> … the juxtaposition 'feminine libido' is without any justification. Furthermore, it is our impression that more constraint has been applied to the libido when it is pressed into the service of the feminine function, and that – *to speak teleologically* – Nature takes less careful account of its [that function's] demands than in the case of masculinity. And the reason for this may lie – thinking once again *teleologically* – in the fact that the accomplishment of the aim of biology has been entrusted to the aggressiveness of men and has been made to some extent independent of women's consent.

'Femininity', in *New Introductory Lectures on Psychoanalysis*, vol. 2 in *The Penguin Freud Library*, trans. James Strachey (London: Penguin, 1991), 166 (my emphasis).

9   See Donna Haraway's Pilgrim Award acceptance comments: 'SF: Science Fiction, Speculative Fabulation, String Figures, So Far', *SFRA Review* 297 (2011): 12–19. Her work frequently appeals to feminist science fiction such as that of Octavia Butler or Ursula LeGuin.

10   I roughly and provisionally distinguish between those scholars associated strongly with deconstruction who have also foregrounded feminist questions, such as Peggy Kamuf or Elissa Marder, from feminist theorists who also incorporate strong readings of Derrida.

11   Sigmund Freud, 'Beyond the Pleasure Principle', in *On Metapsychology*, Vol. 11 in *The Penguin Freud Library*, trans. James Strachey (London: Penguin, 1991), 275.

12   Ibid.

13   Ibid., 334.

14   David Wills suggests it is an 'Order Catastrophically Unknown' in *Mosaic: A Journal for the Interdisciplinary Study of Literature* 44.4 (2011): 21–41.

15   For Freud's famous summation of the primal feast as murder and cannibalism of the father see, *Totem and Taboo: Some Points of Agreement between the Mental Lives of Savages and Neurotics*, trans. James Strachey (London: Routledge, 2001), 164; Sándor Ferenczi, *Thalassa: A Theory of Genitality*, trans. Henry Alden Bunker (London: Karnac, 2005), 99 (hereafter cited in text as *T*).

16   Ferenczi dates his introduction '1923'; Freud's 'Beyond' was first published in 1920. Todd Dufresne notes Ferenczi's claims to priority, see *Tales From the Freudian Crypt: The Death Drive in Text and Context* (Stanford: Stanford University Press, 2000), 62 (hereafter cited in text as *TF*).

17   Elizabeth A. Wilson, 'Gut Feminism', *differences: A Journal of Feminist Cultural Studies* 15.3 (2004): 70 (hereafter cited in text as *GF*). Wilson also remarks on the scant attention to *Thalassa*, however we should note the affirmative introduction written for the French edition by Nicolas Abraham in 1962 (Paris: Editions Payot, 1968).

18   Wilson cites the correspondence published as Sándor Ferenczi and Sigmund Freud, *The Correspondence of Sigmund Freud and Sándor Ferenczi: Vol. 2, 1914–1919*, eds. Ernst Falzeder and Eva Brandt, trans. Peter T. Hoffer (Cambridge: Belknap, 1996). The citation ironically shows up the hierarchy between these proper names when Freud comes before Ferenczi. Wilson's own publications show, also ironically, her efforts to identify herself by virtue of the middle initial, given the host of other established academics also publishing in the humanities under the name 'Elizabeth Wilson'.

19   Emphasis mine. Notes to the essay 'Gut Feminism' inform the reader that this is the name of a wider project, which includes her later essay published as 'Underbelly'.

The other major feminist engagement with Ferenczi, by She Hawke and Anna Gibbs, similarly avoids his heteronormative retrofitting of the thalassal trend even as they connect this trend with Elaine Morgan's subsequent work on *The Aquatic Ape Hypothesis* (1988); see their essay 'The Currency of Water: Ferenczi's Thalassal Trend, the Evolution of Tears and the Role of Affect in the Psychosomatic Relation', in *Thalassa: The Hungarian Journal of Psychoanalysis* 19.1 (2008): 37–57: https://www. academia.edu/769475/Ferenczis_Thalssal_Trend_The_Evolution_of_Tears_and_the_ Role_of_Affect_in_the_Psychosomatic_Relation_t, accessed 24 December 2014.

20 Elizabeth A. Wilson, 'The Brain in the Gut', in *Psychosomatic: Feminism and the Neurological Body* (Durham: Duke University Press, 2004), 31–48. In an interview Wilson indicates her work as feminist enquiry yet not necessarily governed by a focus on 'gender and sex': see 'A Conversation with Vicki Kirby and Elizabeth A. Wilson', *Feminist Theory* 12.2 (2012): 227.

21 Ferenczi quoted in Wilson, 'Gut Feminism', 81; see Ferenczi, *Thalassa*, 12. This is all the more entertaining for those contemporary readers aware of a particular type of American 'personal massager' known precisely as the 'Magic Wand'.

22 Sigmund Freud and Josef Breuer, *Studies on Hysteria*, vol. 3 in *The Penguin Freud Library*, trans. James Strachey (London: Penguin, 1991).

23 Elizabeth A. Wilson, *Neural Geographies: Feminism and the Microstructure of Cognition* (London: Routledge, 1998).

24 Wilson, *Psychosomatic*, 19.

25 Ibid., 20.

26 Freud, 'Femininity', 374.

27 Gayatri Spivak, 'French Feminism in an International Frame', *Yale French Studies* 62 (1981): 118. Spivak finds the insistence on feminine *jouissance* to be the greatest gift of 'French Feminism'.

28 See Luce Irigaray, *Speculum of the Other Woman* [1974], trans. Gillian C. Gill (Ithaca: Cornell University Press, 1985); and also, on '*fort-da*' as a specifically masculine defence reaction, see her 'Gesture in Psychoanalysis' [1985], in *Between Feminism & Psychoanalysis*, ed. Teresa Brennan (New York and London: Routledge, 1989), 127–38. I discuss Irigaray's uncanny repetition of the speculative endeavours of Freud – in terms of the forecasting of a legacy of her own – in 'Unhoming Pigeons: the Postal Principle in Lynn Hershmann-Leeson and Hussein Chalayan', *Derrida Today* 5.1 (2012): 92–110.

29 Irigaray, 'The Blindspot in an Old Dream of Symmetry', in *Speculum of the Other Woman*, 51.

30 'Introjection' is the concept through which Ferenczi's work is more broadly known and appreciated. Nicolas Abraham – who was subsequently to finesse this concept in tandem with Maria Torok – wrote the introduction to the French edition of *Thalassa* (Paris: Payot, 1969).

31 Some mammals have *already* returned to the waters. Their return, however, is not a simple regression. In their recent book, Hal Whitehead and Luke Rendell note that the cetacean return to the sea was radically reshaped by their evolutionary advantage of breathing air, a capacity that supports both speed, by virtue of oxygenation, and vocal communication. See *The Cultural Lives of Whales and Dolphins* (Chicago: University of Chicago Press, 2015).

32 Emily Martin challenges the persistent sexual imaginary of active sperm and passive egg in her article 'The Egg and the Sperm: How Science has Constructed a Romance Based on Stereotypical Male-Female Roles', *Signs: Journal of Women in Culture and Society* 16.3 (1991): 485–501. Derrida readdresses the philosophical imaginary of sperm in *Dissemination*, trans. Barbara Johnson (London: Athlone, 1981).

33 See Irigaray's essay 'The Mechanics of Fluids', in *This Sex Which Is Not One*, trans. Catherine Porter (Ithaca: Cornell University Press, 1985), 106–18.

34 Astrida Neimanis is developing a poetics that is also an ecologic of water (albeit one without any psychoanalytic investment); see her 'Feminist Subjectivity, Watered', *Feminist Review* 103 (2013): 24, italics as original.

35 While Irigaray's poetics speak to the phenomenological feminine body thus refusing its philosophical negation, it is Irina Aristarkhova that insists on more detailed traffic between the biology of the uterus (against its frequent misleading abstraction into an undifferentiated space) and the philosophical concept of *chora*; see her *Hospitality of the Matrix: Philosophy, Biomedicine, Culture* (New York: Columbia University Press, 2012).

36 Wilhelm Bolsche, quoted in Frank J. Sulloway, *Freud, Biologist of the Mind: Beyond the Psychoanalytic Legacy* (Cambridge, MA: Harvard University Press, 1992), 262.

37 Sulloway, *Freud, Biologist of the Mind*, 261–3.

38 Elizabeth A. Wilson, 'Underbelly', in *differences: a journal of feminist cultural studies*, 21.1 (2010): 202 (hereafter cited in text as U). Dufresne notes that Klein supported Ferenczi's interest in phylogenesis and notion of the 'thalassal trend' (see *TF*, 76).

39 Wilson cites Rubin from her 1975 text 'The Traffic in Women': 'The belly's hunger gives no clues as to the complexities of cuisine' (U, 194).

40 Melanie Klein, 'Weaning' [1936], in *Love, Guilt and Reparation and Other Works 1921–1945* (London: Vintage, 1998), 291. Wilson splits up this citation, and uses a previous translation published by the Free Press, 203–4.

41 Jacques Derrida, 'Eating Well or the Calculation of the Subject', in *Points …*, *Interviews 1974–1994*, ed. Elizabeth Weber (Stanford: Stanford University Press, 1995), 281.

42 Prior to 'Eating Well', Derrida had already published 'Foreword: Fors: The Anglish Words of Nicolas Abraham and Maria Torok', in *The Wolf Man's Magic Word: A*

Cryptonomy, trans. Nicholas Rand (Minneapolis: Minnesota University Press, 1986), xi–xlvii.

43   Indexed by Derrida, '*Fors*,' xvi. 'Introjection' doubtless exceeds this genealogy – I merely indicate those most pertinent to this chapter.

44   See my 'Animal Melancholia: On the Scent of Dean Spanley,' in *Animality and the Moving Image*, eds. Laura Macmahon and Michael Lawrence (London: BFI, 2015).

45   Derrida, 'Eating Well', 282.

6

The Obverse Side of Jacques Derrida's 'Freud and the Scene of Writing'

Céline Surprenant

Deconstruction is unintelligible without taking into account Jacques Derrida's sustained interest in psychoanalysis, which he has maintained from the late 1960s until the late 2000s. Psychoanalysis, mostly Freud's and Lacan's writings, is both a resource and the object of critical discussion, while psychoanalytic practice is transformed.[1] Derrida first dealt with Freudian theory through the prism of the deconstruction of logocentrism, and metaphysics, as the metaphysics of presence. He then moved on to theological and ethical concerns more generally, and ended up raising questions regarding psychoanalysis's ability to adapt to the world's unseen forms of violence (to cruelty) in the era of globalization and the World Wide Web, which is the theme of Derrida's last work on psychoanalysis.[2] For forty years, Derrida has re-examined psychoanalytic concepts in relation to writing, the trace, the concepts of inscription, impression and the archive, while acknowledging that the institution of psychoanalysis and its practical rules are in constant evolution, perhaps especially in the face of technological changes.

However, different 'regimes of historicity' would seem to be at work in Derrida's engagement with Freud's discourse.[3] Derrida has emphasized the interrelation between the psyche and its technical and external other, and in doing so, he has granted the possibility of change within psychoanalytic practice. Nevertheless, he has remained attached to Freud's late nineteenth-century, early twentieth-century model of the psyche.

Freud posited that there is no correspondence between the psyche and the brain (which is the matter of the positive sciences). Trained as a neurologist, he took liberties with late nineteenth-century sciences of the brain, while retaining elements from them. Just how important the biological and neurological outlook may have been in the elaboration of psychoanalysis is a moot point in the history and theory of psychoanalysis. Many, such as Frank J. Sulloway in a landmark book polemically entitled *Freud, Biologist of the Mind: Beyond the Psychoanalytic Legend* (1979), have addressed that topic, whereby biology and the neurosciences are meant to provide a standpoint from which to expose the flaws of psychoanalysis.[4] Derrida did not directly engage with those debates. He has tended to view Freudian theory independently from scientific outlooks.

Some thirty years after Sulloway, the philosopher Catherine Malabou's recent work on plasticity in the neurosciences challenges that stance, by calling into question the graphic scheme in which the Freudian theory of the psyche is couched.[5] However, in speaking of 'the obsolescence of writing' for describing the synaptic trace, or in stating that 'the brain is not a writing machine', she would seem to be addressing Derrida's rendering of the Freudian unconscious rather than Freud's.[6] The following essay thus proposes to return to Derrida's highly influential essay 'Freud and the Scene of Writing' (1966), where he provided a synthesis of Freud's use of graphic metaphors to represent the psyche, from late 1895 until 1925, bearing in mind Derrida's position towards not only metaphysics but also positivism, which he described, not very lightly, as two 'complicit menaces within Freud's discourse'.[7] Before doing so, however, it is useful to provide a brief overview of Malabou's arguments on plasticity in the context of the neurosciences. They allow us to open up questions around the opposition between the psyche and technology, Derrida's distance from the sciences (notably the biological and sciences of the brain), topics that might have remained only implicit in Derrida's essay on Freud, as well as in its reception.

'The obsolescence of writing'

Plasticity is for Malabou the 'paradigmatic figure of organization in general', and of the brain in particular.[8] 'From the Greek *plassein*, to model', plasticity 'both means the ability to be formed or "to receive form" and the ability to give form'.[9] In 1979, the neurobiologist Jean-Pierre Changeux had deemed the expansion of the neurosciences 'as important as that of physics at the beginning of the twentieth-century, or as that of molecular biology around the nineteen-fifties. In view of its important consequences, he claimed, the discovery of the synapse and of its functions recalls that of the atom or of the deoxyribonucleic acid.'[10] Inspired among others by Changeux, who believed that philosophers had neglected recent understanding of the nervous system, Malabou has turned to 'cerebral plasticity' as an object of philosophical enquiry. In the context of the neurosciences, plasticity comes together with a concern for history because the brain does not only have a history but it is *a* history, that is, it has a specific way of 'developing, working and *doing*.'[11] Plasticity is the 'neurosciences' federative term' because it allows us to describe and conceive of the brain 'as a dynamic, an organization, and a hitherto unknown structure.'[12] It is in view of 'cerebral plasticity' that plasticity is for Malabou the 'style of [our] epoch.'[13]

In her questioning of the alleged rift between psychoanalysis and neurosciences, Malabou has encountered neuropsychoanalysis, a term introduced by the American neurologist and psychoanalyst Mark Solms in the 1990s to describe the work of neurobiologists, who believe that it is possible to return to Freud, while taking into account the cerebral, biological aetiology of psychical problems, so as to bring brain mechanisms and psychical life together.[14] Neuropsychoanalysis would seem to fulfil Freud's oft-quoted anticipation of the development of psychoanalysis in *Beyond the Pleasure Principle* (1920), and hopes to treat by psychoanalytic means people having suffered physical damage.[15] Malabou finds an homology between the material, physical disappearance of the subject following cerebral accidents (the subject affected by cerebral damage does disappear, and a new subject emerges which knows nothing of the illness that has caused the disappearance in the first place), on the one hand, and the 1960s philosophical stances about the 'disappearance of the author' or of the subject, on the other, as it was propounded by Foucault in 1966, and more generally, in the human sciences during the following decades (she sends us back to Samuel Beckett's 'empty characters').[16]

Neuropsychoanalysis operates with a non-graphic model of the encoding of neuronal information, namely with the model of 'cell assemblies' which constitute 'a logic of signification, that proceeds from the distribution of phonemes, or of units of meaning'. Yet, even though neuropsychoanalysts speak of neuronal signs, what is at stake is a hitherto unknown kind of sign. There are no imprints as in the Freudian paradigm, where psychical space is formed on the model of printing, and where mnemic-traces are conceived as graphic ones, given that the unconscious is thought to be analogous to a text.[17] Neuronal plasticity is not psychical writing. The shift from one paradigm to the other has an impact on our understanding of traumatic events (and of the place of the physical wound in it), which, Malabou says, we have tended to view through the sexual aetiology propounded in Freudian psychoanalysis. Taking into account the physical brain or what she calls cerebrality makes us change our understanding of physical traumatic events, and of the persons who have suffered from them. Malabou is interested in the ethical implications: it 'opens up psychoanalysis to the possibility of catastrophe, the one that can happen any time, which does not trigger anything other than itself, and does not awaken a more ancient conflict'.[18] Tenets of Freudian theory, such as the role of the psychical conflict and of sexuality in the aetiology of psychical illness, are thus seriously challenged.

For Malabou, then, 'the choice of metaphor [from the graphic to the cell assemblies one] changes everything'. She asks: 'Can we keep the notion of the unconscious if we call into question the graphic metaphor?' In other words, is there anything left 'of psychoanalysis and of the psyche as Freud defined it, if plasticity gives rise to a non-textual encoding'? For the neuropsychoanalysts something obviously remains of it, but a different kind of hermeneutic is needed for dealing with neuronal plasticity, one that 'proceeds to a greater extent from the demographic dynamics [the 'cell assemblies'] than from the deciphering of hieroglyphs'.[19]

'Freud and the Scene of Writing'

Derrida delivered 'Freud and the Scene of Writing' at the psychiatrist and psychoanalyst André Green's seminar (1966), and the essay was later included in *Writing and Difference* in 1967. Green's seminar, held at the Institute of Psychoanalysis (of the Paris Psychoanalytic Society [SPP]), provided an opportunity for members of the analytic community to meet up with philosophers and human sciences scholars. Other speakers during that year included Michel Serres, René Girard, Jean-Pierre Vernant and Marcel Détienne, with the aim of creating a dialogue between analysts and philosophers.[20] In particular, Green wished to open up a debate around some of Derrida's propositions from *Of Grammatology* (the first chapter of which had then just been published in *Critique* in December 1965–January 1966). The question arose as to what the psychoanalytic methods and clinic might have to do with deconstruction? Let us recall that 'Freud and the Scene of Writing' contains some of deconstruction's most programmatic statements, notably around the Freudian concept of delayed temporality (*Nachträglichkeit*), which, for Derrida, is Freud's only genuine foray outside metaphysics. The delayed temporality, as Freud conceived of it, allows for something that is repressed to continue to have an effect well after the subject has ceased to be conscious of it, and to be made to connect with something in the present. It implies that traumatic events make sense only in relation to other events.

This does not prevent Derrida from distancing himself from Freud's concepts, at least in a famous aphorism that prefaces the essay: 'despite appearances, the deconstruction of logocentrism is not a psychoanalysis of philosophy' (FSW, 247–8). The deconstructive approach might indeed appear as an attempt to analyse the 'repression' of writing in the philosophical tradition, or to track down the symptomatic form of the return of the repressed in the philosophical tradition. Yet, Freudian concepts, such as repression, can be used only in quotation marks, Derrida argued, because they all 'without exception, belong to the history of metaphysics, that is, to the system of logocentric repression which was organized in order to exclude or to lower (to put outside or below), the body of the written trace as a didactic and technical metaphor, as servile matter or excrement' (246).

Let us briefly recall the essay's main arguments, so as to draw out Derrida's emphasis on the graphic model in Freud, which he presents as a differential principle that becomes more and more prominent as Freud's work develops. This process coincides with Derrida's progressive translation or sort of Freudian concepts into the language of deconstruction.

The four sections of 'Freud and the Scene of Writing' present the 'strange progression' that the successive metaphorical models draw. At first sight, what is at stake is an almost unbroken chronological succession of discursive events up until we reach the 'hypothetical construction' expounded in Freud's 'A Note upon the "Mystic Writing Pad"' (1925 [1924]). We are dealing with the gradual consolidation of the psyche as writing:

> a problematic of breaching [*Bahnung*] is elaborated only to conform increasingly to a metaphorics of the written trace. From a system of traces functioning according to a model which Freud would have preferred to be a natural one, and from which writing is entirely absent, we proceed toward a configuration of traces which can no longer be represented except by the structure and functioning of writing. At the same time, the structural model of writing, which Freud invokes immediately after the *Project* [*for a Scientific Psychology* (1895)], will be persistently differentiated and refined in its originality. All the mechanical models will be tested and abandoned, until the discovery of the *Wunderblock*, a writing machine of marvellous complexity into which the whole of the psychical apparatus will be projected. (251)

Derrida is, however, interested in discontinuity. The Freudian psyche undermines the idea of congruence between the representation of the content of the psyche and that of its functioning. Another set of questions is needed, in so far as metaphor is a matter of the relationship between 'psyche, writing and spacing' or difference, not only in Freud's discourse, but in the 'history of the psyche, text, and technology'. One of the right questions to ask is 'what the imitation, projected and liberated in a machine, of something like psychical writing might mean', and another: 'what is a text, and what must the psyche be if it can be represented by a text? For if there is neither machine nor text without psychical origin, there is no domain of the psychic without text' (250).

Metaphor for Derrida points to 'the possibility of the representational relation' between the psyche and its technical models (287). There are two series of metaphors: the one pertaining to content and the other to a machine. That there should be two series shows that Freud holds an instrumental view of metaphor and of the machine, even though his model is differential. Derrida thus begins by analysing the neurological model in Freud's earliest description of memory in the *Project for a Scientific Psychology*, in which Freud borrows abundantly from late nineteenth-century neurology.[21] It is initially defined as 'the capacity for being permanently altered by single occurrences'. However, a problem arises: 'on the one hand … neurones are permanently different after an excitation from what they were before' and conversely 'fresh excitations meet with the same conditions of reception as did the earlier ones'. This means that 'neurones must be both influenced and also unaltered' (P, 299). In Derrida's voice: memory simultaneously entails the permanence of the trace and 'the virginity of the receiving substance' (FSW, 251). The hypothesis of the contact-barriers [*Kontaktschranken*] and of facilitation or breaching [*Bahnung*] introduces a principle of resistance that accommodates that dual functioning.

The *Project* establishes that 'neuronal excitation [can be described] as quantity [Qn] in a state of flow' and that nervous activity functions according to the principle of inertia. That is to say that the nervous system aims towards the discharge of quantity, that it seeks to avoid 'being burdened by a Qn' (P, 296).[22] This aim is called the primary function. When the nervous system is faced with 'the major needs: hunger, respiration, sexuality' – 'it must put up with [maintaining] a store of Qn sufficient to meet the demand for a specific action [by virtue of which the major needs can be appeased]' (297). This accumulation of Qn is the secondary function. 'All the functions of the nervous system can be comprised either under [these two aspects]' (ibid.). The primary function (discharge) becomes inseparable from something that is opposed to it. The secondary function, the accumulation of quantity, requires 'the resistances [which] are all to be located in the contacts [*Kontakte*]' between the neurones and which 'assume the value of barriers [*Schranken*]'.

Freud thus assigns the contradictory functions of memory to two categories of neurones: 'there are permeable neurones (offering no resistance and retaining nothing) ... and impermeable ones (loaded with resistance, and holding back Qn)' (300). Memory is situated in the latter. The capacity of receptivity and of retention must still be accounted for. The contact-barriers of these neurones thus permanently modified are yet submitted to change in so far as remembering gradually eases the passage of quantity, up to the point where these neurones may become more and more similar to the neurones 'offering no resistance and retaining nothing' (ibid.).

How can neurons be further differentiated? In view of the changing power of the contact-barriers, memory cannot be explained by the fact that some neurones offer a capacity of resistance while others do not. Rather, memory can best be 'represented by the differences in the facilitations between the ψ neurones' (ibid.), differences which, for Derrida, are 'the true origin of memory, and thus of the psyche' (FSW, 252). Given that the breachings are produced by 'the Qn which passes through the neurone' (P, 300), the difference between breachings comes to depend upon that between quantities and the number of repetitions of the passing through. Moreover, a breaching resulting from the passage of quantity can be added to the quantity and can itself become an operative factor in their production. For Derrida, this means that breachings are both analogous to quantity and 'other than it as well' (FSW, 253).

There are no scriptural metaphors in Freud's neurological model. However, it is here that difference between breachings and resistances will be central to writing and metaphoricity. Thanks to them Derrida identifies a principle of difference at work in Freud. For the primary functions (of discharge, of life), of perception, or of receptivity, cannot be conceived apart from what resists them. The functioning of the psyche involves what Derrida calls 'originary repetition' as the opposition of forces of differing amounts of excitations (254). The origin is from the outset duplication, or to put it in Freud's lexicon, the discharge of quantities only makes sense in relation to their accumulation. Derrida interprets this system of difference in terms of writing. Given Freud's conception of the psyche is thus 'a topography of traces, a map of breaches', it is not surprising if no existing type of writing is adequate for representing it (258). 'Psychical writing' is not a metaphorical way of describing the psyche according to Derrida. It is writing 'in the world' that becomes a metaphor in view of the structure of 'psychical writing' (but how to describe 'psychical *writing*' without speaking of writing 'in the world'?).

In *The Interpretation of Dreams* (1900) too the traditional conception of writing as 'an irreversible, linear consecution, moving from present point to present point' cannot represent the Freudian psychical topography, and above all, its temporality (272). Memory's capacity 'for indefinite preservation and an unlimited capacity for reception' is described with reference to inscriptions (*Niederschriften*), and involves differences between inscriptions (277). Still, no existing model of writing is suitable, because each type of inscription is associated with a psychical locality (never to be confused with cerebral anatomy, for Freud), or to a system (*Ics.*, *Pcs.*, *Cs.*). Between each locality, it is never a matter of a simple transcription, or of the translation of an inscription from the one to the other. We find originary repetition not only in the neurological fable of the *Project*, but also in *Beyond the Pleasure Principle*, to which Derrida also sends us back, and in which he 'reinterprets' repetition as moments of *différance*, and links it with an economy of death:

> All these differences in the production of the trace may be reinterpreted as moments of deferring [*moments de la différance*]. In accordance with a motif which will continue to dominate Freud's thinking, this movement is described as the effort of life to protect itself by *deferring* a dangerous cathexis [*l'investissement dangereux*], that is, by constituting a *reserve* (*Vorrat*). The threatening expenditure or presence [what produces breachings] are deferred with the help of breaching or repetition. Is this not already the detour (*Aufschub*, lit. delay), which institutes the relation of pleasure to reality (*Beyond the Pleasure Principle*)? Is it not already death at the origin of a life which can defend itself against death only through an economy of death, through deferment, repetition, reserve? For repetition does not happen to an initial impression; its possibility is already there in the resistance offered the first time by the psychical neurones … it is the idea of a first time which becomes enigmatic. (253–4)

Derrida paraphrases each of Freud's attempts to describe the psyche metaphorically in what will become the language of deconstruction: the trace, différance, originary prints, archives, supplement and the deferred temporality of the unconscious. As long as Freud distinguishes between *psychical content* and the *apparatus* and seeks separate models for them, he will be unable to find an adequate metaphor. Freud's differential conception requires him to link the two together (258). With the model of the 'Note upon a "Mystic Writing Pad"', the two are finally brought together in Freud's discourse by means of a writing machine, an 'apparatus of originary recording or inscription' (Freud's material description of the instrument contrasts with Derrida's gloss of the passage):

The Mystic Pad is a slab of dark brown resin or wax with a paper edging; over the slab is laid a thin transparent sheet, the top end of which is firmly secured to the slab while its bottom end rests upon it without being fixed to it. This transparent sheet is the more interesting part of the little device. It itself consists of two layers which can be detached from each other except at their two ends. The upper layer is a transparent piece of celluloid; the lower layer is made of thin translucent waxed paper. When the apparatus is not in use, the lower surface of the waxed paper adheres lightly to the upper surface of the wax slab.

To make use of the Mystic Pad, one writes upon the celluloid portion of the covering-sheet which rests on the wax slab. For this purpose no pencil or chalk is necessary, since the writing does not depend on material being deposited on the receptive surface. It is a return to the ancient method of writing on tablets of clay or wax: a pointed stylus scratches the surface, the pressions upon which constitute the 'writing'. In the case of the Mystic Pad this scratching is not effected directly, but through the medium of the covering-sheet. At the points which the stylus touches, it presses the lower surface of the waxed paper on to the wax slab, and the grooves are visible as dark writing upon the otherwise smooth whitish-grey surface of the celluloid. If one wishes to destroy what has been written, all that is necessary is to raise the double covering-sheet from the wax slab by a light pull, starting from the free lower end. The close contact between the waxed paper and the wax slab at the places which have been scratched (upon which the visibility of the writing depended) is thus brought to an end and it does not recur when the two surfaces come together once more. The Mystic Pad is now clear of writing and ready to receive fresh notes.[23]

The design of the *Wunderblock* combines the double system that Freud had tried to represent with reference to the nervous system. It embodies the original temporality of the Freudian unconscious. Freud draws out three analogies between the various elements of the Mystic Pad and the psychical apparatus (the pad includes 'what Kant describes as the three modes of time in the *three analogies of experience*: permanence, succession, simultaneity' [FSW, 283]). One element can be likened to the function of perception ('the layer which receives the stimuli' which 'forms no permanent trace') and another to the unconscious (the 'wax slab') where the 'permanent trace of what was written is retained ... and is legible in suitable lights' (ibid.). These two analogies, Derrida argues, concern the 'space of writing, its extension and volume', while the third one is related to the fact that writing is visible only when the two surfaces come together (ibid.). That discontinuous temporality corresponds to the functioning of the psychical apparatus; consciousness is an episodic phenomenon. The machine realizes what was earlier described as the trace or writing. Yet, it is not Freud that would seem to have found the right scriptural model, but rather Derrida, in so far as the writing machine for him materializes (or acts as the model of?) 'a system of gestures … an organized multiplicity of origins', the 'original relation to the other' (FSW, 284). In Derrida's presentation of it, the machine is transfigured:

> Traces thus produce the space of their inscription only by acceding to the period of their erasure. From the beginning, in the 'present' of their first impression, they are constituted by the double force of repetition and erasure, legibility and illegibility. A two-handed machine, a multiplicity of agencies or origins – is this not the original relation to the other and the original temporality of writing, its 'primary' complication: an originary spacing, deferring, and erasure of the simple origin, and polemics on the very threshold if what we persist in calling perception? (ibid.)

It notably gives shape to the process of metaphorical representation, which Derrida calls 'metaphoricity'. 'Mystic Writing Pad' thus attracts notice to the relation of the psyche to technology. From the technical description of a machine (in Freud's language), we move to an abstract register. We are no longer dealing with psychical writing, or writing in the world, but *writing* as duplication, and this opens up for Derrida the question of the relation between the psyche and technology.

Derrida summed up his analysis of the 'Mystic Writing Pad' in *Mal d'archives. Une impression freudienne* (1995), as an attempt to analyse the relation between the psyche and the model of archiving, technology, time and death. Death appears in two ways: on the one hand it is linked with originary repetition, in so far as the differential principle through which Freud conceives of the psyche introduces death *inside* the psyche. On the other hand, for Freud, according to Derrida, the machine remains an external mechanical tool at the service of psychical memory. In spite of his original views, Freud was unable to conceive of the machine as being internal to the psyche, or to acknowledge the mechanical nature of the psyche. He could not, in Derrida's language, imagine the institution of an 'internal prosthesis'.[24]

Heredity

The question arises, however, as to whether the Freudian metaphors of path, trace and breach, the 'unbelievable mythology', to use Derrida's words about the *Project*, might not act as a model for the Derridean concept of trace and of writing? This question is all the more pressing that Derrida excludes from his discussion of Freud's notion of memory the concept of 'the hereditary mnemic-trace', concurring with the rejection of the evolutionist overtones of aspects of Freudian thought. When introducing his aims in 'Freud and the Scene of Writing', he writes: 'it is a question neither of following Jung, nor of following the Freudian concept of the hereditary mnemic-trace' (FSW, 248). The concept of mnemic-traces stems from the phylogenetic dimension of Freud's theory, where he envisages the transmission of unconscious contents and structures, even though he has no experimental proofs that there is a material support for it. It is Freud's attempts to conceive of unconscious transmission by resorting to biology, yet rejecting the biological meaning of heredity. He also calls that process the 'transmission of an archaic heritage', even though he remains doubtful about the concept. He says for example in *The Ego and the Id* (1923), that to try and deal with phylogenesis makes him fear that 'the inadequacy of [his] whole effort' will be laid bare.[25] The hypothesis is at stake almost everywhere in Freud, from *The Interpretation of Dreams*, to *Totem and Taboo* (1912–13), up until 'The Outline of Psychoanalysis' (1940 [1938]), and it deserves a work in itself.[26]

Even though Derrida pushes it aside from the outset, he nevertheless believes that Freud has exploited his genuine discovery about temporality 'beyond the psychoanalysis of the individual' (FSW, 254–5). Derrida relates traces, inscriptions and breachings to 'sociality' (as we saw, with reference to the structure of the multi-layered writing machine). That is to say, by relating them to 'sociality' he is bringing them close to the 'hereditary mnemic-trace'. How is sociality, the 'more than one', to be understood? Is 'sociality' a metaphor for illustrating originary repetition, *différance*, the trace and spacing?

Now, the hypothesis of an archaic heritage, or of 'hereditary mnemic-trace', is precisely one of Freud's means for understanding the sociality of the psyche 'in its ultimate consequences'. Moving 'beyond the psychoanalysis of the individual' makes Freud use his own concepts analogically so as to give an account of collective processes, even though he has only observed these processes at the level of the individual.[27] Just as Freud resorted to neurological models for describing mnemic-traces at the level of the individual psyche, he treats heredity and phylogenesis as fictional aids for representing a transmission without biological and material supports. It is indeed when Freud is moving away from any observable phenomenon that he needs the greatest metaphorical resources. If, in the *Project*, the preservation of psychical contents depends upon the conflicting receptive and non-receptive functions of neurones that are taken to be fictional, in *Moses and Monotheism* (1939), the preservation of psychical content depends upon the human masses which condense 'the residues of the existence of countless egos', to borrow what Freud says of the id in *The Ego and the Id*. It is thus peculiar that Derrida should have granted a (non-figurative?) status to heredity beforehand in introducing the essay, perhaps because heredity had too explicit a biological content to serve as metaphor. Derrida believed that Freud renewed the traditional separation between memory and technical instruments in his discussion of 'A Note upon the "Mystic Writing Pad"', because he associated mechanical instruments with death. However, Derrida's exclusion of the '*hereditary* mnemic-trace' perhaps suggests that it is uneasy for him to grant a metaphorical status to the 'living' – the human masses, the 'countless egos' – or perhaps even the 'demographic dynamics', dear to contemporary neurosciences.

As Freud extends the idea of the unconscious to the human masses, the transmission of psychical contents that was already problematic at the level of the individual, and that leads him to elaborate a differential conception of the psyche, becomes even more acute. The need to renew models and find yet other metaphors becomes even more pressing when we move 'beyond the psychoanalysis of the individual' (288). Derrida's dismissal of the 'hereditary mnemic-trace' from his analysis of Freud's discourse excludes the problematic discontinuities between the individual and the 'collective' that pose problems in Freud's theory.

Techno-sciences and the neurosciences

We can relate Derrida's dismissal of hereditary mnemic-traces to his willingness, in 1994 at the Freud Museum in London, to imagine the future of techno-sciences (when it is a matter of techniques of archiving, and of transmission in relation to psychoanalysis) on the one hand, and his refusal, in 2000, of the neurosciences, on the other. In *Mal d'archives*, Derrida indeed grants that the evolution of techniques of archiving will affect the structure of the psyche, and asks whether the resemblance between the psyche and the machine might not continue to evolve, be ever more striking and no longer be a matter of representative logic.[28] However, Derrida envisaged the expansion of the techno-sciences independently to that of the neurosciences, because he believed that they could be of interest only to analytic philosophers, and that they owed too much to positivist models.

In relation to Derrida's prediction about the future of techno-sciences, however, the psyche (which would be affected by them) seemed to be an invariant, to have remained unchanged since Freud's description of it (from 1895 until 1939). The permanence of the Freudian model of the psyche in Derrida can be compared to the way in which, in Stanley Kubrick's *2001: A Space Odyssey* (1968) the characters still need to eat meals no matter how everything else has been transformed, or no matter how synthetic and futuristic the food has become. Derrida would seem to have kept apart the development of informatics (of the techniques of archiving, memorization and transmission which he deemed were relevant to the future of psychoanalysis) and that of the knowledge of the brain, and advances in neurobiological sciences that go with it. In any case, in his discussion of techno-sciences, he seems to have correlated not contemporary knowledge of the brain and the most recent development of informatics, but rather the late nineteenth-century model of the psyche, as Freud conceived of it, and informatics. It is as though biological functioning could not be dealt with as provisional and technical, as though it were kept apart from the technological realm, because the machine is linked with repetition and death.

In 'Freud and the Scene of Writing', Derrida aimed to move away from the linguistic interpretation of the unconscious, which was controversial on theoretical and institutional grounds because it was linked with Jacques Lacan's various dissident stances during the 1960s. From Derrida's point of view, it was necessary to deconstruct linguistic categories, which renewed the 'ancient phonologism' (the seminar on Freud follows on closely from the first chapter of *De la grammatologie*), before they could help us make sense of the Freudian theory of the unconscious (FSW, 276). The emphasis on the metaphor of writing and its deconstruction was thus aimed at deconstructing the dominance of linguistics in the human sciences.

Malabou's contemporary interventions following the recent development of neuropsychoanalysis suggests that the antagonism between the psychoanalytic community and the neurosciences might be fairly recent, as are Derrida's dismissive stances towards them in his late work on psychoanalysis mentioned at the beginning of this chapter. Yet, the neurosciences were already a concern for the psychoanalytic community in 1966, at the time of Derrida's intervention in Green's seminar. Witness that a large section of the influential sixth *Colloque de Bonneval* is devoted to a discussion, not only of the much debated relation between language and psychoanalysis, but also of that between psychoanalysis and the neurosciences.[29] This is so with reference notably to the pioneering work of Alfred Fessard, the first professor of General Neurophysiology at the Collège de France (1949–71), who developed encephalographic techniques to record the electrical activity of the brain (Jean-Pierre Changeux followed Fessard's professorship by being nominated in 1975 at a chair in Cellular Communications).[30]

It is therefore puzzling that one side of the contemporary debates – that of the confrontation between psychoanalysis and the neurosciences – should be entirely absent from 'Freud and the Scene of Writing'. Were metaphors and writing indeed not foreign to the biological questions raised by the then emerging sciences of the brain? Was the emphasis on Freud's metaphor of writing not a *desire* to save Freud from biology, from the positive sciences of the brain?

We saw that Derrida's early take on Freud itself raises problems around what counts or not as metaphors. If, for Derrida, the analysis of the metaphor of writing, in fact of writing machines, in Freud is a means of thwarting the menace of metaphysics within Freud's discourse, what can allow us to thwart that of positivism? In Freud's conception of the psyche the latter is dependent on the machine, or technology, that is, on an inherently changing world. But the psyche in Freud's account is also bound to evolving scientific outlooks (Freud goes so far as to imagine a path from psychoanalysis to biology, as we saw). Derrida's discussion of the metaphor of writing does not seem to allow for that level or that kind of change, even though it implies a mobile view of technologies of writing.

This is the question that returning to Derrida's early essay in the light of Malabou's criticism has allowed us to raise. Derrida seems to have more willingly associated Freud's conception of the psyche with technologies of writing than with biological processes, even though Freud drew metaphors from biology as much as from technologies of writing when defining the psyche. Derrida's *blindness* towards biological processes in Freud or towards the metaphorical potential of biology, if one may say so, with the evolutionary overtones, might have determined his lack of interest in contemporary neurosciences.

The concern with the relation between the psyche and technology guided Derrida's early encounter with Freud. Given this bias, then, and perhaps rather than seeing in the essay an avoidance, it seems perhaps more useful to say that paying attention to metaphor in Freud, as a relation between the psyche and technology, is a way of appropriating, albeit indirectly, the questions that arose in the neurosciences during the 1960s, namely the relation between the brain and the techniques for discovering the functioning of the brain.[31] If so, 'Freud and the Scene of Writing' does not only give us a means of understanding Derrida's attachment to Freudian concepts, but also leads us to questions raised in the neurosciences between the psyche, the brain and technology that Derrida apparently ignored, but with which he eminently dealt in the context of the deconstruction of metaphysics. Apparently detached from any concern with the neurosciences, 'Freud and the Scene of Writing' in fact sends us right back to them, and document a climate of research, just as the speculation about the past and the future of psychoanalysis in view of technologies of memorization and communication in *Mal d'archives* makes us relive the birth of the internet and that of electronic communication through email. Between these two sides of the history of the psyche, there was apparently no easy passage for Derrida.

Notes

1   For the history of psychoanalysis in France in the post-war period up until the mid-sixties, see Alain de Mijolla, *Freud et la France, 1885–1945* (Paris: Presses universitaires de France, 2010), *La France et Freud* vol. 1, *Une pénible renaissance 1946–1953* and vol. 2, *D'une scission à l'autre, 1954–1964* (Paris: Presses universitaires de France, 2012).

2   Jacques Derrida, *États d'âmes de la psychanalyse: l'impossible au-delà d'une souveraine cruauté* (Paris: Galilée, 2000).

3   I borrow the notion of 'regimes of historicity' from François Hartog, *Régimes d'historicité, Présentisme et experiences du temps* (Paris: Seuil, 2003).

4   Frank J. Sulloway, *Freud, Biologist of the Mind: Beyond the Psychoanalytic Legend* (New York: Basic Books, 1979).

5   This philosopher's critical analyses of the Freudian psychoanalytic paradigm through the concept of plasticity were partly prompted by the recurrent attacks on psychoanalysis that we find in the *Livre noir de la psychanalyse*, one of many other polemical works against psychoanalysis borne out of advances in the neurosciences. See Catherine Meyer, Mikel Borch-Jacobsen, Jean Cottraux et al., *Le livre noir de la psychanalyse: vivre, penser, aller mieux sans Freud* (Paris: les Arènes, 2005).

6   Catherine Malabou, 'Trace psychique et trace synaptique parlent-elles la même langue', in *Neurosciences et psychanalyse*, eds. Pierre Magistretti and François Ansermet (Paris: Éditions Odile Jacob/Collège de France, 2010), 55.

7   Jacques Derrida, 'Freud and the Scene of Writing', in *Writing and Difference*, trans. Alan Bass (London: Routledge, [1967] 1978; 2001), 249 (hereafter cited in text as FSW).

8   Malabou tells the story of her elaboration of the concept in *La plasticité au soir de l'écriture. Dialectique, destruction, déconstruction* (Paris: Léo Scheer, 2005).

9   Catherine Malabou, *Que faire de notre cerveau?*, 2nd ed. (Montrouge: Bayard, [2004] 2011), 43.

10   Jean-Pierre Changeux, *L'Homme neuronal* (Paris: Arthème Fayard/Pluriel [1983] 2012), quoted in Malabou, *Que faire de notre cerveau?*, 37.

11   Ibid., 36–7.

12   Ibid., 41.

13   Catherine Malabou, *Les nouveaux blessés: de Freud à la neurologie, penser les traumatismes contemporains* (Paris: Bayard, 2007), 11; 110.

14   See Malabou, 'Trace psychique', 51–72; 54.

15   Sigmund Freud, *Beyond the Pleasure Principle* (1920) (*The Standard Edition of the Complete Psychological Works of Sigmund Freud*, Vol. XVIII [London: Hogarth Press, 1957]). Jean Nageotte, Professor of Comparative Histology (1912–37) at the Collège de France, was stating the reverse in his Inaugural Lecture delivered in 1912: he called for the elaboration of a psychology that would complement the findings in histology. See Alain Berthoz and Marie-Hélène Grosbras, *Leçons sur le corps, le cerveau et l'esprit: les racines des sciences de la cognition au Collège de France* (Paris: Éditions Odile Jacob/Collège de France, 1999), 269.

16   See Malabou, *Les nouveaux blessés,* 329–39.

17   See Malabou, 'Trace psychique', 55.

18   Ibid., 71.

19   Ibid., 56

20   For contextual data on the Paris Psychoanalytic Society, see among many other works, Alain de Mijolla's *Freud et la France.*

21   Sigmund Freud, 'Project for a Scientific Psychology' (1950 [1895], in *The Standard Edition*, Vol. I, 299 (hereafter cited in text as P).

22   On the definition of affect in Freud as a quantum, see A. Green, *Le discours vivant. La conception psychanalytique de l'affect* (Paris: Presses Universitaires de France, 1973) and 'De L'Esquisse à L'*Interprétation des rêves*: coupure et clôture,' *Nouvelle Revue de Psychanalyse*, no. 5 (1972).

23   Sigmund Freud, 'A Note upon a "Mystic Writing Pad"', in *The Standard Edition*, Vol. XIX, 228–9, quoted in 'Freud and the Scene of Writing', 284.

24   Jacques Derrida, *Mal d'archives. Une impression freudienne* (Paris: Galilée, 1995), 37–8.

25   See Freud, *The Standard Edition*, Vol. XIX, 38.

26   Freud, *The Standard Edition*, Vol. XXIII, 102. See Marie Moscovici's description of phylogenesis in 'Un meurtre construit par les produits de son oubli' (*Écrits du Temps* 10 [1985]) as 'a controversial and enigmatic aspect' (127), which is either left aside or considered to be inessential (129). See among other discussions of the issue, A. Green, *Cent ans après* (Paris: Gallimard, 1998), 112–25.

27   Freud uses quotation marks abundantly and conspicuously, particularly around his own concepts. See Céline Surprenant, *Freud's Mass Psychology. Questions of Scale* (London: Palgrave/Macmillan, 2003), Ch. 4. I have developed part of the

analyses presented here in Chapter 1 of that book, which I propose to revisit in relation to the history of the sciences of the brain contemporary with Derrida's discussion of Freud.

28   See Derrida, *Mal d'archives*, 33.

29   Henri Ey, ed., *L'Inconscient*, VIe Colloque de Bonneval 1960 (Paris: Desclée de Brouwer, Bibliothèque neuro-psychiatrique de langue française, 1966).

30   For a detailed discussion of the inception of the sciences of the brain in France around the figure of Alfred Fessard up until Jean-Pierre Changeux's nomination at the Collège de France, see Pierre Buser, 'Alfred Fessard, neurophysiologiste: influence nationale et internationale', in Claude Debru, Jean-Gaël Barbara and Céline Cherici (eds), *L'essor des neurosciences France, 1945–1975* (Paris: Hermann, Histoire des Sciences, Paris, 2008), esp. 11–13. On the debate concerning the neurosciences in the psychoanalytic community, see Claude Blanc, 'Conscience et Inconscient dans la pensée neurobiologique actuelle. Quelques réflexions sur les faits et les méthodes', in *L'Inconscient*.

31   Chris Johnson argues that cybernetics provide a model for Derrida's analysis of Freud in 'Freud and the Scene of Writing'. See 'Derrida and Science', *Revue Internationale de Philosophie*, 52, 205, 3 (1998).

7

The Desire for Survival?

Kas Saghafi

How are we to contend with the provocation that has presented itself as 'the desire for *survival*'? Could Derrida's work be characterized as describing, representing or calling for a 'desire for survival'? Is what Derrida calls survival, or *survivance* as he prefers to refer to it in his later work, even something that can be *desired*? Is not surviving, or survivance, in addition to referring to the finitude of a mortal being, also a structural feature, of, for example, writing, the date and the name? Recent attention has been paid to the notion of desire in relation to Derrida's work by Martin Hägglund, whose *Radical Atheism* has garnered much critical attention. Foregrounding a notion of desire in *Radical Atheism*, Hägglund asserts that 'Derrida himself did not provide a systematic account of his notion of desire, and it has remained unexplored by his commentators, but I will argue that it is altogether crucial for his thinking' (*H*, 32).[1] Embarking upon 'a sustained attempt to reassess the entire trajectory of Derrida's work'– no small feat – in *Radical Atheism*, Hägglund refutes a notion, which Derrida never endorsed or promulgated, of 'an ethical or religious "turn" in his thinking' (1). Using as his pivot the notion of desire, Hägglund expresses a need for a systematic account in order to provide a shopping list of what is and what is not desirable. Since what has traditionally been designated as desirable, the absolute being of God or the immutability of the soul, fails to meet Hägglund's criteria, he provides an alternative: 'everything that can be desired is mortal in its essence' (111). Life, on his account, is 'essentially mortal, which means that there can be no instance' that is immortal, as immortality is equated with an existence uncontaminated by time (8).

According to Hägglund, what is desired is in its essence finite, which seems to designate the opposite of infinite and is thus something that terminates, ends or dies. Employing a Lacanian definition of desire inspired by Plato, Hägglund takes desire to be an attempt to attain fullness. In the account of desire (*epithumia*) in the *Symposium* Socrates declares that the desiring subject 'desires what it does not have' (Griffith) or 'lacks' [*endeés*] (Lamb) (200b) and wants 'to continue to possess in the future what he possesses now' (Griffith) (200d).[2] As Diotima tells Socrates, what is mortal tries to be everlasting and immortal. This 'love [*eros*]' with a view to 'immortality [*athanasias*]', also translated as 'desire for immortality' (Griffith), is how a mortal being partakes of (Lamb), or tastes [*metexei*] (Griffith), immortality (208b).[3] For Lacan, the lack of fullness – the fact that desire cannot be fulfilled – is what gives rise to desire. What is ultimately desired, Hägglund reasons, is the desire for survival and not the desire for immortality. Thus the desire to survive is the desire to live on as a mortal being – hence Hägglund's relentless refutation and refusal of immortality and insistence in favour of a 'radical atheism'.

Hägglund approaches his reading of Derrida, which he opposes to those providing a 'theological account' of Derrida's work, from the perspective of the problem of atheism. Taking issue with traditional atheism in his crusading fervour and zealous denial of the existence of God and immortality, Hägglund aims to strongly rebuke those critics who write about Derrida from a 'religious framework'. Stating that there is nothing beyond mortality and that life is 'essentially mortal' (an oft-repeated phrase), Hägglund argues that 'the so-called desire for immortality' displays an 'internal contradiction' with a desire that 'precedes it and contradicts it from within' (*H*, 1). In fact, the desire for immortality disguises 'a desire for survival' (ibid.).

In Hägglund's view, the notion of survival defines life as '*essentially* mortal' (48) and inherently divided by time (33). He defines 'to survive' as 'to remain after a past that is no longer and to keep the memory of this past for a future that is not yet' (1). (Isn't this a very classical and conventional definition of 'to survive'? Would one need to appeal to Derrida to come up with such a definition?) He argues hyperbolically – although one cannot but think here of the tone of an advertising slogan or a religious exhortation – that 'every moment of life is a matter of survival' (ibid.). Hägglund's notion of 'survival' is, at best, a Nietzschean affirmation of mortal existence, rejecting the desire for anything that exceeds or transcends finite human life. Life, for Hägglund, is predicated on the idea that it may come to an end at any moment (pathos or panic?). The fact of living should then be an affirmation of finitude. It is hard to see how this account differs from classical existentialism, peddled for decades in American philosophy departments urging young minds to take up the virtues of *carpe diem*. Why would we need Derrida to tell us what Nietzsche, Heidegger, Sartre and others seem to have told us already – unless Derrida is saying something else entirely?

Presenting a purely formal account of Derrida's work shorn of subtlety, elegance and complexity, Hägglund, like a good analytic philosopher, points out inconsistencies, incoherences, fallacies and logical contradictions in Derrida's readers and interpreters, finding 'untenability' and incompatibility everywhere. Providing a systematic account of Derrida's notion of desire, an account that Derrida himself did not provide, and developing arguments in directions deemed by Hägglund as 'crucial' for Derrida's thinking, Hägglund seeks to explicate 'the logic of deconstruction' (as if there is such a thing, as if deconstruction is simply a logic and as if a younger generation, who may have never heard of Gasché and Bennington – who meticulously laid out the logical intricacies and [infra]structural aspects of Derrida's thought – is in need of being instructed about its logical operations) (82). Hägglund, who seems to mistake deconstruction's task as simply providing systematic accounts, treats deconstruction, according to Michael Naas, as 'a discourse of ontology or episte-mology', restricting deconstruction to merely ontological claims.[4]

Displaying a dogged attachment to mortal life and a tenacious opposition to all that is immortal or smacks of it, Hägglund is adamant that as human beings we live on by remaining 'subjected to temporal finitude' (*H*, 2). His privileging of temporality can be discerned throughout *Radical Atheism*: for Hägglund, everything in Derrida seems to follow from 'the constitution of time' (in what sense of *follow*? Come after? Logically proceed from? And why just time and not space as well?[5] In what sense does 'the structure of the trace *follow* from the constitution of time?') (*H*, 1). Hägglund refers to 'the trace structure of time' (9), but why is Derrida said to have had an insight simply into 'the trace structure' of *time*? Nothing is exempt from 'temporal finitude', Hägglund argues (2–3), yet all he seems to understand by 'the time of mortal life' is the fact we are 'finite', that is, that we die (2). This is how we are to understand the statement that immor-tality would annihilate the time of mortal life.

What is surprising is that in none of Hägglund's work, whether in *Radical Atheism* (2008) or in subsequently published texts, is there a mention of the notion of 'radical atheism' in Derrida's own work.[6] In 'Penser ce qui vient', a talk initially given at the Sorbonne in 1994 following the publication of *Specters of Marx* and published a year before Hägglund's book, during the course of thinking about the event and what comes, Derrida raises the notion of 'radical atheism' when he asks himself whether he is an atheist or a radical atheist.[7] Derrida broaches the topic of an atheism, not as a personal conviction that can or cannot be shared, but an atheism or a secularism [*laïcité*] or some kind of 'structural agnosticism' that characterizes *a priori* every relation to what comes and who comes (21). Derrida's atheism differs from Hägglund's, whose atheism is fervently in opposition to religiosity or any belief that bears a resemblance to it. For Derrida, as he explains in 'Penser ce qui vient', to think the future is to be able to be an atheist. However, even if his atheism is a 'structural' atheism, Derrida wonders whether he is not a 'singular' atheist 'who remembers God and who loves to remember God' (ibid.). In his brief remarks Derrida states that he would like to think further about 'a hypermnesic atheism' that brings together the messianic promise, revolutionary spirit, the spirit of justice and emancipation. For, the concept and thinking of the political is, for Derrida, inseparable from this singular atheism (23).

In what follows, I would like to pursue several elements or themes of Hägglund's discourse of 'radical atheism', namely desire, finitude, immortality and survival, in order to examine in more detail his reading of Derrida's work.

Desire in Derrida

There are many instances where the word 'desire [*désir*]' appears in Derrida's texts, but can it be said that desire as such is an operative concept in Derrida's work, as it is, for example, in Lacan? The usage of the term, which commonly denotes a wish, a want or an inclination for what is beneficial, useful, etc., is very complex in Derrida's writings and does not lend itself to easy summarizing. In his early writings, Derrida writes about philosophy's desire or the desire of metaphysics: references abound to the desire of logocentrism and the metaphysics of presence (*DLG*, 71), philosophy's 'desire for sense' (*ED*, 349), the desire or wish to believe in the remaining of the thing itself (*VP*, 117), the suspicion of writing as a perfectly coherent desire of ethnocentrism (*DLG*, 161) and the desire of and for reason in Kant (*Ver P*, 45/38). One can also find references to metaphysical desires that Derrida puts into question, such as the desire for the origin (*DLG*, 345), the desire for presence (206), the desire for the centre (411), the desire for a 'centered structure' (*ED*, 410/279), the desire to exclude the foreigner/stranger (*SM*, 273), as well as the desire for the archive (*Mal*, 38/19) and the archive's desire (52/19). The appearance of the word at times refers to another thinker's desire, for example, Rousseau's desire for a rehabilitation of speech and condemnation of writing (*DLG*, 204), or to a concept in a thinker's writings, for example, the notion of desire in the work of Levinas (*ED*) or Fukuyama's usage of Hegelian desire (*SM*). On other occasions, desire is accompanied by another term in a pair, as in the desire and the disorder [*trouble*] of the archive in *Mal d'archive* (*Mal*, 128/81), or terror and desire of being buried alive in *The Beast and the Sovereign, volume II*. It seems, one would be hard pressed to find many places where Derrida uses the term for his own purposes.

While the references in the earlier texts cast a suspicious eye on the notion of desire, in his later works Derrida is more likely to use the term favorably. For example, in 'Psyche: Inventions of the Other' he comments on the desire for invention (*Psy*, 34–5); in *Donner le temps* he writes of the desire to think and to give the impossible (*DT*, 52/35), in 'Faith and Knowledge' he writes of 'an invincible desire for justice' (FS, 31/18); in *Echographies*, he refers to what he calls 'exappropriation', where 'it is necessary' that I try to make what I desire mine, while it remains other enough for me to desire it (*E*, 125/111); in *Sauf le nom* he writes of the desire of God [*désir de Dieu*], double genitive (*SN*, 18–20/37) and the desire of the desert ('the desert as the other name, if not the proper place, of *desire*') (103/80); and in *The Death Penalty* seminar he notes that the death sentence is desired 'as desire itself' (*PM*, 339/249). It would be safe to say that the way desire functions in these Derridean texts does not adhere to any traditional concept of this term, whether Platonic or psychoanalytic, and would have to be assessed contextually and carefully read in relation to a notion of need.

Finitude

Throughout his early writings, from an appraisal of 'originary' or 'primordial' finitude in Husserl in *The Problem of Genesis in Husserl's Philosophy* (1953–4) (*PG*, 171 n.91/98 n.91; 257 n.8/163 n.8) and *Introduction to Husserl's Origin of Geometry* (1962) (*OG*, 108/105–6; 151 n.1/138 n.164) to an investigation of the thinking of Levinas, Freud, Husserl and Heidegger in various essays in *Writing and Difference*, Derrida engaged with the thought of finitude. Yet, given what Rodolphe Gasché in *The Tain of the Mirror* refers to as 'Derrida's persistent critique of the notion of finitude', Derrida cannot simply be branded as a thinker of finitude since the latter has meaning only within the philosophy of presence.[8] In fact, the very idea of finitude is derived from the movement of supplementarity, Derrida tells us in the essay 'Freud and the Scene of Writing' in *Writing and Difference* (*ED*, 337/228). In *Of Grammatology* he describes *différance* as 'something other than finitude' (*DLG*, 99/68) and in *Voice and Phenomenon*, published the same year, he informs us that we cannot think *différance* within the opposition of the finite and the infinite (*VP*, 114/87). As late as *Le Toucher*,

Jean-Luc Nancy (2000), a voice in Derrida's text half-jokingly, some would say sarcastically, refers to Nancy's notion of touching or *le toucher* as simply a thought of finitude: 'Touching is finitude, period [*Le toucher, c'est la finitude, un point c'est tout*]' (*LT*, 160).

Thus Derrida's thinking of *différance* is not simply a thinking of finitude, whether radical or not, whether temporal or not, but a thinking together of the finite and the infinite. In 'Derridabase' Geoffrey Bennington refers to 'the inextricable complication of the finite and the infinite that *différance* gives us to think' while admitting that 'the terms "finite" and "infinite" function in a disturbing way in Derrida's texts'.[9] Bennington, commenting on the notoriously difficult and misunderstood phrase (what he also refers to as 'a line' or 'a slogan, a motto, a maxim, a sentence, even perhaps a witticism' [75]) 'infinite differance is finite' from *Voice and Phenomenon* (*VP*, 114/87), observes in *Not Half No End* that the infinite and the finite are 'wrapped in a paradoxical relation'.[10] This indicates that the thinking of the infinite and the finite cannot be simply reduced to oppositions and that their complex and intricate relation would have to be carefully unfolded and explained.

Granted, Hägglund may be making efforts in this direction by describing *différance* as a thought of 'infinite finitude' (*H*, 220 n.14). Yet this notion, which is insufficiently developed, combined with his vociferous defence of and emphasis on finitude – however radical – still places the *stress* on a certain notion of finitude. Perhaps Hägglund's inspiration comes from Derrida's tangential question in 'Violence and Metaphysics' when he asks 'can one think "spurious infinity [*le «faux-infini»*]" as such (*time, in a word*)' (*ED*, 176/120, my emphasis)? Hägglund appeals to 'Violence and Metaphysics' to explain the difference between spurious and positive infinity and to show how *différance* is a form of non-totalization that contests a notion of positive infinity, as the latter reduces or 'sublimates' the trace. Contrary to the Hegelian true or genuine infinity (*Unendlichkeit*), which is an all-embracing totality, Derrida's thinking of infinity is non-Hegelian. Even though Derrida's thinking of the trace, the text and the infinite substitution of quasi-transcendental terms or non-concepts has been compared to a form of infinity, Derrida's infinite is not any form of endlessness.

Here it would be worth briefly referring to some of the central historical sources of the relation between finitude and infinity. The thought of what has been called examining 'positive infinity', according to Rodolphe Gasché, begins with Plato culminating via Spinoza in Hegel's theology of the absolute concept as logos.[11] Spinoza rejected the conception of the infinite that represents it as an amount or series that is not completed, while Hegel also argued against spurious infinity for a genuine notion of infinity. For Hegel, the true or genuine infinite, associated with reason, is unconditioned and self-contained whereas the bad infinite, associated with understanding, is merely endless. Spurious infinity (*das schlechte Unendliche*), 'the indefinite, a *negative* form of infinity', associated with an infinitist metaphysics, is only another form of the finite (*ED*, 175/119). True infinity includes itself and its other. As he writes in the *Science of Logic*, true infinity must be an infinite that 'embraces both itself and finitude – and is therefore the infinite in a different sense from that which the finite regarded as separated and set apart from the infinite'.[12]

An echo of Heidegger's emphasis on finitude as temporal may be found in Hägglund's stance: for Heidegger finitude (*Endlichkeit*) is temporal finitude. Neither infinite nor immortal, Dasein exists as finite, exposed to its end. Dasein does not have an end (*Ende*), but 'exists finitely' (*SZ*, 378/329). As *Being and Time* demonstrates 'primordial time is finite' (379/331), while infinite time is derived or secondary. Primordiality, then, is not infinity. It is in his reading of Kant in *Kant and the Problem of Metaphysics* that Heidegger demonstrates that humankind is finite.[13] Finitude is the source of the understanding of Being and of all 'infinity'. Furthermore, from *The Concept of Time* (1924) to *On Time and Being* (1962) Heidegger distinguishes the thinking of time from the thinking of eternity. In contrast to the theological problematic of eternity, to think time is not to think eternity. The finitude of Dasein does not mean that it will die one day, but that it exists as dying. Finitude is connected to the limit, but for Heidegger the limit is not that at which something stops but that from which something begins.

Immortality

Radical Atheism and subsequent publications set up an opposition between mortality and immortality, in which 'the desire for immortality' is contrasted with the mortal condition, thoroughly and unapologetically lived in time. What causes Hägglund's ire and draws his criticism is a conception of immortality, which he associates with religiously inclined interpreters of Derrida, as perfect and indivisible, not situated in time and having no relation to an outside. In contrast, Derrida is portrayed as espousing a thinking of radical finitude. So caught up is Hägglund in opposing or fighting those he sees as conservative religious advocates that he falls back on traditional conceptions of immortality and eternity in the history of Western thought as discrete concepts and neglects to consider how mortality and immortality have been treated in Derrida's own work. Not only is there no clear-cut opposition or demarcation in Derrida's writings between immortality and mortality, as Hägglund would like to have it, but also Derrida's is a thought of the strange, paradoxical imbrication of mortality and immortality. Immortality is not a state reserved for the deathless but rather it is only the dead who become immortal.

However, before turning to his treatment of immortality, it would be helpful to very briefly see how immortality has been treated in the Western tradition. It has been shown by a number of scholars that as early as Heraclitus, mortality and immortality were not considered to be rigorously separated or demarcated from each other. Marcel Conche in his commentary on Heraclitus's fragment 62 argues that, for Heraclitus, 'the mortals [*thnetoi*]' and 'the immortals [*athanatoi*]' are not treated in separation from or in opposition to each other. In fact, immortality is thought by Heraclitus *in relation* to mortality.[14] There is an undoubted affinity between this fragment and certain mystic doctrines associated with the Orphic or Pythagorean tradition, indications of which may also be found in Empedocles' *Katharmoi* or 'Purifications'. From Homeric survival where the name and the renown of heroes who had shown valour in battle would be remembered and memorialized, Pericles' funeral oration bestowing immortality on patriots, the Pindaric *threnos* or lament for the dead and its related eschatology, to the Empedoclean *daimon* and the thought of the pre-existence of the soul and its transmigration into other beings, and the Orphic and Pythagorean beliefs about asceticism and inner life, notions of immortality in Greek thought are inseparable from the development of a notion of the *psuchē* or the soul. The Platonic notion, where the soul constitutes one's real being in the interior recesses of each individual, is a late development in Greek thinking. For Plato, the *psuchē* is immortal, permanent and unchanging, detaching itself from the body at death, while the living body is considered to be insubstantial and illusory. It is not until later that the pagan concept of immortality becomes contaminated by the Christian idea of resurrection.

Perhaps the notion of immortality in the Western tradition would best be considered in the context of survival, as a form of survival, as Derrida once did in *Aporias* (1993) when he referred to 'the theme of immortality like that of any form of survival [*survie*] or return [*revenance*]' (A, 103/55–6). While considering Heidegger's account of Dasein's relation to death and assessing the relationship between mortality and immortality in *Aporias*, Derrida writes that Dasein remains immortal, in other words, 'without end [*sans fin*]', in the sense of *verenden*, and imperishable in its originary being-to-death. As Dasein, I do not end, I never end (76/40–1). In fact, Derrida will write later on, underscoring the inextricable relationship between mortality and immortality and the necessity of not thinking them in opposition to each other, 'only a living-to-death can think, desire, project, indeed "live" immortality *as such*' (102/55). He adds that in fact one cannot 'think being-to-death without starting from immortality' (103/55). More importantly for a consideration of Hägglund's work, Derrida emphasizes that 'the theme of immortality like that of any form of survival or *revenance* ... is *not opposed to being-toward-death, it does not contradict it*, it is not symmetrical with it, because it is conditioned by being-toward-death and confirms it at every moment' (103/55–6, my emphasis).

Demeure

In order to further examine Derrida's thinking of immortality and its complicated relation to mortality, I would like to turn to one of his texts, *Demeure, Maurice Blanchot*, in which he pursues a probing, intricate reading of what he names 'immortality as death'. In the midst of a meticulous and painstakingly close analysis of Blanchot's *L'instant de ma mort*, the autobiographical account of the narrator's close call with death, in *Demeure*, Derrida refers to a stark phrase, what he calls a 'sentence without sentence [*phrase sans phrase*]': 'Dead-Immortal [*Mort-immortel*]' (D, 86/67). Two words held together and separated by a hyphen [*trait d'union*], a sole line [*un seul trait*] of union and separation (ibid.). (It is worth noting here that in the English translation, what is referred to as a hyphen by Derrida appears as a dash. Therefore, 'Dead-immortal' is one, hyphenated composite word.) In what follows I would like to comment on Derrida's description of this phrase and suggest that it can be used as an example of how he treats the question of immortality. Even though it is embedded in a text devoted to a close reading of a narrative, one could argue that Derrida generalizes this notion, as he often does when it comes to something that appears to be absolutely singular (like one's own language in *Monolingualism of the Other*, for example), to provide an account of 'immortality *as death*'. It will become clear that Derrida does not ever believe in a clear opposition between immortality and mortality or finitude, and his reading of mortality and immortality does not conform to any traditional definition.

Blanchot's text *L'instant de ma mort* ostensibly consists of an account provided by the narrator about a witness, who may be the narrator, involved in certain events leading to the experience of being almost executed. Even though the reader may wish to assume that the text is the account of the narrator-witness – and much of the structure of the text seems to lead one to believe this – it is important to note that, as Derrida writes, there is a 'null and uncrossable' distance between the one who says 'I' and the 'I' of the young man of whom he speaks and who is himself (84/65). In other words, the reader must not forget that a distance separates the narrator from the witness and from the signatory of the text.

I would like to focus my attention on a couple of passages in this notoriously elliptical narrative in which the young man, about whom the narrator writes, and the female members of his family are forced by the invading troops to leave their home preparing to face a firing squad. As the young man pleads to have the members of his family, all female, be spared, he ends the sentence mentioning their long, slow procession suggesting that death had already taken place, that it had already happened (79/62). Death has already arrived because it is 'inescapable' (79/62–3). It is an experience from which one is not 'resuscitated … even if one survives it' (79/63). For, 'one can only survive [this death] without surviving it' (80/63). Yet this survival should not be mistaken for a resurrection. In Derrida's view, the entire scene mimics and displaces the Passion, the Resurrection and absolute knowledge. There can be no knowledge, for in 'the life without life of this survivance' all knowledge would tremble (ibid.).

Blanchot then makes a reference to 'the encounter of death with death', perhaps the encounter between what has already arrived and what is going to come (82/64). The two deaths meet, a death that is 'both virtual and real', at the tip of the 'instant' (ibid.). Death 'has come to pass insofar as it comes; it has come as soon as it is going to come' (82–3/65). 'Death encounters *itself* in this 'arrival of death at itself' (83/65). This death that never arrives and never happens to me, Blanchot writes, is the event of an 'unexperienced experience [*expérience inéprouvée*]' (quoted on 83/65).

Not only is death not an event that can be experienced but also one death cannot replace the other: the one who says 'I' cannot take the place of the young man he has been, substitute or speak for him or relive what has been lived, and consequently is not capable of describing this very 'odd experience' or what he felt at that moment. The two 'egological identities' are separated by nothing but death (85/66). The young man is 'offered unto death' (85/67). Blanchot's text describes him as 'Dead-Immortal' (86/67).

Derrida glosses this phrase as

Dead and yet [*et cependant*] immortal, dead because [*parce qu'*] immortal, dead insofar as [*en tant qu'*] immortal (an immortal does not live), immortal from the moment that [*dès lors que*] and insofar as [*en tant que*] dead, although and for as long as [*tandis que et aussi longtemps que*] dead; because once dead one no longer dies ... one has become immortal. (ibid.)

As Derrida explains a little further on: 'an immortal is someone who is dead [*c'est un mort*]', for only 'someone who is dead can be immortal' (ibid.). 'What happens to him is immortality, with death and as death at the same instant' (ibid.). The immortals are dead, but this immortality, Derrida explains, is 'not a Platonic or Christian immortality in the moment of death or of the Passion when the soul finally gathers together as it leaves the body, having already been at work there in philosophy according to the *ēpimeleia tou thanatou* of a pre-Christian *Phaedo*' (86–7/67). Rather, it is in the instant of death, in death, that 'immortality yields to [*se livre*] an 'unexperienced experience' (87/67). Death arrives 'where one is not yet dead in order to be already dead, at the same instant' (86/67–8). At the same instant, I am dead *and* not dead (87/68). 'I am immortal because I am dead: death can no longer happen to me' (ibid.).

Blanchot designates this experience as 'the happiness of not being immortal or eternal' (quoted in 89/69). Even though 'dead-immortal' may appear to be the reverse of the above description, it does not, Derrida notes, in the least signify eternity (89/69). The condition that Derrida describes in *Demeure* – that of one who is dead and yet immortal, dead because immortal and dead insofar as immortal – is far from designating what has been understood as immortality in the Western tradition. 'The immortality of death is anything save the eternity of the present' (ibid.).[15] For, what Derrida designates as 'abidance [*demeurance*]' 'does not *remain* [reste] like the permanence of an eternity' but rather 'is time itself' (ibid.). Not timelessness or eternity of the present, but the time of an interminable lapse [*laps*] or interval. Not an ongoing or perduring state of timelessness, abidance [*demeurance*] would be an awaiting, a waiting for, a withstanding, an enduring, a bearing patiently. To abide somewhere is to sojourn or to continue in a place. What Derrida draws out of Blanchot's text is what he describes as a 'non-philosophical and non-religious experience of immortality as death [*l'immortalité comme mort*]' (ibid.). This experience 'gives [*donne*] ... the happiness, this time' of being neither immortal nor eternal (ibid.). In 'the immortality of death', there is 'a bond without bond, the disjointing [*désajointement*], the disadjusting [*désajustement*] of a social bond [with other mortals] that binds only ... to death, and on condition of death' (89–90/69).

Returning to the narrative of *The Instant of My Death* we find that 'at that instant' death happened to the young man. But death had already taken place. The moment that the young man had begun to wait for 'the final order' of 'Fire', he had left the world

> dying before dying, not for another world, but for a non-world beyond life, not for a transcendent beyond or the beyond that religions and metaphysics tell us about, but for a here-below without world [*ici-bas sans monde*], for a beyond here-below [*un au-delà ici-bas*], a without-world [*un sans-monde*] from which he who is already dead already returns [*déjà revient*], like a ghost [*comme un revenant*]. (91/70–71)

Like a ghost that returns.

The young man has left the world for a non-world that is not beyond this world or transcendent to it. Far from it. He is without world, in this non-world here-below. His being without world signifies that he is already dead. The dead one is not elsewhere but here-below. The beyond here-below differs from a transcendent beyond, since it is a beyond here from which the already dead returns. Survival or *survivance* is thus a ghostly returning, *revenance*.

The reference to immortality as death in *Demeure* hearkens back to Blanchot's ruminations on mortality and immortality in 'Literature and the Right to Death', which are taken up again by Derrida in *The Death Penalty, vol. 1*, Seminar of 1999–2000. In the fourth session of that seminar, while discussing the writer's role and literature's relation to revolution, Derrida sheds further light on the notion of death as the impossibility of dying or on sur-viving as dying by citing Blanchot's famous phrase from 'Literature and the Right to Death':

> As long as I live, I'm a mortal man, but when I die, by ceasing to be a man, I also cease to be mortal, I am no longer capable of dying, and my impending death horrifies me because I see it as it is: no longer death but the impossibility of dying.[16]

It would be instructive here to look at Blanchot's early interpretation of Kafka, particularly in the essays 'Reading Kafka' (1943), 'Literature and the Right to Death' (1948) and 'The Language of Fiction' (1949), all published in *The Work of Fire* (1949), in order to draw out themes from Blanchot's reading and to show the force that a reading of these essays has exercised on Derrida's thinking of mortality and immortality. It cannot be underestimated how uncannily consonant Derrida's terminology – motifs such as 'buried alive', 'survival', etc. – and conceptualization are with Blanchot's. Derrida's affinity with, and development of, Blanchot's reading of Kafka would have to be stressed here.

There is no end, there is no possibility of being done with the day, Blanchot writes in 'Reading Kafka'. Such is the truth that Western man has made 'a symbol of felicity' (*PF*, 15/8). He has tried to make the fact that there is no end 'bearable by bringing out [*en dégageant*] the positive side, that of immortality, a survival that would compensate for life'. But, rather than compensating for it, 'this survival [*survivance*] is our life itself' (15/8). We do not die but we do not live either, as Blanchot writes. 'We are dead as we live [*nous sommes mort de notre vivant*], we are essentially survivors' (16/8). Even though death 'ends our life', 'it does not end our possibility of dying' (ibid.). 'Dying', here as well as in Blanchot's other writings, is understood intransitively as an ongoing process while one is living. It is also worth recalling that in a later text, *The Writing of the Disaster*, Blanchot, referring to the 'passivity' of dying (*Ec D*, 29), describes dying as 'without power' (67). In Hegel death is 'at work [*à l'oeuvre*]', linked with the power of negation (76), whereas for Blanchot dying is associated with 'non-power' (81). 'Dying outside of oneself [*hors de soi*]' (50) is described as something that is 'without goal' (67).

In 'Literature and the Right to Death' Blanchot observes that when we die we leave death behind. To die is to be absent from one's own death. It is the loss of death, 'the loss of what in it and for me made it death' (*PF*, 325/337). As alive, I am dying, but 'when I die, I cease to be mortal. I am no longer capable of dying' (ibid.). Death, then, occasions the impossibility of dying. Certain religions have taken this impossibility of death and have tried to 'humanise' it by calling it 'immortality' (ibid.). This means that by losing the advantage of being mortal, I also lose the possibility of being man. 'To be man beyond death' is 'to be, in spite of death, still capable of dying, to go on as though nothing happened' (ibid.). Other religions call this 'the curse of being reborn [*la malediction de renaissance*]' (ibid.). 'You die because you have lived badly, you are condemned to live again, and you live again' (325/338). 'In dying you become a truly blessed man –a man who is really dead' (325/337–8). According to Blanchot, Kafka inherited this idea from the Kabbalah and Eastern traditions. Whether, strictly speaking, it is understood as reincarnation or not, it nevertheless involves a kind of transformation or metamorphosis. Blanchot illustrates this wryly and succinctly: 'A man enters the night, but the night ends in awakening [*conduit au reveil*], and there he is, an insect' (ibid.).

In 'The Language of Fiction' (1949) Blanchot comes back to this idea reiterating that Kafka 'probably under the influence of Eastern traditions seems to have recognized in the impossibility of dying the extreme curse of man' (87/81). 'Man cannot escape unhappiness, because he cannot escape existence [and it is in vain that he heads toward death because] … he dies only to survive. He leaves existence, but only to enter the cycle of metamorphoses.' (ibid.) Thus, for Blanchot, there can be 'no actual death in Kafka, or more exactly, there is never an end' (ibid.). This is perhaps because Blanchot, in agreement with Levinas, believes that one cannot exit existence. The thought of the 'impossibility of dying' is derived from the interminability of existence – like the Ancient *apeiron*, existence is without beginning or end. Thus, most of 'Kafka's heroes are engaged in an intermediate moment between life and death' (ibid.). Blanchot observes that this strange condition of 'the dead who do not die' is expressed by Kafka in a couple of stories: 'The Hunter Gracchus', in which the Black Forest Hunter is alive *and* dead, and 'The Guest of the Dead'. Defining ambiguity, wherein 'assertion and negation are in continuous threat of reciprocity', Blanchot describes the ambiguity of the condition that he calls being *'buried alive'* in the following way: 'death that is life, that is death as soon as it survives [*dès qu'elle survit*]' (89/84). One dies only to survive. If death is not a possibility, then life can only be described as the ambiguous survival of a 'death that is life, that is death'. An examination of Blanchot's thought has shown that rather than depicting a death-bound finitude, the condition that Blanchot terms 'buried alive' or survival speaks of the 'ambiguous' relation between life and death.

Survivance

The rather mysterious notion of survivance makes an early appearance in Derrida's work. In one of its first instances, in 'Freud and the Scene of Writing', it emerges in relation to writing (*l'écriture*), which is described as a 'surviving trace' (*ED*, 331/224). Later in 'Circumfession' writing is again portrayed as that 'intense relation to survivance' (Cir, 178/191). In *Shibboleth*, the 1986 text devoted to Paul Celan, the signature of the date is designated as capable of surviving and calling the disappeared or the vanished [*disparu*] (*Sch*, 59/32), while in *Memoires for Paul de Man*, from the same year, we learn that the name *'already survives'* the name holder, bearing his death each time it is pronounced (*MPdM*, 63/49).

In an interview given in the mid-1980s Derrida explains that *survivre* is not a matter of survival in the sense of posterity.[17] Rather, surviving treats this 'strange dimension' of *plus de vie*, both 'more life' and 'no more life'. In the interview Derrida uses another expression *plus que vie*, more than life, to add to his descriptions of what he means by *survie*. So, he remarks that for him *survivre* is a matter of both *plus de vie* and *plus que vie*. In response to a question about translation Derrida refers to the relation between the original text and the translated text as an *augmentation*. Translations, he explains, produce augmentations or new textual bodies. This augmentation is precisely *survivance*, not in the sense of merely allowing the original to survive but allowing it to have another life, as it were, in another language, a more invigorated, perhaps even richer, life. In *Mal d'archive* Derrida describes surviving in a similar way, referring to 'the surviving of an excess of life' (*Mal*, 96).

In the most extensive treatment – though not the systematic account desired by Hägglund – of *survie* in *Parages* (from 1986 again), Derrida writes of a survival and a ghostly return beyond the straight line of one's lifeline: 'Survival [*survivance*] and *revenance*, living on and ghostly returning. Living on [*survivre*] goes beyond [*déborde*] both living and dying' (*Par*, 153/134). (It 'goes beyond' but also overflows [*déborde*] as the entire text of 'Living On [*Survivre*]' treats the relation of shorelines to bodies of water.) Living 'beyond' one's death, *sur-vivre* is not to be mistaken with a life *after* death but rather sur-viving means life intensified, *more* life *still*. Sur- does not indicate superiority, supremacy, height, altitude or height above life (*BS II*, 194/131). In 'Living On' Derrida describes *sur-vie*, which Michael Naas renders as a 'sur-life', 'a surplus of life', for this '*more-than-life* [sur-vie], marks … a survival in the time of life, in the form of a reprieve [*sursis*]' in which the survivor lives 'more than a lifetime [*plus qu'une vie*]' in the short span of a few moments (*Par*, 168/147, tr mod.).[18]

In *Politics of Friendship* Derrida writes that what is called *philia*, or friendship, begins with the possibility of survival. Friendship is a relationship that structurally necessitates that the friend 'already bear my death and inherit it as the last survivor' (*PA*, 30/13). The friend bears, carries [*porter*] my own death (which is expropriated in advance). In a way, he is the only one to bear it. '*Surviving* [*survivre*]' would thus be 'another name of a mourning whose possibility is never to be awaited', since mourning, its anguished apprehension, will have begun before death (31/13). One does not survive without mourning – without literally bearing or carrying this grief [*porter le deuil*] (30/31). For Derrida, *survivre* is 'the essence, the origin, and the possibility, the condition of possibility of friendship' (31/14). The time of surviving thus gives the time of friendship. Such a time gives itself in withdrawing, it occurs through effacing itself. Its *contretemps* 'disjoins the presence of the present' inscribing 'intemporality and untimeliness [*intemporalité et intempestivité*]' in friendship (ibid.). In giving time and taking time friendship 'survives the living present' (32/15).

For Derrida, this bereaved survivance is to be distinguished from the stability, constancy or firm permanence of Aristotelian primary friendship (31–32/13). Friendship, as Derrida writes, is promised to testamentary revenance, the haunting return, of a more (no more) life, of a surviving [*le revenance testamentaire d'un plus-de vie, d'un survivre*]' (20/3).

In a late discussion with Jean-Luc Nancy and Philippe Lacoue-Labarthe in 2004, Derrida describes his feelings regarding the anticipation of his death. In his relation to the death to come, knowing that it will annihilate him, he acknowledges that there is beneath the surface 'a testamentary desire' that '*something* survive, be left, be transmitted – an inheritance' that will not come back to him 'but that, perhaps, will remain'.[19] There is a feeling that haunts him about what will remain, not simply things that are in the public domain but also private things. This feeling, which he calls testamentary and is linked to the structure of the trace, is part of the experience of death.[20]

In his last years, in published texts, seminars and interviews Derrida publicly expressed his struggle with his so-called mortality, with the fact that he had come to terms with death or had to 'learn how to die'. The fact that he was not able to accept death for Derrida did not mean that his fatal illness was met by a 'refusal' to die, but rather that it caused a thoughtful consideration of how mortality has been defined throughout the philosophical tradition. Perhaps this 'refusal' to learn to die, as every philosopher must learn to do in order to properly be a philosopher, was itself a 'refusal', on the part of Derrida, of philosophy as a way of life that leads to the *soteria* of the soul and as a discipline or practice *of* and *for* death (and hence as a discipline for immortality). As demonstrated above, Derrida's thinking of survivance from the very beginning questioned the easy distinction between mortality and immortality. When, in his interview with Jean Birnbaum in 2004, initially published in *Le monde*, he said that he was at war with himself or against himself, this was because he could not believe that death was simply an end.[21] If surviving begins before death and not merely after it, as it is commonly thought, then life itself *is* originarily survival: 'life *is* living on, life *is* survival [La vie *est* survie]' (*AV*, 26).

As we have seen, *survivance* does not simply refer to what remains and endures for posterity nor does it signify surviving, or somehow living on after death in an afterlife or a life-everlasting in an afterworld, but the *sur-* in *survivre* indicates 'more living', *plus de vie*, a more than life, *plus que la vie*, in life.[22] For, life and death, which are not separable as such, are themselves both traces of a *sur-vie* or irreducible survivance that dislocates the self-presence of the living present. The possibility of this *sur-vivre* does not wait for death 'to make life and death indissociable', it comes in advance before death, to disjoin and dislocate the self-identity of the living present (*BS II*, 176/117). The living present is divided, divides itself, between its life and its survival, bearing death within itself. Survivance, then, is or says the complication, the inextricable alliance of the dead and the living. However, in order to adequately analyse the notion of survivance and its complex temporality, one would have to think it in relation to *revenance*, *restance* and *arrivance*. Alas, this is for another time.[23]

List of abbreviations

Note: Where no page references to the published translations have been given, the translations are my own.

Works by Jacques Derrida

A   *Apories*. Paris: Galilée, 1996. Translated by Thomas Dutoit as *Aporias*. Stanford: Stanford University Press, 1993. [English version is a translation of the chapter 'Apories: Mourir-s'attendre aux limites de la vérité', published in *Le passage des frontières: autour du travail de Jacques Derrida*. Paris: Galilée, 1993.]

AV   *Apprendre à vivre enfin: Entretien avec Jean Birnbaum*. Paris: Galilée, 2005. Translated by Michael Naas and Pascale-Anne Brault as *Learning to Live Finally: The Last Interview*. Hoboken, NJ: Melville House, 2007.

BS II   *Séminaire La bête et le souverain. Volume II (2002-2003)*, edited by Michel Lisse, Marie-Louise Mallet and Ginette Michaud. Paris: Galilée, 2010. Translated by Geoffrey Bennington as *The Beast and the Sovereign*, volume 1. Chicago: University of Chicago Press, 2011.

Cir   'Circonfession', in *Jacques Derrida* [with Geoffrey Bennington]. Paris: Seuil, 1991. *Jacques Derrida*. Translated by Geoffrey Bennington as 'Circumfession', in *Jacques Derrida*. Chicago: University of Chicago Press, 1993.

D   *Demeure, Maurice Blanchot*. Paris: Galilée, 1998. Translated by Elizabeth Rottenberg as *Demeure: Fiction and Testimony*. Stanford: Stanford University Press, 2000 [Published with a translation of Maurice Blanchot's *The Instant of My Death*].

DLG   *De la grammatologie.* Paris: Minuit, 1967. Translated by Gayatri
       Chakravorty Spivak as *Of Grammatology.* Baltimore: Johns Hopkins
       University, 1974, 2nd corrected edn 1998.

DT   *Donner le temps: 1. La fausse monnaie.* Paris: Galilée, 1991. Translated
       by Peggy Kamuf as *Given Time: 1. Counterfeit Money.* Chicago:
       University of Chicago Press, 1992.

E   *Echographies—de la télévision (Entretiens filmés avec Bernard Stiegler).*
       Paris: Galilée, 1996. Translated by Jennifer Bajorek as *Echographies of
       Television: Filmed Interviews.* Malden, MA: Blackwell, 2002.

ED   *L'Ecriture et la différence.* Paris: Seuil, 1967. Translated by Alan Bass as
       Writing and Difference. Chicago: University of Chicago Press, 1978.

FS   'Foi et savoir: Les deux sources de la "religion" aux limites de la
       simple raison', in *La Religion,* edited by Jacques Derrida and Gianni
       Vattimo. Paris: Seuil, 1996. Translated by Samuel Weber as 'Faith and
       Knowledge: The Two sources of "Religion" within the Limits of Mere
       Reason', in *Religion,* edited by Jacques Derrida and Gianni Vattimo.
       Stanford: Stanford University Press, 1998, 1–78.

LT   *Le toucher, Jean-Luc Nancy.* Paris: Galilée, 2000. Translated by
       Christine Irizarry as *On Touching—Jean-Luc Nancy.* Stanford:
       Stanford University Press, 2003.

M   *Marges de la philosophie.* Paris: Minuit, 1972. Translated by Alan Bass
       as *Margins of Philosophy.* Chicago: University of Chicago Press, 1982.

Mal   *Mal d'archive. Une impression freudienne.* Paris: Galilée, 1995.
       Translated by Eric Prenowitz as *Archive Fever.* Chicago: University of
       Chicago Press, 1996.

MPdM   *Mémoires: pour Paul de Man.* Paris: Galilée, 1988. Translated by
       Cecile Lindsay, Jonathan Culler, Eduardo Cadava and Peggy Kamuf
       as *Memoires: For Paul de Man.* New York: Columbia University Press,
       1986, 2nd revised edn 1989.

OG   *Introduction à 'L'Origine de la géométrie' de Husserl.* Paris: Presses
       Universitaires de France, 1962, 2nd edn 1974. Translated by John P.
       Leavey, Jr. as *Edmund Husserl's 'Origin of Geometry': An Introduction.*
       Lincoln: University of Nebraska Press, 1978, 2nd edn 1989.

PA *Politiques de l'amitié.* Paris: Galilée, 1994. Translated by George
   Collins as *Politics of Friendship.* New York: Verso, 1997.

Par *Parages.* Nouvelle édition revue et augmentée. Paris: Galilée, 2003.
   Translated by Tom Conley, James Hulbert, John P. Leavey and Avital
   Ronell as *Parages,* edited by John P. Leavey. Stanford: Stanford
   University Press, 2011.

PG *Le problème de la genèse dans la philosophie de Husserl.* Paris: Presses
   Universitaires de France, 1990. Translated by Marian Hobson as *The
   Problem of Genesis in Husserl's Philosophy.* Chicago: University of
   Chicago Press, 2003.

PM *La peine de mort. Volume I (1999-2000).* Paris: Galilée, 2012.
   Translated by Peggy Kamuf as *The Death Penalty. Volume I.* Chicago:
   University of Chicago Press, 2014.

Psy *Psyché, Invention de l'autre, t. 1 (nouvelle édition augmentée).* Paris:
   Galilée, 1998.

Sch *Schibboleth: Pour Paul Celan.* Paris: Galilée, 1986. Translated by
   Joshua Wilner as 'Shibboleth: For Paul Celan', in *Word Traces:
   Readings of Paul Celan,* edited by Aris Fioretos. Baltimore: Johns
   Hopkins University Press, 1994.

SM *Spectres de Marx: l'etat de la dette, le travail du deuil et la nouvelle
   internationale.* Paris: Galilée, 1993. Translated by Peggy Kamuf as
   *Specters of Marx: the State of the Debt, the Work of Mourning, and the
   New International.* New York: Routledge, 1993.

SN *Sauf le nom.* Paris: Galilée, 1993. Translated by John P. Leavey, Jr. as
   'Sauf le nom', in *On the Name,* edited by Thomas Dutoit. Stanford:
   Stanford University Press, 1995.

Ver P *La vérité en peinture.* Paris: Aubier-Flammarion, 1978. Translated
   by Geoffrey Bennington and Ian McLeod as *The Truth in Painting.*
   Chicago: University of Chicago Press, 1987.

VP *La voix et le phénomène.* Paris: Presses Universitaires de France, 1967.
   Translated by Leonard Lawler as *Voice and Phenomenon.* Evanston,
   IL: Northwestern University Press, 1973.

Works by Blanchot

EcD   *L'écriture du désastre*. Paris: Gallimard, 1980. Translated by Ann Smock as *The Writing of the Disaster*. Lincoln: University of Nebraska Press, 1986.

PF   *La part du feu*. Paris: Gallimard, 1949. Translated by Charlotte Mandell as *The Work of Fire*. Stanford: Stanford University Press, 1995.

Other works

H   Hägglund, Martin. *Radical Atheism: Derrida and the Time of Life*. Stanford: Stanford University Press, 2008.

SL   Hegel, G. W. F. *Wissenschaft der Logik I*, ed. E. Moldenhauer and K. M. Michel, in *Werke in zwanzig Bänden*, vol. 5. Frankfurt am Main: Suhrkamp Verlag, 1969. Translated by A. V. Miller as *Hegel's Science of Logic*. Amherst, NY: Humanity Books, 1999.

SZ   Heidegger, Martin. *Sein und Zeit*. 12th edn. Tübingen: M. Niemeyer, 1972. Translated by John Macquarrie and Edward Robinson as *Being and Time*. New York: Harper & Row, 1962.

Notes

1   I have benefited from the astute analysis of Hägglund's work by the following commentators: Michael Naas, 'An Atheism that (*Dieu merci!*) Still Leaves Something to be Desired', *New Centennial Review* 9, 1 (2009): 45–68; Jacques de Ville, *Jacques Derrida: Law as Absolute Hospitality* (New York: Routledge, 2011); Ernesto Laclau, 'Is Radical Atheism a Good Name for Deconstruction?', *Diacritics* 38, 1–2 (Spring–Summer 2008): 180–89; and Danielle Sands, Review article in *Parrhesia* 6 (2009): 73–8.

2   Plato, *Symposium and Phaedrus*, trans. Tom Griffith (New York: Everyman's Library/Knopf, 2000) and Plato, *Lysis, Symposium, Gorgias*, trans. M. R. M. Lamb (Cambridge, MA: Harvard University Press, 1996), Loeb Classical Library. Lamb renders the latter passage as: 'I wish these things now present to be present also in the future'.

3   We should note the Latinate vocabulary of immortality, which would be better rendered as 'deathless' in the Greek context.

4   Michael Naas, 'An Atheism that (*Dieu merci!*) Still Leaves Something to be Desired', 49.

5   Hägglund does not pay adequate attention to spacing, even though he mentions its importance in *H*, 72.

6   Derrida mentions 'radical atheism' in *Sauf le nom* (*SN*, 103/80).

7   Jacques Derrida, 'Penser ce qui vient', in *Derrida pour le temps à venir*, ed. René Major (Paris: Stock, 2007).

8   Rodolphe Gasché, *The Tain of the Mirror: Derrida and the Philosophy of Reflection* (Cambridge, MA: Harvard University Press, 1988), 317.

9   Geoffrey Bennington, 'Derridabase', in *Jacques Derrida*, trans. Geoffrey Bennington (Chicago: University of Chicago Press, 1993), 117 and 115.

10   Geoffrey Bennington, *Not Half No End: Militantly Melancholic Essays in Memory of Jacques Derrida* (Edinburgh: Edinburgh University Press, 2010), 85.

11   Rodolphe Gasché, 'Structural Infinity', in *Inventions of Difference* (Cambridge, MA: Harvard University Press, 1994).

12   G. W. F. Hegel, *Science of Logic*, trans. A. V. Miller (Atlantic Highlands: Humanities Press, 1989), 144.

13   In a footnote in 'Violence and Metaphysics', Derrida writes that Henri Birault's study 'Heidegger et la pensée de la finitude' shows that the theme of *Endlichkeit* is progressively abandoned by Heidegger (*ED*, 207 n.2/141 n.70). Birault claims that Heidegger no longer mentions finitude after *Kant and the Problem of Metaphysics*.

14   Héraclite, *Fragments*, text established, translated and commented on by Marcel Conche (Paris: Presses Universitaires de France, 1986), 369–71. *DK* frag. 162; Frag. 106 of the Conche edition.

15   Derrida defines eternity, the best treatment of which is found in 'Ousia and Grammē: Note on a Note from *Being and Time*', as another name for the presence of the present (*M*, 34/32). In *Being and Time* Heidegger announces 'the determination of the meaning of being as *parousia* or as *ousia*, which in the ontologico-temporal order means "presence" (*Anwesenheit*)' (33–4). The ontological *project* can be understood in relation to time. 'The entity is grasped in its being as 'presence' (*Anwesenheit*), that is, it is understood by a reference to a determined mode of time, the present (*Gegenwart*)' (34). In a note, Derrida continues quoting Heidegger from *Kant and the Problem of Metaphysics*, who states that metaphysics has understood the Being of the entity as *permanence* and *persistence (Beständigkeit)*. The project relative to time lies at the basis of the comprehension of Being. Even eternity, taken as *nunc stans*, the eternal now, is conceivable as 'now' and 'persistent' only on the basis of time. Being is synonymous with 'permanence in presence' (33–4/32). In the essay Derrida

explains that, for Hegel, everything that receives the predicate of eternity (the Idea, Spirit, the True, etc.) must not be thought outside (or necessarily inside) time (50/45). 'Eternity as presence is neither temporal nor intemporal. Presence is intemporality in time or time in intemporality' (51/45–6). Eternity, then, is another name of the presence of the present. Though, as Derrida notes, Hegel distinguishes this presence from the present as now (50–51/45–6).

16   Jacques Derrida, *La peine de mort. Volume I (1999–2000)* (Paris: Galilée, 2012); *The Death Penalty, Volume I*, trans Peggy Kamuf (Chicago: University of Chicago Press, 2014), 174/119. The quote is from 'Literature and the Right to Death', translated by Lydia Davis, which appears in Maurice Blanchot, *La part du feu* (Paris: Gallimard, 1949), 325; *The Work of Fire*, trans. Charlotte Mandell (Stanford: Stanford University Press, 1995), 337, trans. modified throughout.

17   Jacques Derrida, 'Deconstruction in America: An Interview with Jacques Derrida', in *Critical Exchange* 17 (Winter 1985): 1–33.

18   Michael Naas, *Miracle and Machine: Jacques Derrida and the Two Sources of Religion, Science, and the Media* (New York: Fordham University Press, 2012), 214. On survival, see Michael Naas, especially the chapter entitled 'The Passion of Literature', and Geoffrey Bennington, in *Not Half No End* throughout.

19   'Dialogue entre Jacques Derrida, Philippe Lacoue-Labarthe et Jean-Luc Nancy', *Rue Descartes* 52 (2004): 86–99, 93.

20   Ibid.

21   Jacques Derrida, 'Je suis en guerre contre moi-même', *Le monde*, October 12, 2004: VI–VII.

22   In *A Taste for the Secret*, a book-length interview with Maurizio Ferraris, Derrida noted that 'I do not believe that one lives on post mortem', in Jacques Derrida and Maurizio Ferraris, *A Taste for the Secret* (Malden: Polity Press, 2001), 88.

23   I have attempted elsewhere, in a companion essay, to discuss survivance in relation to what Derrida in *The Beast and the Sovereign, vol. II* calls a strange 'cycle' of *survivre*. See my 'Dying Alive', *Mosaic*, forthcoming.

8

The King Is Dead! Long Live the King!

Chiara Alfano

The king's two bodies

The king is dead! What happens after singularity? A wound 'no doubt comes in (the) place of the point signed by singularity, in (the) place of its very instant (*stigmē*), at its point, its tip'.[1] After the singularity of a life, the pain of mourning. Yes, but not only. The loss is always compensated for: 'But *in (the) place of* this event, place is given over, for the same wound, to substitution, which repeats itself there, retaining of the irreplaceable only a past desire' (*WM*, 67). Thus, after every 'the king is dead!' there will be a resounding 'long live the king!' The *king* is dead – the *king* lives. After death there is at once repetition and substitution, but not, mind, of the irreplaceable, which remains irretrievable. What is substituted is something different, in which nonetheless, writes Jacques Derrida, something of the irreplaceable lives on like a past desire. This strange incantation – the king is dead, long live the king – therefore unites both loss and substitution, both ashes and desire. Most importantly, however, it speaks of desire. But desire for whom or desire for what?

We have known at least since Ernst H. Kantorowicz that the king has two bodies: a natural body and a body politic.[2] These two bodies are both con- and disjoined, both dependent on and outstripping the other. Coming second the body politic is, in the words of renowned Tudor legal scholar Edmund Plowden, on whose reports Kantorowicz's study draws heavily, 'conjoined' to the body natural. At the same time, this secondary political body 'includes' the corporeal body.[3] Included by the body politic, the body natural is 'lesser', and yet the greater body depends on the lesser for its consolidation.[4]

The body politic needs a body natural. But whilst death may ravage the body natural, it has no power over the body politic. The body politic is, again in Plowden's words:

> Not subject to Passions as the other is, nor to Death, for as to this Body the King never dies, and his natural Death is not called in our Law (as *Harper* said) the Death of the King, but the Demise of the King, not signifying by the Word (*Demise*) that the Body politic of the King is dead, but that there is a Separation of the two Bodies, and that the Body politic is transferred and conveyed over from the Body natural now dead, or now removed from the Dignity royal, to another Body natural.[5]

The king's body politic, his actual body, one feels tempted to say, the body that makes him *king*, does not die, it demises. Demise: 1. 'a person's death' or 'the end or failure of an enterprise or institution'; 2. 'conveyance or transfer of title by will or lease'.[6] In this sense, the natural body's death does not spell the end for the body politic, it merely separates the king's two bodies, but only for the time it takes to say 'The king is dead! Long live the king!' Thus, when the body natural dies – 'the king is dead' – the body politic is conveyed or transferred, transsubstantiated perhaps, in the silent fraction it takes to insert an exclamation mark or a breath, to a different mortal body: Long live the king! Never perhaps were the remarkable acrobatics by which sovereignty shores itself up encapsulated in so elegant and effective a slogan.

This idea of 'twin-born majesty' secures the continuity of the monarchy's sovereign, and, if it must be, it does so also beyond the bloodline.[7] 'King,' Plowden writes notably omitting the article – not *the* king or *a* king but *King* – 'is a Name of Continuance, which shall always endure as the Head and Governor of the People (as the Law presumes) as long as the People continue ... and in this Name the King never dies'.[8] This notion, in other words, severs the fragility and precariousness of mortal flesh from the very idea of sovereignty, giving it stability. In doing so, it also inoculates sovereignty against human weakness. The body natural may be subject to passions or misjudgments, but the body politic is incapable of folly or weakness.[9] In fact, this bit of mediaeval alchemy brings about not merely a separation between body politic and body natural; this severing of bodies is also transformative. Not merely does the king's body politic become perfect, but this perfection also extends to his body natural, no matter what follies may have beset it previously. The body politic can 'reduce, or even remove, the imperfections of the fragile human nature'.[10] Attracting and absorbing, as it were, the stuff of human impurity, the body natural leaves a pure, almost divine, essence of king, what was also called the king's '*character angelicus*'.[11]

As Kantorowicz's subtitle – *A Study in Mediaeval Political Theology* – suggests, very real issues necessitated the notion of the king's two bodies. Far from voicing a lofty idealism, the idea of sovereignty thus wore the marks of the grind of the political machine. It is, in fact, a mediaeval idea Elizabethan jurists fell back on to solve issues relating to the continuity of sovereignty, thus also ensuring a regulated circulation of power, as well as, for instance, making sure that the distribution of justice was seen as lawful. The notion of the two bodies in this sense explained why the king was, despite not being able to distribute justice personally, still present in all his courts. As it does in the case of the issue of the continuity of the line (showing how the king can live long although the king just died), here the notion of the king's two bodies solves a problem of multitudes (showing how one royal body can be in more places at the same time) by introducing unity and ubiquity. Paradoxically then, the severing of the king into two bodies triggers not effects of multiplication but of unification, even of incorporation.

To incorporate, from the Latin *incorporare* (literally, to form into one body, to embody), means to 'take in or contain (something) as part of a whole' and to 'combine (ingredients) into one substance'.[12] We also use this word to describe the incorporation of several bodies or persons into the fictive, unified body that is a corporation. Just as the body natural's follies are purged by the incorporation into the body royal, the actions of a member of the corporation will no longer be her own but the actions of the corporation. The dissection of the sovereign into body natural and body politic and subsequent re-incorporation of these two bodies into the royal corporation safeguards the unity of King, the absolute and transcendent body of King, preserves King Incorporated if you will.

King Inc. of course has more than one royal member. Apart from all the proceeding kings (now demised) and the king's corporal body, which is always con- and disjoined to his corporation body, it also incorporates the king's subjects:

> And as to this it was argued on this Side that the King has two Capacities, for he has two Bodies, the one whereof is a Body natural ... the other is a Body politic, and the Members thereof are his Subjects, and he and his Subjects together compose the Corporation, as *Southcote* said, and he is incorporated with them, and they with him, and he is the Head, and they are the Members, and he has the sole Government of them.[13]

Besides assuring the continuity of kingship, the notion of the king's two bodies solidifies the state itself into a Leviathanesque body which works towards the greater good – as defined by the sovereign who heads it, of course. Therefore, whilst the king and his subjects are part of this corporation, they do not have an equal standing in it. The king is greater than his subjects; his Majesty is, in fact, the greatest. It would seem that what this notion of the king's two bodies safeguards, beyond the sovereignty of a particular king or royal lineage or the containment of a particular circuit of power, is the very *idea* of sovereignty, not understood as the self-determination of a state and its citizens, but, quite on the contrary, as a sovereign's dominion *over* a corporation. What is safeguarded are, going even further, the very strategies by which man may claim mastery over a realm and by which man consequently places himself above other members of a corporation to which he professes to belong.

Dissecting sovereignty

Derrida touches on the idea of the king's two bodies when thinking about the dissection of sovereignty in the Tenth and Eleventh sessions of *The Beast & the Sovereign Volume I*. Here too we find an uncanny body-twinning, albeit not between the king's two bodies, but between a living king and a dead animal of no less majesty. In 1681 in the Menagerie of Versailles Louis le Grand, the Sun King himself, attended an anatomical dissection of an elephant. In front of 'the living body of a king', there lay then 'the submissive cadaver laid out, exposed, carved up, explored' of 'one of the greatest, if not the greatest, animal in the world'.[14] The king is not only present in person, in *his* person, but also in his person*s*, in that he has 'at his disposal another body, that double body' (*BS*, 285). Derrida's paraphrase of the notion of the king's two bodies follows: 'these two persons and these two bodies are united during life but separated after death'; 'the "sovereignty" or the "majesty" of the king' survives his mortal body and 'is inherited from one king to another'; during a king's lifetime, however, 'the two bodies, the two royalties, the personal and the ideal, dignity and majestic sovereignty, are united' (286). For Derrida, this co-presence of the (dead) beast and the sovereign recalls, even illustrates, the unification of King through a division into two bodies.

Autopsy means seeing for one-self. In 1681 Louis the Grand saw the autopsy of the elephant for *himself*, but through that witnessing he not merely participated in the autopsy, he also took part or partook in the dissected cadaver. For Derrida, in fact, the animal's dead body represents 'the denied, averted, vaguely totemic representation of the dead king, the mortal king, the king dead from a death of the king that everyone both fears and hopes for, and that every subject projects into the autopsy or the necropsy of sovereignty' (294). Standing in front of the cadaver – which is also the totemic representation of the king's natural, mortal body – the King is also standing in front of his own mortality. And sure enough, at the time of the dissection Louis the Grand was himself being subjected to his doctors's dissecting gazes due to his ill health (287–7). What is being autopsied is, in other words, both the elephant's and the king's body natural. What is of interest, therefore, is not merely the 'physio-zoological knowledge as to the functioning of the animal organism, but was already a comparative knowledge that was to clarify the analogies between human anatomy and physiology and animal physiology' (283). Put differently, the dissection of the elephant is aimed at preserving the king's life, at, if not averting then at least postponing his feared-for demise and the subsequent transfer of sovereignty onto a different body natural.

A beast's death for the sovereign's life. The co-presence of the king and the elephant is, according to Derrida, a *corps à corps*, a close body combat, for the beast had to be hunted, captured and killed for the sovereign to attend and profit from its autopsy (281). 'Anatomical inspection', Derrida writes, 'always presupposes some cadaver docile to autopsy' (282). This dissection of the elephant happens not merely under the gaze or for the profit of the sovereign, but also under the order of the sovereign (280). And again the metonymic character of this tableau, as Derrida describes it, implies that this is not a single or singular violent exertion of the sovereign's power. The violence represented in this *corps à corps* is part and parcel of the exertion of power. There is no sovereignty, no majesty, no mastery without violence.

Who wields such power? What or who demands such total and deadly docility? Yes, Louis le Grand was present, as head of the state-corporation, head of his limb-subjects; but if we consider the theatre of this dissection, namely the Menagerie which under its founder Louis XIV had also become a research institution, he is also present as a sort of principal investigator, the sovereign-head of the pursuit of knowledge. The autopsy table is also a 'cathedra' and the anatomy itself also a lesson where knowledge may be transmitted from a teacher to her students (276). For Derrida, therefore, the elephant's dissection under the gaze and for the king serves an even greater sovereign than the king's sovereignty; the elephant is not only 'at the disposal' of the 'absolute monarch', but more importantly also at the disposal of 'absolute knowledge' (280). Like the monarch, knowledge wants to be 'all-powerful' and 'have possession and mastery of its object' (ibid.). Even more than the monarch, whose life, remember, depends on the knowledge gained in this investigation, 'knowledge is sovereign' (ibid.).

In this 'autopsy of autopsy' Derrida hence dissects both the sovereignty of majesty, as well as the majesty of a different kind of sovereignty, which, as it in fact did, can survive even the decapitation of a monarch. 'What is it to "know"?' (278). In dissecting the sovereignty of knowledge, which itself dissects and thus masters its object, Derrida wishes, I believe, first and foremost to think of a different way of knowing that whilst not denying the inherent violence of knowledge does not seek to elevate itself by its cut but which remains vulnerable and open to the wounds it must necessarily inflict.

Professor Tulp's lesson

As Derrida himself concedes, in order to bring knowledge, as we know it, to its limits, one would have to coordinate this dissection of dissecting knowledge with the entire history of medicine, as well as with the history 'of anatomical painting and drawing of the human body at that time and previously' (292). Derrida is here thinking for example of all the *Anatomy Lessons* Rembrandt painted, in which a science book replaced the Bible, in which in other words the sovereignty of God and of his anointed king is replaced by the sovereignty of knowledge (ibid.).

Derrida is specifically thinking about Rembrandt's 1632 anatomical painting depicting, and here the philosopher misremembers, 'Professor Nicholas Tulp' (ibid.). Rembrandt's *The Anatomy Lesson of Doctor Nicolaes Tulp* (1623) is a curious painting. At the centre of the composition is the object of the lesson: a marble-white, spectrally radiant cadaver. Around him are eight men, all except one – the most nosy one, who is bending over the body and whose light reddish brown silky jacket echoes the tone of the wound Tulp is opening – are dressed in dark colours, blending with the dusky surroundings of what appears to be the vault of a subterranean anatomical theatre. The only source of light is, it seems, the whiteness of the body itself, which (very much like Christ in Rembrandt's *Descent From the Cross*, 1633) is amplified by the white cloth draped over his genitals and reflected in the white, starched ruffs of the eight men, as well as in Tulp's white cuffs. What Rembrandt's use of chiaroscuro demands could not be more clear. Our gazes are drawn from light to light: from the corpse, to the collars and almost disembodied, floating heads of Tulp and his audience, to the Doctor's hands – the only ones framed by white ruffles of fabric – and finally to the book that is resting at the feet of the cadaver.

Despite the almost clandestine characterization of the dissection, Rembrandt's painting was part of a healthy and strong tradition of the depiction of anatomy lessons. Since Vasalius, each year the head of the surgeon's guild in Amsterdam, the Praelector Anatomiae, would give a lecture to the members of his guild and often he would commission an artist to immortalize this occasion.[15] Such portraits would usually find the members of the guild facing the painter. In contrast, Rembrandt has his subjects, more or less intently of course, follow Tulp's lesson. Only three men lock eyes with us. Of the other four, one is looking at Tulp and three are looking over the body to the book at its feet. Given that the subject of this moment of Dr Tulp's lesson is the anatomy of the forearm and hand, it seems remarkable that most hands and arms in the painting are either entirely or partially hidden from view. Dr Tulp's hands, however, like the corpse's, can be seen clearly. Tulp is looking into the mid-distance. Pointing to the tendons in the cadaver's left arm with a forceps he holds in his right hand, the thumb and index finger of his elevated left hand touch. Perhaps this is a didactic gesture, or, as Svetlana Alpers has argued, he is demonstrating the use of the tendons he is pointing to.[16]

Whilst Derrida only briefly points us toward this anatomy lesson in *The Beast & the Sovereign*, he does speak about it in more detail in *The Work of Mourning*, in the context of his discussion of Sarah Kofman's posthumously published last piece 'Conjuring Death: Remarks on *The Anatomy Lesson of Doctor Nicolas Tulp* (1632)'. In as much as Dr Tulp is first and foremost a professor professing and sharing his knowledge with his students, Derrida's slip of the tongue in referring to the anatomy lesson of Professor and not Doctor Tulp is apt. Although Tulp's students are not all looking in the same direction, they are united by the same 'intense curiosity animated by the singular desire to learn and to know' (CD, 237). 'Theirs are luminous eyes', Kofman writes, 'turned toward the light of truth' (238). The men share, so writes Kofman, a scientific gaze, but it is not in fact directed at the body that lies before them (237). Following the gazes of Tulp's students, Kofman remarks that although the body is in plain view it is overlooked in favour of the book at the cadaver's feet.

It is not entirely true that the body is in full view: a white cloth is carefully draped over the dead man's genitals. Like Derrida, Kofman stays a little while with the word anatomy, pointing out three of its meanings: nudity or sex; dissection; and analytical discourse or structure of a work (293). Tulp does not merely speak about the anatomy of the man lying dead on the table in front of him, nor does he speak about the sexual difference that the carefully hidden anatomy of the man points us to; what he says also follows a certain anatomy or structure governed by the rules of scientific discourse, as orchestrated by the book at the cadaver's feet. In Kofman's way of looking at the painting, the three meanings of the word anatomy point us toward a mechanism of suppression and displacement that undergirds the men's pursuit of knowledge. Rembrandt's use of light directs his viewers' gazes from the body's whiteness – amplified by the loin-cloth – to the men's starched ruffs, to the white pages of the book. It is, indeed, as if the body's luminosity were amplified by the very covering of the corpse's genitals. The whiteness of the loin-cloth is picked up in the men's stiff-white ruffs which, slicing through the dimness of the composition, seemingly sever the men's heads from their bodies. In this way of looking at the painting, Rembrandt's chiaroscuro and composition depict the divorce of body and knowledge, which is at the heart of the anatomy, or structure, of this scientific discourse. What is covered with the man's genitals, what in other words endangers the men's pursuit, are two things. First, what is covered up is sexual difference. It is as if there was no room for it in this corporation's pursuit of knowledge. There are in fact no women in this painting, but given that it depicts the medical profession in 1632 this is hardly shocking. I shall return to the role of sexual difference in this corporation later. The second thing that is hidden from view is the body's soma in general and the idiomaticity of *that* rather than any other body. As in statues where the smooth white surface does not belie even the tiniest bulge, the effect is one of generalization, as if what were depicted was not *his* or *her* body, not even *a* body but *body*. Left uncovered, the corpse's genitals would get in the way because they would resist the sublimating and generalizing thrust of the men's pursuit of knowledge.

Kofman's reading of Rembrandt's *The Anatomy Lesson of Doctor Nicolaes Tulp* as depicting the displacement of the body through the book is captured beautifully in her image of the cadaver's feet serving as a lectern for the book. Derrida, too, must have found this image striking because he quotes it not once but twice in his essay on Kofman in *The Work of Mourning*. Saying that the body is a lectern for the book does not merely indicate that the body props the book up, makes it possible to read, but also that the book frames or filters the body, that it is what Tulp's students have foremost in their minds. In Kofman's reading of Rembrandt the book, in fact, frames, directs and orchestrates their perception of the body. As Derrida sums up: 'This open book organizes: an organ detached from the body, it has an organizing mission' (*WM*, 176). For Derrida, Kofman's text, like Rembrandt's painting, makes us wonder why 'a book always comes to take the place of the body', about our tendency to replace bodies with books or to displace bodies by books (169).

Kofman writes that what 'attracts the gazes, much more even than does the point of the scissors that has begun to peel away the skin from the body stretched out there' is the book 'and the opening it provides onto the science of life and its mastery' (CD, 238). As the ambiguous grammar of 'its mastery' suggests, what is at stake in this deciphering of the body is both a deeper understanding of the mastery of the body and the grasping of the mastery of the book and of knowledge itself. Like in the elephant's autopsy, there is an unifying doubling of bodies. There the dead beast and the living sovereign embody the king's two bodies, his mortal body natural and his transcendent body politic, which is usually hidden from view. In Rembrandt's painting, too, there is such a unifying multiplication of bodies: the corpse and the book, both anatomies though of a different order, and the corporation of doctors gathered around them. Teasing out this strange relationship between 'the book and the body' will thus involve not merely thinking about the relationship between the body and the book, but also between the corpse and the body describing its anatomy, in other words 'the body or corporation of doctors gathered there' (*WM*, 175). And it is of course, as already suggested, the men's repression of the corpse's sexual anatomy that ignites their '"scientific" gaze' (CD, 237). It is, in short, thanks to this displacement from body to book, from one sense of anatomy (sex) to another (scientific rigour), and also, Kofman suggests, through the separation of one sex from the other, that the men 'belon[g] to the same corporation or practicing body' and '*form one body [font corps]*' (ibid.).

Knowledge reigns sovereign over this scene as it did over the elephant's dissection described in *The Beast & the Sovereign*. What role the body may have in this is, however, unclear. To the men the corpse is, Kofman writes, 'a purely technical instrument that one of them manipulates in order to get a hold on the truth of life' (238). The body is the lesson's object, but it is not its subject. Blinded by the light of truth, the men seemed to have forgotten that what they are studying is an 'image of what they themselves will one day be' (ibid.). Like the doctors in the Menagerie of Versailles in 1681, they are not fascinated by the mortality the corpse embodies; quite the contrary, they are fascinated by what their knowledge of this body can reveal about life. For Kofman (who is here very much arguing against traditional readings of Dutch paintings of this period that highlight their prominent use of *vanitas*), the corpse, therefore, signifies not the triumph of death or a *memento mori*, but the triumph over death, to be more precise, the triumph of knowledge over death (239).

For Kofman, this placement of body and book is a careful ordering but also a replacement, a dissimulation and a displacement.

> The fascination is displaced, and with this displacement, the anxiety is repressed, the intolerable made tolerable, from the sight of the cadaver to that of the book wide open at the foot of the deceased, who might now serve as a lectern. (238)

The reliance on the speculative, on what illuminates, on the realm of knowledge, is, for Kofman, a function of occultation; what remains hidden behind the clinical and illuminating dissection of the cadaver is 'the cadaveresque that each living being, already from the origin, carries within itself' (239). As in the autopsy of the elephant, this move to knowledge is thus motivated ultimately by the desire to deny or at least avert mortality. This is then, to recapitulate, also the function of the loin-cloth: with the covering of its sex, the smooth marble-white body is shielded from any friction that its idiomacity may provide. A particular and mortal man's body becomes a general body, valuable to the doctors precisely because it is no longer unique but representative of the body in general, a body so general, so sublimated that it has no place for sexual difference. A body can die, but *body* is the name of continuance. It would therefore seem that sovereignty (whether it be of King Inc. or Knowledge Inc.) is subject to an even greater majesty than its own which it seeks to defend against: death, oblivion and obscurity.

The philosopher's two bodies

Just like the king, the philosopher – who is also sovereign albeit of a different realm – has two bodies. These two bodies are both con- and disjoined, both dependent on and outstripping the other: her body and her philosophical body, or corpus. Coming second, the philosophical body is 'conjoined' to the philosopher's body; the philosophical body needs the philosopher's body and yet it survives it. The philosophical body is not, as Plowden might have said, subject to death. A philosophy does not die, it 'demises', is transferred to an heir, who secures its continuity. As with royalty, should such heirs be absent or insufficiently influential a particular philosophy will be usurped by a different house. But even in this case, as in the case of monarchy, sovereignty assures itself beyond the trickling out of a blood-line: *a* philosophy might fall out of fashion, but philosophy or knowledge (or rather what is understood as 'philosophy' or 'knowledge') still reigns sovereign, albeit fighting under a different banner.

In contrast to the king's two bodies, the philosopher's two bodies are, however, both subject to passion and folly. The philosophical body is by no means free from human weakness, be it misjudged intellectual alliances or mistakes of argument or reason. Philosophy can think and do wrong; in fact, its sovereignty is established very much by pointing out its previous mistakes. More importantly, both bodies are equally and often in the same gesture, as *ad hominem* arguments illustrate, the object of passions and of desire, ignited perhaps by the strange relationship between the philosopher's two bodies. Like in Rembrandt's painting, when doing philosophy we partake, whether we will or not, in a strange replacement: 'a *corpse* replaced by a corpus, a *corpse* yielding its place to the bookish thing' (*WM*, 176).

The strange relationship between the philosopher's body and his corpus – how does the death of a philosopher impinge on the way we read her? – is at the heart of Derrida's *The Work of Mourning*. Each of its fourteen pieces testifies to the many ways in which the philosopher's two bodies are disjoined, but also incorporated. In 'The Deaths of Roland Barthes', Derrida remarks that 'these thoughts are *for him*, for Roland Barthes, meaning that I think of him and about him, not only of or about his work' (35). Thinking in the wake of Barthes, like thinking in the wake of Kofman, would therefore already have to begin with multiples: thinking *for* Barthes – the name we give his philosophical oeuvre – and Barthes Derrida's friend. Writing about a philosopher in his wake is not only a gift or an homage, but also a quest to discover her, as if for the first time. In the essay Derrida indeed speaks about Barthes, for Barthes but also *toward* Barthes, as if Barthes were a destination thoughts had not yet reached (ibid.).

Who or what, however, is the destination and the object of our desire when we write about, for and towards a philosopher? Barthes philosopher, or Barthes man and friend? Kofman philosopher, or Kofman woman and friend? It seems that often our gazes follow the direction of the glances of Tulp's students: we read a corpus also in the hope of discovering more about the person – his or her beliefs, convictions, doubts, desires – who wrote them. Equally, we look from body to the book. And although there is always a prurience to our desire to know more about a philosopher's life, we also believe that knowing the man or woman will ultimately bring us closer to the work.

Although Derrida's text is written *to* Barthes it is also written in the knowledge that Barthes can no longer read the text that Derrida has written for him. If 'Roland Barthes is the name of someone who can no longer hear or bear it', if 'he will receive nothing of what I say here of him, for him, to him', it is also because Barthes, still living, already was no longer his name (45). Not only is Barthes always plural, as the final s of his name implies, his deaths are also plural, because his 'actual' death was already preceded by another death (46–7).

Indeed, when Derrida says 'Roland Barthes' he names him 'beyond the name', and reflects on the fact that Barthes the man already split off from Barthes the philosopher, as soon as he put pen to paper (45). As Derrida writes in relation to Kofman, 'death cut[s] the name off in the midst of life', death already detaches or '[tears] the name away from the body' every time 'we speak, write, and publish' (178–9). Whenever we write, whenever we give birth to a body of a text there is, like in Rembrandt's depiction of Tulp's anatomy lesson, an 'insistence on anonymity, on the loss of the name in the being-right-there of the *corpse*', or rather the corpse-corpus, the text that has *ab initio* been cut off from life (178). Derrida's mediation on the plurality of Barthes is not merely another riff on différance; it is a meditation on the philosopher's two bodies, the fact that as soon as Barthes became *Barthes*, or Kofman *Kofman*, the philosopher's body of work splits away from his or her body natural, demanding immortality of its heirs.

Whether we wish to know more about the man or his work, our thirst for knowledge, our desire to keep the other alive is often, despite our best intentions, a desire for mastery. It is also, and more importantly, a desire to place ourselves over others by means of an appropriation. All the essays in *The Work of Mourning* are acutely aware of the difficulties involved in speaking of, for and to the dead, and in particular of the danger of machinating 'an abusive interpretative framing or narcissistic reappropriation' in the name of mourning (168). Derrida writes, still about Barthes: 'Since he himself is now inaccessible to his appellation, since this nomination cannot become a vocation, address, or apostrophe (supposing that this possibility revoked today could have ever been pure), it is him in me that I name, toward him in me, in you, in us that I pass through his name' (46). When we speak about or towards a philosopher, we thus also always run the risk of speaking for him, of appropriating him for our own uses. Such mimesis in which one '[takes] him into oneself, to identify with him in order to let him speak within oneself, to make him present and faithfully to represent him' is, as Derrida writes, 'at once a duty' and the 'worst', 'most indecent and most murderous' of temptations (38). Thus an homage, or a 'personal testimony', Derrida writes now in the context of his remarks on Lyotard, by which one sought to keep the other alive, by which one sought to make the other speak can turn into 'an indecent way of saying "we", or worse, "me"' (225).

Again the parallels with the 1681 elephant autopsy and Tulp's lesson are remarkable. As Derrida suggests in *The Beast & the Sovereign*, it was the fear of his own death and the demise of his sovereignty to a different body natural that informed Louis's attendance and participation in that autopsy. Tulp's students, too, shift the focus to book and only then to body because they are afraid of their own mortality: the 'doctors having eyes only for the book facing them, as if, by reading, by observing the signs on the drawn sheet of paper, they were trying to forget, repress, deny, or conjure away death – and the anxiety before death' (176). When writing to, for, about and towards a philosopher, as Derrida goes on to show in his essay on Barthes, the desire to appropriate the philosopher and thus to place him beyond all suspicion is also caused by a fear of death, not primarily of our own death, but of the death, or the consignment to obscurity, of the corporation to which both we and the philosopher's corpus belong.

Like the king's two bodies, a philosopher's two bodies are incorporated or conjoined to each other; but as with the king's two bodies, this incorporation is a function of a corporation whose business it is to keep alive sovereignty. Whilst we may pledge allegiance to a certain corpus or corporation or declare ourselves part of a tradition, we wish, like the sovereign, not merely to be part but to be the head of this corporation. The name of the philosopher becomes like an invocation, his corpus like a talisman from which we draw 'supplementary force to be turned against the living', whether they are part of the philosopher's corporation or antagonistic towards it. We thus use the philosopher 'to denounce or insult' others, as well as 'to authorize and legitimate' ourselves. In raising the philosopher 'beyond all suspicion', in immortalizing him, we also follow our desire for mastery which dissimulates our fear not merely of our corporation's but also of our own obscurity (51). Thinking in the wake of a philosopher, we are thus often besieged by three distinct but interrelated worries: about our own standing within the corporation (belying the fear of our mortality), about the fate of the corporation itself (speaking of an anxiety about irrelevance) and about the future of philosophy or knowledge as we know it (voicing our dread of chaos). The first fear, which is perhaps the strongest, underlies the other two. Like Tulp's students we hang on to knowledge to avoid our human mortality and fallibility. This is not merely suggested by Kofman's reading of Rembrandt, but is also Stanley Cavell's account of the sceptic philosopher's predicament.

Derrida's corpus

Rembrandt, it seems, knew about the strange relationship between the corpse and the corpus. The men's scientific gazes go, Kofman writes, 'from the sight of the cadaver to that of the book wide open at the foot of the deceased, who might now serve as a lectern (CD, 238). Whilst both Kofman and Derrida remark on the peculiar but eloquent redirection of the men's gazes, Derrida does not pick up on the fact that Kofman's striking description of the cadaver's feet as a lectern for the book is not entirely accurate. The open pages of the book face towards the corpse and its spine rests on what seem to be two or three stacked books working as a make-shift book-stand. The corpse's feet could serve as a lectern only if the book's back rested on them and the book's open pages faced us, the viewers.

By way of this inventive inversion of the book, Kofman has performed our involvement in this reading scene. She has drawn us in, or rather has made us aware that we were already involved. We are not merely dispassionately observing this reading scene – watching how Rembrandt's scientists dissimulate the body and its mortality, noting how the men's strange fascination with the book and then the body echoes knowledge's sovereignty in the 1681 elephantine autopsy and noting how both illuminate the strange dynamic between a philosopher's body and corpus – Kofman shows us that Derrida as well as you or I are part of the corporation's scientific gaze. Put differently: that strange relationship between the book and the body which Kofman finds depicted in Rembrandt's painting is not merely the subject or part of Derrida's essay on Kofman in *The Work of Mourning*; it also orchestrates his delicate negotiation between her body and her work.

Negotiating the legacy of Derrida's corpus now more than ten years after his death, we too are complicit in the corporation glancing from book to body and back. It does, in fact, sometimes seem that in the last ten years Derrida Inc. has spent little time doing anything else. If, as Derrida writes in his last interview, *Learning How To Live Finally*, 'to philosophize is to learn to die', it would seem that in order to understand how to philosophize with, about, to and for Derrida we must make sense of what his death means for the way we read and write about him.[17] It may also mean to learn to let philosophy, as we know it, die.

Derrida knew, of course, that his corpus would be subjected to this strange relationship between the body and the book that he speaks about in relation to Kofman's reading of Rembrandt. 'Circumfession' is, for example, supremely aware of the constant slippage between the twin-bodies of Derrida and his corpus and of what will happen to the latter after the former's death; it is also aware that this problematic relationship between body and book starts before his death and that all his writing is to some extent posthumous. 'I posthume as I breathe', Derrida writes.[18] Arguing along the same lines in his final interview, he says: 'I leave a piece of paper behind, I go away, I die: it is impossible to escape this structure, it is the unchanging form of my life. Each time I let something go, each time some trace leaves me, "proceeds" from me, unable to be reappropriated, I live my death in writing' (*LLF*, 32–3). At the same time as writing's trace signifies 'at once my death, either to come or already come upon me', it inaugurates a hope that this trace 'survives me' (32).

Derrida knew that all writing is a corporation waiting to happen, and that whatever this corpus does, whether it lives on or is forgotten, it does so independently from us. He knew well that every time one writes and 'expropriates oneself', one does so 'without knowing exactly who is being entrusted with what is left behind. Who is going to inherit, and how? Will there even be any heirs?' (33). The philosopher, therefore, partakes in his corporation's anxiety about and dissimulation of obscurity. Derrida has:

> The *double feeling* that, on the one hand, to put it playfully and with a certain immodesty, one has not yet begun to read me, that even though there are, to be sure, many very good readers (a few dozen in the world perhaps, people who are also writer-thinkers, poets), in the end it is later on that all this has a chance of appearing; but also, on the other hand, and thus simultaneously, I have the feeling that two weeks or a month after my death *there will be nothing left*. Nothing except what has been copyrighted and deposited in libraries. (33–4)

Derrida here makes an interesting distinction between the part of his work that will be deposited in libraries and that which will be read and picked up by writer-thinkers or poets. Given Derrida's suggestion that there are only perhaps a few dozen readers of his work who are also writer-thinkers or poets and thus would be able to ensure the abidance of his work beyond what is copyrighted and deposited in libraries, one is no doubt justified in wondering where this leaves the scores of scholars who count themselves as part of 'his' corporation.

Derrida's division of his work into two, which by implication also cleaves his readership in two (those few writer-thinkers and poets, and the rest of us), raises two further questions for me. Who is the corporation and is Derrida's distinction an accurate description of what it does with his corpus? Although we are part of one corporation, our strategies for looking are, like they are after all for Tulp's students, different. Geoffrey Bennington, who in our corporation perhaps takes on a bit of a tulpish role, wrote a book whose title (*Jacques Derrida*) and cover work (a photograph of Derrida as an adult on the front and a photograph of Jacques the child on the back cover) seemed to speak of a desire of holding the work of and the philosopher Jacques Derrida in its entirety. Bennington's text notably does not contain a single of Derrida's quotes, limiting itself rather to speak about the corpus or thought in general and thus also in its totality. In the pursuit of knowledge Tulp's students look over and beyond the body to the book; in *Jacques Derrida* too, Derrida's thought is literally and typographically placed above the idiom of Derrida's corpus. In 'Circumfession' – a text which is in constant conversation with Bennington's and which is printed in the lower page margin of *Jacques Derrida* – Derrida remarks, echoing it would seem his text on Barthes, that although 'G. will have written up there, beside or above me, *on* me, but also *for* me, in my favor, toward me and in my place', he has made the choice of quoting not one word 'from what might be called in the university my corpus' (C, 26–7). Is not this a strange choice 'when one is writing a book *on* someone who writes books' not to have 'retained intact a single fragment of my corpus', and instead to have 'cut or lifted out some pieces', to have 'erased' or 'incinerate[d]' them, as if to lift from their ashes something transcendent, living beyond these words (27–8)?

This protestation is naturally only half-meant because Bennington of course knows that any book such as the one that he is writing must negotiate 'the relationship between commentary and interpretation', between the 'identification and delimitation of a corpus or a work', with 'the respect ... owed to the singularity ... or the event of a work in its idiom ... its signature ... its date'.[19] It is, in fact, no coincidence that Derrida's thinking about the corpus and quotation comes beneath or next to the part of Bennington's text on the sign and the signifier, which stands as a reminder for the difference between a philosopher's paraphraseable tenets and his idiom.[20]

Like any philosopher, the philosopher Derrida, therefore, does not merely have a corpus, understood as his generalized contributions to a particular field of philosophy, but also, what Derrida calls, 'my corpus, the set of sentences I have signed' (C, 27). Whilst this idiomatic corpus of the philosopher seems to retain something of the body which wrote it – in *The Work of Mourning* Derrida as a matter of fact speaks of Barthes' 'inimitable *habitus* of a unique body' or '*manner*' – it is also, like the criminal's cadaver in Rembrandt's painting, cut off from it and thus retains an essential anonymity (*WM*, 39; 40). Derrida's '*double feeling*' that although 'one has not yet begun to read me', and that despite, or perhaps just because of, that there will be nothing left, 'except what has been copyrighted and deposited in libraries', can be explained by his double understanding of corpus as both totality of thought and idiom (*LLF*, 34). What will be left in libraries is what 'universities may call his corpus', and yet we still have not begun to read his idiom.

What then do we do with his idiom? We have, as Derrida puts it in *The Work of Mourning*, two 'impossible' choices. The first is to remain silent and thus (perhaps 'out of zealous devotion or gratitude') to be 'content with just quoting', in other words to preserve the philosopher by preserving the sentences he has signed like so many relics (*WM*, 45). Far from revitalizing the corpus, such fidelity would, however, run the risk of circulating the dead as living. Derrida writes: 'this excess of fidelity would end up saying and exchanging nothing. It returns to death. It points to death, sending death back to death' (ibid.). The other is to 'avoid' all quotation, as well as 'identification', so that 'what is addressed to or spoken of [the philosopher] truly comes from the other' (ibid.). In scholarly terms, this might mean to try and ignore what Derrida's idiom does (and what it does to other idioms) in favour of what his 'philosophical arguments' are. Again, this would be a betrayal because this overlooking of the idiom 'risks making him disappear again' (ibid.). Surely, if we take away anything from Derrida's work, it is that philosophical thoughts, tenets or arguments cannot easily be distilled from the context from which they emerge. This means that we cannot hope to get a clear understanding of what he is saying if we ignore his idiom. Not to understand this about Derrida means not to understand Derrida.

To return to the question of what to do with Derrida's idiom, neither strategy – the overindulgence or avoidance of the Derridean idiom – would be immune from the dangers of re-appropriation, from fantasies of mastery accompanying our pursuits of knowledge. As soon as there is the desire for absolute knowledge (be it of the body, of mortality, or of a philosopher), everything becomes pre-scripted, pre-calculated: 'everything moves as though mechanically, everything unwinds as one unwinds or holds tight on to a string, and thereby on to a marionette' (*BS*, 228). Here thinking in Derrida's sense of thinking-poetry – a *poiesis*, something that creates – stops. How can these marionette strings be cut? Derrida gives us a clue in his notion of writer-thinkers or poets (*LLF*, 34). To know how to read Derrida would not only mean to learn how to negotiate the dynamic between the body and the book (both corpus-thought and corpus-idiom). Such negotiation would furthermore have to be conditioned by an understanding of what it is to read poetry.

The majesty of the present

That poetry is key to rethinking not merely the sovereignties of a particular philo-sophical corpus but that it is also vital to rattle the sovereignties of philosophy as we know it is suggested in *The Beast & the Sovereign*. Poetry, indeed, makes a strange appearance just at the moment when Derrida dissects the sovereignty of knowledge. In the Eleventh session of *The Beast & the Sovereign* there is a whole clustering of twin-bodies: the king's natural body and his body politic, which is totemically represented in the twin-bodies of elephant and king. The other twinned bodies Derrida picks out are the bodies participating in the dissection and the corporation in whose sovereign name this dissection is taking place, a corporation that, as we have seen, bows to knowledge. Long live sovereign knowledge! It is just at this juncture in *The Beast & the Sovereign* that Derrida draws our attention to yet another invocation, Lucile's 'Long live the king!' in *Danton's Death*. It is this invocation – written by Georg Büchner and reported by Paul Celan – on which Derrida stakes the fissuring of knowledge that he is working towards. This exclamation takes us to the very end of Georg Büchner's *Danton's Death*, right to the Place de la Révolution on which two henchmen are still clearing up after a day's work. Danton and Camille have been guillotined. Camille's wife Lucile sits down on the steps in front of the guillotine and shouts: 'Es lebe der König!' (4.9.21).[21] Lucile's shout, sealing her fate, as she seemingly pledges allegiance to the beheaded monarch at the symbolic heart of the revolution, in truth pledges allegiance, so argues Paul Celan on accepting the Georg-Büchner-Prize in 1960, to a different sovereignty.

The characters in *Dantons Tod* have a lot to say about art. In Danton and Camille's famous *Kunstgespräch* in Act 2, Scene 3, Camille expounds lengthily on Büchner's *Fundamentalrealismus*. Like the young playwright, Camille criticizes his contemporaries' predilection of art over realism:

> I tell you, if they don't get things in wooden copies, all neatly labeled, in theatres, concerts, or art shows, they've got neither eyes nor ears for them. But carve a puppet, show them the hole where the string goes in, give it a pull so that its joints creak in blank verse with every step it takes – and then, what character-drawing, what verisimilitude! (2.3; 33)[22]

Put that same audience on the common street, Camille continues, and they will not be able to perceive how 'red-hot creation thunders and lightens in and around them at every moment' (2.3; 33). Their art is, he concludes, artificial and fruitless. No wonder then that although Pygmalion's statue may have come to life, it bore no children. Danton agrees. Great minds!

Then, suddenly, Lucile, who although we hear nothing appears to have said something, interrupts this corporation of men. Camille: 'Was sagst du, Lucile?' or 'What do you say, Lucile?' (2.3.4/2.3; 33). Lucile: 'Nichts, ich sehe dich so gern sprechen' (2.3.5). 'Nothing, I so love watching you when you speak' (2.3; 33). Lucile has said nothing but yet this nothing has interrupted, if only for a moment, the corporation's learned discussion. Lucile's silent interruption is multiple: she interrupts the men but, or so the men wish to believe, her understanding is equally interrupted by her inability to grasp what it is they are saying. Lucile, whom Celan calls the 'Kunstblinde' (she who cannot see art), is actually 'die Kunsttaube' (she who cannot hear art) – she hears Camille but she does not understand him. She is just a woman, after all. Camille: 'Sei ruhig, lieb Kind' (2.3.30). 'Hush, my dear' (2.3; 34). I cannot help but notice that the sexual difference within the corporation, which Derrida spoke of in relation to Kofman's interpretation of Rembrandt, is also at work in Büchner's play.

With its rich tapestry of allusions, the first paragraph of Celan's famous 'The Meridian' points us precisely to Danton and Camille's conversation on the nature of art: 'Art, you will remember, is a puppet-like, iambically five-footed and ... a childless being'.[23] Camille and Danton's conversation could, Celan concedes, 'be continued indefinitely, if nothing interfered' (*TM*, 2). But 'something does interfere' (ibid.). 'Es kommt etwas dazwischen'.[24] During their conversation about the nature of art Danton had been called out of the room and told that the *comité de salut public* wants his head. Thus politics collides with literature not merely in Büchner's political play, but also in Celan's speech which, amongst its numerous and also often unfathomable gestures, seeks to reclaim a politics for literature, albeit in a different way than Büchner.

Politics is, however, not the only thing that interrupts Camille and Danton's musings on art: '– ach, die Kunst!' (*DM*, 4). Certainly, it is easy to philosophize about art, Celan admits to his audience who presumably expects him to do precisely that (*TM*, 2). But there is also Lucile. With the corporation whose business it is to think about art, perhaps to drag art into the realm of what can be understood and talked about reasonably or with reason, there is someone like Lucile who 'listens and looks ... and then doesn't know what the talk was all about' (3). But does Lucile really not know what the men's conversation was all about?

> Camille: Do you listen as well?
> Lucile: Of course!
> Camille: Well, am I right? Do you really know what I said?
> Lucile: To tell you the truth, no. (2.3; 34)

Although her husband hears in Lucile's 'no' an admittance of her lack of understanding, her 'no' could also be read as her answer to whether she thinks Camille is right or not. Lucile's silent interruption can thus be read as a radical interruption of this discourse on art, as well as the sovereignty of the sort of knowledge the men promulgate; radical precisely because it does not merely question the men's argument but the very mode or ground of their argumentation. The blind or deaf ones are then, perhaps, the men who are not able to acknowledge Lucile's silent interruption for what it is because it does not fit into their modes of thinking, because they do not recognize it *as* thinking. What happens to a royal lineage when its body politic changes from one gender to the other? The king is dead! Long live the queen! What happens to the body philosophical if the knowledge on which it bases its sovereignty changes modality?

Lucile works yet another interruption in the play. Yes, she interrupts the *Kunstgespräch*, but her improbable pledge of allegiance is also a rupture. For Celan it is just this not-quite-almost-silent *Dazwischengekommene* ('what had inserted itself') that speaks in Lucile's exclamation in front of the guillotine (*TM*, 3). Both of Lucile's interruptions – her seemingly counter-revolutionary exclamation at the end of the play and her silent interruption of her husband's musings on art – have, therefore, to be thought together. Radically different than all that was said before, Lucile's is, Celan argues, a 'Gegenwort', a 'counterword', an 'act of freedom' (ibid.). Like Celan, Derrida got stuck on Lucile's 'Long live the king!' perhaps also because, like Celan, Derrida wishes to fathom 'a certain poetic signature', as distinct from a 'poetics' or an '*ars poetica*', in other words, as distinct from learned conversations about poetry in the manner of Danton and Camille's *Kunstgespräch* (*BS*, 227). In order to do so, Celan must work a modulation of registers and must 'withdraw[ing]' Lucile's cry 'from its political code' (229). What Lucile's profession salutes, therefore, is not the monarchy. Lucile's shout also does not profess allegiance to the majesty of art, be it the kind of art (or the understanding of art?) that Camille deplores – remember, her counterword cuts through the marionette strings – or Büchner's sovereignty of the real. Neither does she, like Tulp, profess knowledge. For Celan, Lucile's cry has no political or philosophical master; it also does not serve knowledge, as we know it: it is itself sovereign.

What speaks in Lucile's counterword is, Derrida agrees in *The Beast & the Sovereign*, a different majesty. Derrida quotes Celan in full: 'Homage is being paid to the majesty of the absurd as witness for the presence of the human' (*TM*, 3). 'Gehuldigt wird hier der für die Gegenwart des Menschlichen zeugenden Majestät des Absurden' (*DM*, 3). 'Upping the ante with respect to sovereignty', the poet elevates one majesty over the other (*BS*, 230). Derrida paraphrases: 'There is the sovereign majesty of the sovereign, the King, and there is, more majestic or differently majestic, more sovereign or differently sovereign, the majesty of poetry, or the majesty of the absurd insofar as it bears witness to the presence of the human.' (ibid.) Celan, however, also ups the ante on Büchner who with Camille upped the ante on art. Thus the majesty of the absurd, bearing witness, as it were, to the presence of what makes man man (for Celan speaks not of *Mensch* but of *des Menschlichen*), trumps realism, which in turn trumps the wooden fakeries of a marionette-like conception of art. What then is the majesty of the absurd? Celan: 'This, ladies and gentlemen, has no name fixed once and for all, but I believe that this is ... poetry' (*TM*, 4).

What does the majesty of the absurd have to do with poetry? Celan, being the poet of darkness that he is, does not tell us. Derrida intervenes and offers an interpretation: 'Majesty is here majestic, and it is poetry, insofar as it bears witness to the present, the now, the "presence", as Launay translates it, of the human' (*BS*, 231). Put differently: Lucile's '*Gegenwort*' speaks in favor of the majesty of the *Gegenwart*' (229).[25] For Celan, too, the poem is presentness itself, in that it is 'one person's-language-become-shape ... according to its essence, presentness and presence' (*TM*, 9). Despite these insistences on presence, it is all a question of divisions, and not merely between Lucile's poetry and Büchner's understanding of art on the one hand, and the sovereignty of Lucile's poetry and the sovereignty of the monarch on the other hand. What matters is the division to which Lucile's *Dichtung* owes its majesty, namely the division of the present itself, what, returning to Celan's 'Meridian' in the Tenth session, Derrida calls 'the division in the point, the pinpoint, the very punctuality of the now' (*BS*, 259).

The sovereignty of poetry has to do with this very punctuality of the now, because it is this division which opens up poetry to the other. In fissuring self-presence, it can become a 'conversation', a conversation moreover that inaugurates its interlocutor (*TM*, 9). Thus, in the space of the poem, Celan writes, the addressed 'constitutes' itself, albeit not in such a way as to overwhelm the addressing one, but to preserve its otherness. 'But the addressed which though naming has, as it were, become a you, brings its otherness into this present' (ibid.). For Derrida, then, the punctuality of the present constitutes the poematic because it opens up any being, any presence – at its heart – to alterity. This is what Derrida takes away from Celan:

> He specifies that this now-present of the poem, *my* now-present, the punctual now-present of a punctual *I*, my now-present must *allow* the now-present of the other, the time of the other, *to speak*. It must *leave* time, *give* time to the other.
>
> To the other, it must leave or give *its* time. *Its own time.* (*BS*, 232)

In his reading of Büchner's 'Long live the king!' Derrida thus pledges to the sovereignty of the punctuality of the now of poetry. It is this division which ultimately, according to Derrida's reading of Celan, rocks sovereignty – the political sovereignty of the monarch and, as we shall see, the even more insidious sovereignty of 'knowledge' – by fissuring the assumption of 'self-present ipseity' in which the very concept of majesty and of mastery is rooted (270).

The punctuality of the present that Derrida hears in Celan governs the reading of philosophy, just as much as it governs the reading of poetry. A strikingly similar discussion of punctuality can in fact be found in 'The Deaths of Roland Barthes' in *The Work of Mourning*. Again, like in his reading of 'The Meridian', the reader-thinker or poet Derrida takes the philosopher by his idiom, an idiom, however, that gives space to the other. Thus Barthes's notion of the punctum becomes for Derrida the very punctuality of the idiom, the punctuated now-present which allows for his reading of Barthes. It is 'a point of singularity that punctures the surface of the reproduction – and even the production – of analogies, likenessness, and codes. It pierces, strikes me, wounds me and bruises me, and, first of all, seems to concern only me. Its very definition is that it addresses itself to me.' (*WM*, 39) The punctum's point of singularity interrupts. Most importantly, it concerns and wounds only me, the me, to be precise, that is reading *at this very moment*.

Governed by the idiom, Derrida's readings present a scene in which neither body nor book become subservient either to each other, or to the corporation whose business is the continuity of a thought in, for and towards the name of a Celan or Barthes. The idiom does not belong either to the philosopher's body or book, because the idiom, that irreducible poematic signature, gives time to the other and any other. In inviting endless appropriation the idiom cannot be appropriated and cannot be put to use to any sovereignty but its own. Derrida's insistence on the punctuality of the idiom therefore side-steps the knowledge-corporation's fantasies of mastery and appropriation.

The idiom must leave or give its time. This formulation is, Derrida immediately concedes, 'not literally Celan's', just like Barthes might not have had the punctuality of the now in mind when coining his notion of the punctum. But in not quite being Celan's it is a crucial meta-critical, even performative, moment in his reading of 'The Meridian'. Derrida's reading of Celan accounts for itself; in other words, his insertion of alterity at the heart of the now-present allows for him reading Celan 'not literally'; it demonstrates how 'The Meridian', which Derrida also calls a poem, can give space to Derrida's reading. To put it perhaps somewhat simplistically: in describing this alterity, Derrida performs it. This is Derrida's counterword, his step towards freedom, taken with, but also most importantly beyond, those whose wake he is in.

'Es lebe der König!'

If 'each book is a pedagogy aimed at forming its reader', what lessons does Derrida's work on other philosophers and philosopher-poets hold for us (*LLF*, 31)? They are to be sure lessons and not how-to-guides: they demand not mimesis but something different. Again the question of fidelity, of the purity or illegitimacy of a bloodline, rears its head. All the choices we have before us are, Derrida himself admits, impossible: 'zealous devotion' to Derrida's idiom or an avoidance of the latter, in favour of a grasp of his corpus, the idea that there even is an entirety of his thought. Our choices may even be more impossible than he anticipated, in that each thinking *in, for* and *towards* his name would scarce escape the machinations of sovereign knowledge that he circumvented. Put differently, whilst Derrida's insistence on the punctuality of the idiom allowed him to side-step the corporations of knowledge, any such side-stepping on our part would ultimately still belong to the corporation that he, in so doing, founded. What was original for him is what we have come to learn to expect. From our hands the same gestures will not perform the same unprecedented interruption of the sovereignty of knowledge, but its consolidation. For us, the same patterns of thought will not do.

The assertion that our modes of reading have to change means first of all that the fundamental rationale on which those readings are based must change. It cannot only be a question of positioning our reading in different contexts or junctures; whatever we do next must be informed by a rethinking at the fundament of Derrida's work and his idiom. What we need then is another counterword, a step into a different direction. There are many steps we could take. By way of conclusion, I would like to adumbrate merely one, which merits further exploration than I can give it here. In the 'hic and nunc' of Lucile's silent interruption, which is also poetry's silent interruption, Werner Hamacher – following to be sure not merely Derrida but also Benjamin and Heidegger – hears not différance but a 'linguistic being ... in which language reaches out to its own nothingness, to the nothingness of its reference, its meaning, and its determination'.[26] What would speak in Lucile's silent interruption, but also in Celan's and Büchner's and Derrida's own, would thus not be the différanced now-present, but a linguistic being, what Hamacher's Benjamin might have called pure language and which Hamacher himself might call language's intensity: something that although positing presence itself can itself not be posited, unless perhaps in silence. Staying longer with this nothing, thinking about how it works with but also resists a Derridean notion of différance, would perhaps be one way of cutting the marionette-strings, to which, in our attempt to compensate for something irreplaceable, we have fastened our habits of thought. Admittedly such a cutting of strings may also be a cutting of ties with our corporation, perhaps even a betrayal. But would that be so terrible?

Notes

I would like to thank Simon Morgan Wortham and Sarah Doebbert Epstein for their valuable comments on earlier drafts of this chapter. A warm thank you also to Catriona Murray for our conversations about Rembrandt.

1   Jacques Derrida, *The Work of Mourning*, eds. Pascale-Anne Brault and Michael Naas (Chicago and London: University of Chicago Press, 2001), 67 (hereafter cited in text as *WM*).

2   Ernst H. Kantorowicz, *The King's Two Bodies: A Study in Mediaeval Political Theology* (Princeton: Princeton University Press, 1957).

3   Edmund Plowden, *The Commentary or Reports of Edmund Plowden* (London, 1816), 213.

4   Ibid.

5   Ibid., 233a.

6   *Oxford English Dictionary*, 2nd edn, s.v. 'demise'.

7   Kantorowicz, *The King's Two Bodies*, 5.

8   Plowden, *Reports*, 177a.

9   Kantorowicz, *The King's Two Bodies*, 4.

10   Ibid., 9.

11   Ibid., 8.

12   *Oxford English Dictionary*, 2nd edn, s.v. 'incorporate'.

13   Plowden, *Reports*, 233a.

14   Jacques Derrida, *The Beast & the Sovereign Volume I*, trans. Geoffrey Bennington (Chicago and London: The University of Chicago Press, 2009), 285 (hereafter cited in text as *BS*).

15   For more on the history and tradition of painted anatomy lessons please refer to Sarah Kofman, 'Conjuring Death: Remarks on *The Anatomy Lesson of Doctor Nicolas Tulp* (1632)', trans. Pascale-Anne Brault, in *Selected Writings*, eds. Thomas Albrecht, with Georgia Albert and Elizabeth Rottenberg (Stanford: Stanford California Press, 2007), 294 (hereafter cited in text as *CD*).

16   Svetlana Alpers, *Rembrandt's Enterprise: The Studio and The Market* (Chicago and London: University of Chicago Press, 1988), 27.

17   Jacques Derrida, *Learning to Live Finally: An Interview with Jean Birnbaum*, trans. Pascale-Anne Brault and Michael Naas (Hoboken: Melville House Publishing, 2007), 24 (hereafter cited in text as *LLF*).

18　Jacques Derrida, 'Circumfession', trans. Geoffrey Bennington, in Geoffrey Bennington, *Jacques Derrida* (Chicago and London: The University of Chicago Press, 1993), 26 (hereafter cited in text as C).

19　Geoffrey Bennington, *Jacques Derrida* (London and Chicago: The University of Chicago Press, 1993), 9.

20　Ibid., 26–7.

21　Georg Büchner, *Dantons Tod: Ein Drama* (Stuttgart: Reclam, 1998) (text references are to act, scene and line of this edition).

22　Georg Büchner, '*Danton's Death*', in *The Plays of Georg Büchner*, trans. Victor Price (London: Oxford University Press, 1971) (text references are to act, scene and page of this edition). Büchner's original German reads: 'Schnitzt einer eine Marionette, wo man den Strick hereinhängen sieht, an dem sie gezerrt wird und deren Gelenke bei jedem Schritt in funfüssigen Jamben krachen – welch ein Charakter, welche Konsequenz!' (2.3.12–15).

23　Paul Celan, 'The Meridian', trans. Pierre Joris, in *The Meridian: Final Version – Drafts – Material*, eds. Bernhard Böschenstein and Heino Schmull (Stanford: Stanford University Press, 2011), 2 (hereafter cited in text as *TM*).

24　Paul Celan, 'Der Meridian', in *Der Meridian. Endfassung – Entwürfe – Materialien*, eds Bernhard Böschenstein and Heino Schmull (Frankfurt: Suhrkamp Verlag, 1999), 2 (hereafter cited in text as *DM*).

25　*Die Gegenwart* means the present; *das Gegenwort* is Celan's term and indicates the counterword.

26　Werner Hamacher, *Premises: Essays on Philosophy and Literature from Kant to Celan*, trans. Peter Fenves (Cambridge, MA and London: Harvard University Press, 1996), 371.

Index